DUBLIN BE PROUD

DEDICATION

To my lovely children Anne Marie and toddlers Brendan and Padraig in the hope that this book may help to make Dublin a better place for them to grow up in.

Dublin Be Proud

PAT LIDDY

In celebration of
Dublin's Millennium Year 1988

CHADWORTH LIMITED
DUBLIN

First published October 1987
Chadworth Limited

Text and Drawings © Chadworth Ltd. and Pat Liddy
Jacket Design © Pat Liddy
Layout and Design Sean and Rory McNeela
Co-ordination and Distribution Chadworth Ltd.
Colour plates Master Photo Ltd.

Typeset and Printed in Ireland by
Cahill Printers Ltd., Dublin

Paperbound ISBN 0 9512510 07
Case bound ISBN 0 9512510 15
Special bound Limited Edition ISBN 0 9512510 23

TRUSTEE SAVINGS BANK DUBLIN

Trustee Savings Bank Dublin had its origins as the School Street Savings Bank on February 11th, 1818. Its first Chairman was Percy La Touche of the famous banking family.

The Bank's business soon outgrew its initial premises and following a number of different locations, it opened a branch in Marlborough Street where today stands our famed Abbey Theatre. This premises in turn proved too small and in October 1840 the Bank moved its headquarters to the present Lower Abbey Street branch. This building remained the Bank's headquarters until 1983 when the Bank purchased and renovated 114/115 Lower Grafton Street and occupied the building as its headquarters.

In Ireland, the first Savings Bank was founded in Kilkenny on the 20th of May 1816 and the movement prospered so rapidly that by 1829 there were 60 separate Savings Banks. This proved to be the peak for numbers of Savings Banks as in the next 60 years there was a constant decline caused by periods of economic stagnation and civil strife. By the time the Irish Free State was founded in 1922, five Savings Banks survived and indeed were flourishing in the country.

Today, Trustee Savings Bank Dublin, an independent Bank governed by its own Board of Trustees, is a member of the Association of Trustee Savings Banks in Ireland. This body, made up of Trustee Savings Bank Dublin, Trustee Savings Bank Waterford and the combined Cork and Limerick Savings Banks, is the representative for the Savings Banks movement in this country.

Through the years the Bank has played an integral role in the life of the city. It has expanded and prospered with the city and as such is proud to be associated with the publication of this superb book on Dublin.

The Author and Publishers wish to thank the Trustee Savings Bank Dublin, for their encouragement and generous support towards the publication of this book.

ACKNOWLEDGEMENTS

In a special way I want to acknowledge Master Photo Ltd. who supplied the colour separations as their contribution towards the Dublin Millennium Year. Cahill Printers Ltd. deserve plaudits for tremendous support in helping us to meet the publishing deadline. I am very grateful to the Minister for the Environment, Padraig Flynn, the former Lord Mayor, Bertie Ahern and to Denis Shelly, Tom Coffey and Bill Nowlan for their own written contributions to this book. My thanks also for the support we received from Aer Lingus, the City Centre Business Association and the Dublin Chamber of Commerce.

Gathering the historical material was made both easy and pleasurable by the kindness shown to me everywhere I went. I couldn't possibly thank everyone I met in Dublin Corporation, the Office of Public Works, *The Irish Times* and in various companies and institutions.

Neither can I adequately thank Carol Fitzsimons who put in long hours during her school holidays to make sense out of my filing non-system and youthful neighbour Louise Briscoe who was always at hand when I needed her. But for Sean, Rory, Paraic and Donal McNeela who displayed daring, drive, initiative, imagination and a capacity for hard work this book would have been but a pipe-dream.

Finally, without the unselfish and patient support of my wife Josephine not to mention the unremunerated secretarial duties she performed even the pipe-dream would not have been possible.

Also thanks to the developers and architectural firms who supplied material for Chapter 13, and to everyone who lent support in one form or another.

BIBLIOGRAPHY

Guide to Historic Dublin, Adrian MacLoughlin, Gill & Macmillan Ltd., Dublin, 1979.
DUBLIN, Peter Somerville-Large, Granada Publishing Ltd., London 1979.
Dublin 1660-1860, Maurice Craig, Allen Figgis & Co. Ltd., Dublin 1980.
Dublin, Desmond Clarke, B. T. Batsford Ltd., Dublin, 1977.
Lost Dublin, Frederick O'Dwyer, Gill & Macmillan Ltd., Dublin, 1977.
Me Jewel and Darlin' Dublin, Eamonn Mac Thomais, The O'Brien Press, Dublin, 1980.
The Liberties of Dublin, Edited by Elgy Gillespie, The O'Brien Press Ltd., Dublin, 1973.
The Course of Irish History, Edited by T. W. Moody and F. X. Martin, RTE and Mercier Press, 1984.
North Dublin City and Environs by Dillon Cosgrove, published C.T.S., 1909.

CONTENTS

COLOUR PLATES

PREFACE

Dublin has the topography, the fabric and the potential to achieve greatness again. I use "again" deliberately because the city once enjoyed an international status for its architecture and elegance but it has since slipped into a state of some neglect and shabbiness. Admittedly the degenerative process started 150 years ago but in recent decades it was hastened by bad planning decisions, greed, carelessness, misunderstandings, disregard for the law, double standards, opportunism and plain lack of awareness.

It is certainly not too late to reverse the decline. Public debate has raised the level of consciousness and commitment and as a direct result there are already a goodly number of magnificent projects either recently completed or now under way.

Only a change in the attitude of the people themselves can make the real difference and raise Dublin from the ranks of the mediocre. We will have to care for our property as advocated by Thomas Drummond when he said "property has its duties as well as its rights". We will have to respect the public streets as extensions of our livingrooms. Only then can Dublin regain its stature and become the capital city that we can all be proud of.

Perhaps in some small way this book might help to attain this ambition.

Teach an Árd-Mhaoir,
Baile Átha Cliath 2,
Éire.
Telefón: 761845, 712402.

Mansion House,
Dublin 2,
Ireland.
Telephone: 761845, 712402.

The Rt. Hon. The Lord Mayor Alderman Bertie Ahern T.D.

Resilience is the primary characteristic of Dublin. The Capital City of Ireland has had its share of abuse over the centuries. Equally it has had its share of moaners and groaners. In spite of all that it has endured and endured well.

Dublin to-day is making yet another come-back. In 1988 it will celebrate 1,000 years of its past, this celebration will reflect on the past and will even more so concentrate on investment in the future. However noble a past the city may have had the call of the future is more compelling. The City must evolve and adapt but it must also do so with care and sensitivity.

We must therefore allow our city to renew itself. We must have the confidence to believe in our resilience and to welcome rather than fear renewal and re-development.

To take this more mature view of Dublin is what is needed to-day. In such an approach we always run the risk of being misunderstood and misrepresented. Being optimistic and hopeful is not fashionable in Dublin.

The great virtue of Pat Liddy's work is that it is saturated with hope and optimism. He is not afraid to praise, encourage and welcome. He appreciates the physical features of our great city and equally appreciates the pressures and realities of age, cost, use and economic circumstances.

This book is the food of pride, it is a source of great knowledge and great hope. It is because of writers like Pat Liddy that Dublin will recognise its past as it plots its future. Our city will survive, of that there is no doubt, but that it will survive well is due, in large measures, to the appreciative and caring work of Pat Liddy.

ALDERMAN BERTIE AHERN T.D.,
LORD MAYOR OF DUBLIN.

DALKEY ISLAND

Dalkey Island, a craggy extrusion of the submarine geology which inland rises to form the Wicklow Mountains, has a history of habitation reaching far back into the shrouded mists of mesolithic times. Excavations have unearthed the household remains of 5,000 years ago and the arrival of early Christianity four millennia later is marked by the small ruined oratory dedicated to St. Becnat.

The Vikings plundered the little island and from its shelter launched many looting expeditions. During the Middle Ages and right into the 18th century the anchorage protected by the island was popular with captains who were loath to risk passing over the treacherous sand bars blocking the entrances to the Liffey. Cargoes were transferred at Dalkey into barges which were then sailed into Dublin. However, in adverse weather conditions even the relative security of Dalkey sometimes proved inadequate or deceptive and the jagged coastline swallowed up its share of foundered wrecks.

In the 15th and 16th centuries the island was sanctuary to hundreds of refugees who fled to escape the plagues and epidemics which periodically ravaged Dublin. It also provided cover to smugglers who hauled in contraband which, by arrangement, had been tossed overboard from passing ships. These nefarious activities were curtailed during the Napoleonic scare when the islet became a key fortress in the defence of Dublin Bay. The martello tower and other ramparts date from this period as probably also do the famous wild goats who presumably were introduced for the benefit of the garrison.

The island was also famous for the crowning of the King of Dalkey, a wild and disorderly annual occasion which was suppressed in 1797. This travesty of a court was presided over by "His facetious Majesty the King of Dalkey, Emperor of Muglin's, Elector of Lambay and Ireland's Eye, Defender of his own Faith and Respector of all others, Sovereign of the Illustrious Order of the Lobster and the Periwinkle".

Chapter One

The Sands of Time

Ireland was wrenched from the land mass of Britain about 50,000 years ago and was effectively cut off from the probings of early Stone Age migrants. However around 6000 B.C. Mesolithic man emerged from the swirling mists of prehistory and fanned out across the length and breadth of Ireland. We know from excavations that one place they settled was Dalkey Island. Their Neolithic successors likewise descended on Dalkey Island and presumably also chose other agreeable locations around Dublin Bay and its hinterland. These people respected death and raised their tombs such as the Knockmary Cromlech which can still be seen near the grounds of St. Mary's Hospital in the Phoenix Park.

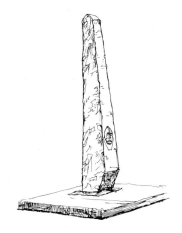

NEOLITHIC CROMLECH

Knockmary, Phoenix Park.

Bronze Age civilisation dawned around 1500 B.C. (remains were found in 1857 under present-day Parliament Street) only to be rudely brushed aside by the various waves of the more advanced Celts.

Ireland still lacked any decent village let alone an urban development. The 2nd. century A.D. Greek astronomer and matematician, Claudius Ptolemy, in his map of the British Isles alluded to a tribe called Eblani in the Dublin area rather than to a city as has often been supposed.

Between the 5th and 9th centuries Christian monasteries were founded on Ireland's Eye, Dalkey Island, Finglas and Tallaght. Other churches were build along the rivers Liffey and Poddle. Small secular communities sprang up around these foundations and probably evolved into villages in their own right.

Two localities where settlements may have grown gave Dublin its Gaelic and Anglicized names. The first, Ath Cliath (meaning Hurdle Ford), was placed beside a causeway crossing of the Liffey and the second, Dubh Linn (Black Pool), was adjacent to a dark lagoon — near where the Olympia was built — formed by the convergence of the Poddle and the Liffey. Dubh Linn became Dyflin in the Viking tongue.

The real story of Dublin begins with the coming of the Viking adventurers. In 837 a fleet of 65 Norwegian ships sailed into Dublin Bay marking their arrival by erecting the Steyne, a symbolic high stone, on sandy ground at the junction of what is now Townsend Street and Hawkins Street. In 841 these sea marauders fortified their harbourage with a wooden stockade. They had come to stay and Dublin was born.

Over the next three centuries successive Viking kings ruled over the fledging town using it as a base for launching sorties on monasteries and campaigns against enemies. They forged alliances with Irish kings to face common rivals but opportunistically switched sides as the humour took them. Their tenuous foothold on Dublin did not go without serious challenge and on one occasion, in 902, they were driven out altogether. But a huge armada of Danish and Norwegian longships returned sixteen years later and the real work of colonising Dublin began. Huge earthen ramparts were thrown around the per-

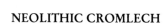

STEYNE STONE

Over 11 feet high this rough hewn stone, erected in 1986, commemorates the original stone which stood on this site from the 9th century until 1720.

The sculptress was Cliodna Cussen.

imeter and clay and wattle houses were erected. Much of the excavated material found at Wood Quay, Fishamble Street and Christchurch Place dates from this period onwards.

Warlike neighbours gave little respite to the Norsemen and Dublin was attacked on several occasions. Mael Seachnaill, King of Leinster captured the town in 981, 989 and 995 and Brian Boru, King of Munster, sacked Dublin in 1000. The Viking King Sitric Silkenbeard backed the losers at the Battle of Clontarf in 1014 when Boru and his Munster army defeated the Leinsterman and their Norse allies from Orkney.

Despite the distractions and ravages of war the struggling community nestling beside the Liffey got on as best they could with their ordinary lives. Commercialism was built up and by the eleventh century Dublin was a key trading centre in the Viking world. Christian dogma began to replace the Nordic gods and in 1036 King Sitric and Donat, the first bishop of Dublin, founded Christ Church Cathedral.

By the 12th century the town was taking on a more distinctive urban appearance with streets, meeting places, churches, market areas, craft centres and a small port of sorts. However, except for some ecclesiastical structures, stone buildings were still a rarity.

In 1162 St. Lawrence O'Toole was made archbishop but his reign was soon to be disturbed by an ominous and cataclysmic wind of change; the coming of the Anglo Normans.

The Middle Ages

The Anglo Normans landed in Wexford in 1169 and a year later captured Dublin. The Vikings were ousted but they resettled across the Liffey in Ostman Town (later Oxmantown). King Henry II, wary of the ambition of his Norman lords, came to Dublin himself in 1171 and in his Charter of the following year granted the city to the citizens of Bristol.

The medieval character of what was now to become Ireland's principal city began to emerge. In 1192 St. Patrick's Cathedral was founded by Archbishop Comyn and 12 years later the building of Dublin Castle was begun. Over the next few decades the city was encompassed by strong defensive walls, the excessive width of the Liffey was narrowed, and more stone churches and secular buildings were erected. Commercial life was better organised and the trade guilds were formed. The great religious orders arrived. . . the Augustinians, Cistercians, Carmelites, Knights Templars and Knights Hospitallers, Dominicans and Franciscans. Municipal organisation began to take shape and in 1229 Henry III decreed the election for the position of Mayor. The population rose to about 8,000 people.

Life in the old town was difficult, to say the least. There was constant aggravation from neighbouring mountain communities such as the O'Tooles and the O'Byrnes. Massacres were perpetrated by both sides. The city endured a seige by Edward Bruce in 1316 and, on a couple of other occasions, had to be rebuilt after devastating fires. Plagues, diseases and famines paid regular and deadly visitations.

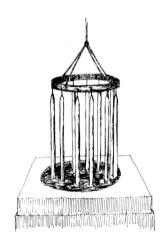

MEDIEVAL MAP OF DUBLIN

This map shows the location of the old city walls, gates and watchtowers.

RATHBORNE'S, EAST WALL ROAD

The Rathbornes came over from Chester in 1488 and established their candle making business in Dublin. One of the oldest firms in Europe in continuous operation, Rathbornes still employ centuries old techniques for making types of candles.

Post Medieval

The citizens of Dublin still had to suffer pestilence and rebellion with the added affliction of religious persecution. The Reformation began to really bite around 1539 when the process started within the "Pale" (a word first used in 1446 to describe the area around Dublin under secure English control) to dissolve the great religious houses and force the surrender of their properties. Over the next century various Penal Laws directed against Roman Catholics were enacted. In 1649 Oliver Cromwell landed with 13,000 troops at Ringsend and he showed scant respect for the revered places of Dublin.

On the other hand there were some very positive developments to come out of the 16th and 17th centuries.

The first record of a book being printed in Dublin dates from 1550 and a decade later the first public clocks were erected on St. Patrick's Cathedral, Dublin Castle and the Tholsel. Trinity College was founded in 1592 and the city's first theatre opened in Werburgh Street in 1637. From the 1660s major works were carried out to the Liffey quays, the Phoenix Park was walled in and stocked with deer, St. Stephen's Green was enclosed and drained and in 1684 the Royal Hospital, an institution for wounded and retired soldiers and the first of its kind in the British Empire, was opened. The revocation of the Edict of Nantes in 1685 increased the influx of refugee French Huguenots who, along with Jewish, Dutch and Palatine immigrants, were to play a major role in the development of the industrial, commercial and architectural life of the city. The population approached the 60,000 mark by 1682, a galloping increase on the 10,000 or so of only a few decades earlier.

ARCHWAY,
TAILORS' HALL

An Age of Refinement

The 18th century ushered in a generally more peaceful era when trade flourished and the great Georgian streetscapes began to unfold, first on the north side of the Liffey and then more expansively on the south side. Rows of elegant town mansions were richly complemented by the splendours of the House of Parliament, Trinity College, the Custom House, the Four Courts and the Rotunda Hospital.

Parliament became properly established and won a certain independence of action from Britain. There were significant advances in the formation or expansion of charitable, cultural, social and medical institutions.

Jonathan Swift was installed as Dean of St. Patrick's in 1713 and Frederick Handel conducted the world's first performance of his Messiah in 1742 in the Music Hall, Fishamble Street.

In 1745 Roman Catholics were again allowed to assemble in public worship and in 1782-93 a number of Catholic Relief Acts were passed.

The Wide Streets Commissioners were established in 1758 and their urban planning was very enlightened for the day. In 1762 Merrion Square was laid out.

In the broad cultural and scientific fields two notable events took place. These were the formation of the (Royal) Dublin Society in 1750 and the Royal Irish Academy in 1758. External communication with the city was eased by the opening of the two canals, the inauguration of mail coaches (1790) and the improvements to Dublin Port. Dubliners

HENRY GRATTAN,
COLLEGE GREEN

Henry Grattan was born in Dublin in 1746 and entered the Irish Parliament when he was 29. He proved to be an able and fiery orator and became leader of the opposition Liberal Party. He wanted Ireland to have a measure of legislative freedom and an end put to trade restrictions. He did not, however, envisage a break with the British Crown as such.

The statue was sculptured by John Foley.

MOUNTED UNIT, DUBLIN METROPOLITAN POLICE

Unlike many other major cities Dublin has had no mounted police since the Dublin Metropolitan Police was amalgamated with the Garda Síochána in 1925. Some day might wiser counsels and a healthier exchequer allow the reintroduction of this resplendent corps?

CUCHULAIN, GPO

The bronze statue by Oliver Sheppard, R.H.A., stands in the public office as a memorial to the participants in the Easter Rising. It depicts the dead Cuchulain, leader of the Red Branch Knights of Irish mythology.

saw their first steam engine operating in 1791. The population had increased to 150,000 by the later half of the 18th century which made Dublin one of the largest cities in Europe.

A high point had been reached but dark clouds were gathering on the horizon which would severely blunt the development of the city, reduce it to the status of a provincial capital and plunge the growing number of the poor working classes into greater despair and deprivation.

The British Government, suspicious and perhaps even jealous of the semi-independent Irish Parliament was jolted further by the bloody insurrection of 1798 and contrived by every means, mostly foul, to bring about its dissolution. Through bribery and corruption the Irish Parliament voted itself out of existence and in 1800 the Act of Union with Great Britain was proclaimed.

The Nineteenth Century

The cultural, social and commercial life of the city did not come to an abrupt halt when the Act of Union became effective from the 1st January, 1801 but rather ran out of steam for a decade or two. Some of the nobility, court followers and those seeking the centre of power did depart for London and the building of fine mansions was virtually discontinued. Enthusiasm was still found, however, to erect a monument or two to the great heroes of British arms. Horatio Nelson was placed on top of his pillar in 1808 and nine years later the foundation stone for the Wellington Testimonial in the Phoenix Park was laid.

The coming of the railways in the 1830s heralded a new period of expansion and hastened the exodus of residents from centre city streets to the balmier climes of Blackrock, Dalkey and Dun Laoghaire. Suburbs sprang up on all sides while places like Henry and Grafton Streets were given over to shopping and business. The British Empire itself was expanding at an ever increasing rate and the impetus this gave to industrial and commercial enterprises spilled over to Dublin. During the latter half of Queen Victoria's reign a great building boom spread across the city. Public and private institutions erected prestigious buildings many of which became significant architectural landmarks.

Dublin became the hub of the country's vast network of railroads and the Dublin Steam Packet Company operated the fastest steamships in the world on the crossing to Britain. To cope with the ever-increasing cross-channel passenger traffic a massive artificial harbour — the world's largest at the time — was constructed at Kingstown (now Dun Laoghaire). In Dublin Port the docks bristled with cargo craft of all shapes, sizes and modes of power. While on the subject of shipping it is worth noting that the Corporation for the Preservation and Improvement of the Port of Dublin Lifeboat Service was the first coordinated lifeboat service in Europe. It was set up in 1801 and within six years there were stations ranged around the whole coastline of Dublin Bay. The Royal National Lifeboat Institution took over the operation in 1861.

THE HALFPENNY BRIDGE

Since the disappearance of Nelson's Pillar in 1966 the Halfpenny Bridge, a hugely popular pedestrian crossing over the Liffey, has become the virtual symbol of the city. Built in 1816 as the Wellington Bridge it is now known officially as the Liffey Bridge. Its more common name derives from the toll that used to be charged until withdrawn in 1919.

The cast iron structure was recently enhanced by Dublin Corporation with period standards and lanterns and by floodlighting at night-time.

SAINT STEPHEN'S GREEN

Sir Arthur Guinness, later Lord Ardilaun, arranged out of his own pocket to have the closed and derelict St. Stephen's Green relandscaped and opened to the public in 1877.

The park, a quarter of a mile long on every side, is a much sought-after refuge from the pressures of the surrounding commercial streets. There is much to enjoy inside it including wooded walks, formal lawns and flower beds, several fountains and a rustic bridge over lakes populated by ducks. Completing the picture is a bandstand, a pavilion, a children's playground and 15 monuments and statues. The lakes are fed directly by underground pipes from the Grand Canal.

WESTMORELAND STEET

This section of streetscape is enhanced by the happy, side-by-side coexistence of three styles of architecture — Italian, Dutch and French and typifies the exuberance expressed by commercial firms in the late Victorian era.

SUNLIGHT CHAMBERS, WELLINGTON QUAY

Built by Lever Brothers at the turn of the century, this remarkable edifice is decorated by terracotta friezes advertising, in an era before radio and television, the benefits of using Sunlight Soap.

Not all trades flourished and the collapse of the textile industry in 1826 brought severe hardship to certain parts of the city which had been dependent on that business. The wretchedness of the poor was aggravated by a typhus epidemic in 1816/17 and an outbreak of asiatic cholera in 1832. The famines of 1845-1847 also left terrible scars. Emigrants flooded through the ports of Ireland, including Dublin, on their way to what they hoped was a better life. One interesting statistic shows that between 1820 and 1970 almost five million people left for the U.S.A. alone.

Life was barely tolerable for the tens of thousands who lived out their wretched lives in overcrowded tenements. More than one family often shared a single, albeit large, room in a decaying Georgian mansion. Personal hygiene was less than basic and more died from privation that from old age. Infant mortality among the poor was considered to be almost the highest in the world.

Yet out of a mix of poverty and adequacy, which often lived side by side, came a literary revival which was to put Dublin on the map. Their names read like a catalogue of the world's greatest writers; James Joyce, Sean O'Casey, George Russell (A.E.), Richard Brinsley Sheridan, Patrick Kavanagh, Brendan Behan, John Millington Synge, Oscar Wilde, W. B. Yeats and Samuel Beckett. Perhaps popular writers such as Bram Stoker (Dracula) and Cornelius Ryan (The Longest Day and A Bridge Too Far) should also be included. No other city has had the honour of producing three separate Nobel prizewinners for literature (Beckett, Shaw and Yeats).

Political rumblings marked the progress of the nineteenth century. Nationalism was expressed openly and subversively, peacefully and with violence. Catholic Emancipation was won in 1829 by Daniel O'Connell and the rise of the Catholic middle classes made the Protestant ascendacy increasingly insular. The British administration failed to effectively grasp what was happening politically and by the turn of the century despite the apparent loyalty of the majority of the population there was a gathering momentum towards open rebellion.

A New Dawn

The twentieth century started harmlessly enough. Queen Victoria, who quite liked to visit Dublin and her feelings were usually reciprocated, arrived in 1900. Over the next few years various large squadrons of battleships paid courtesy calls to Dublin which probably also served as a British show of strength. Nevertheless political and social unrest grew fuelled by the stress of bad housing and poor labour relations. The General Strike of 1913 pitched the citizens against authority and organisations such as the Citizen Army and the Irish Volunteers were formed. Insurrection broke out on Easter Monday 1916 which left Dubliners appalled at the loss of life and the destruction of their city. Their antipathy towards the rebels changed after the leaders of the rebellion were executed and Dublin was to become the scene of ambushes and shoot-outs until the Treaty of 1921.

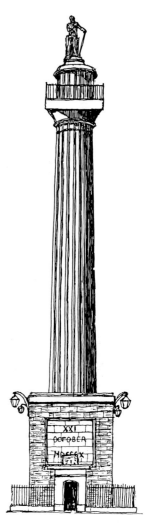

NELSON'S PILLAR

Built in 1808 this towering 121 feet high Doric column surmounted by the 13 feet high statue of Horatio Nelson was blown up on March 8th, 1966. Long the symbol of the city, opinions were divided about the loss.

7

The Civil War of 1922 wreaked further havoc on the city and it was to be another ten years before this latest damage was fully repaired. Except for two or three small raids Dublin was spared the devastation of the Second World War but some would argue that an equally violent but insidious wave of destruction befell the capital in the sixties and seventies. An economic boom brought a seemingly insatiable demand for office blocks and one by one Georgian and Victorian streetscapes were replaced by characterless glass boxes. Admittedly some modern blocks had merits but these were in the minority. To compound the situation road engineers were accused of making insensitive plans to drive motorways through the very heart of the city.

The recession from the late 70s brought a virtual halt to land speculation and office building and a breathing space was gained. Renewal has now become a priority issue and subsequent chapters in this book will show the potential Dublin still has in attaining the status of an exciting, interesting and really beautiful city on a par with the best in Europe.

HOWTH LIFEBOAT

The "City of Dublin" was presented to the RNLI at Howth in May 1987. The 52 feet (16 metres) lifeboat which cost £480,000, and at 18 knots is twice as fast as its predecessor.

GILBEYS

In my mind one of the most unforgivable acts of "Development Vandalism" in O'Connell Street was the destruction in the 1970s of this noble and highly decorative facade. Great was the pity that it could not have been imaginatively incorporated into the office block which replaced it.

VIKING FINDS

It started in High Street in 1962 and continued into Christchurch Place, Winetavern Street and Fishamble Street before concluding at Wood Quay in 1981. It was one of Europe's largest ever urban archaeological excavations and it yielded a greater and more important find of Viking artefacts than any other site including those of York, London, Hamburg and Bergen.

Some of the artefacts are on exhibit at the National Museum Annexe in Merrion Row, which should be visited by anyone with even a remote interest in the origins of Dublin.

The drawing includes a small iron saw shaped to resemble a Viking longboat. It was used to cut bone and antler, as in the examples shown of an 11th-century comb and its carrying case. The Norsemen are credited with introducing the composite comb into Ireland. The comb consists of two side plates between which are gripped a number of individual tooth plates. Antler pegs or iron or copper rivets hold the whole assembly together.

Imported from abroad, the iron sword is 12th-century. The polished bone pins, most likely used to tie up hair or fasten garments, have finely decorated heads which represent real or mythological animals. Also unearthed were hundreds of lead weights, all conforming to units based on the Carolingian ounce. Both folding and rigid scales were used to weigh precious metals. The example here features a 12th-century beam and 13th-century pans.

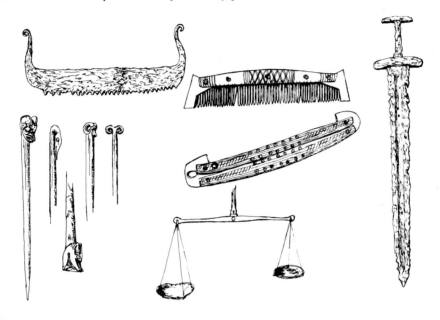

OLD CITY WALLS, COOK STREET

The Normans enclosed Dublin with massive walls which were punctuated with up to 32 fortified gates and towers. One such gate was St. Audeon's which was opened in this earlier stretch of wall in 1275. This is the longest piece of wall to survive the passage of time and it may owe its continued existence to its having been strategically replaced by another outer wall when the Liffey was pushed further back.

In 1975 the wall was restored by the Corporation as their contribution to European Architectural Year. It is now possible to walk up the evocative steps in the gateway and along the ramparts and into the beautiful little historic park. Behind is the tower of St. Audeon's Church which is the city's oldest continuously used parish church. Across the walls is an extensive view of the north city skyline. St. Audeon's Catholic Church is the location of the recreated Viking Fishamble Street

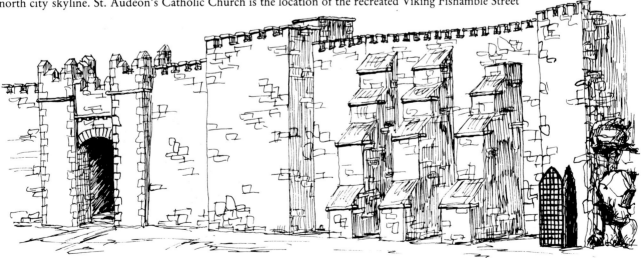

CRYPT, CHRIST CHURCH CATHEDRAL

The crypt, built at the time of Strongbow and Archbishop St. Lawrence O'Toole, is Dublin's oldest surviving building. It is unexpectedly vast and consists of a nave, aisles, apse and three chapels. Although the vaults were obviously religious in their original use, their revenue earning potential was recognised in the seventeenth century and they were let out to shopkeepers.

Years of misuse and neglect had left the underground passages in a ruinous state, but they were refurbished during the general restoration of the Cathedral by the great whiskey distiller, Henry Roe, between 1871 and 1878.

Some very surprising relics and artefacts can be viewed in the various corners of the crypt. They include two of the city's oldest secular statues, possibly of Charles II and James II, which were commissioned for the Tholsel, the one-time assembly house for the Corporation.

Most interesting of all are the official Ancient Stocks of the Liberty of Christ Church, made in 1670, into which the Dean had authority to commit offenders of the law. The air in the vaults is especially preservative and the twelfth century wooden wedges used in the construction are now iron hard.

The crypt is open to the public during normal Cathedral visiting hours.

FISHAMBLE STREET

This winding narrow street owes its name to the medieval fish shambles or markets which were once held here.

In the 17th and 18th centuries it was quite a fashionable street and in 1742 Frederick Handel himself conducted the world's first public airing of his oratorio "The Messiah" in the newly opened Music Hall.

The Music Hall is now the ironworks of Kennan and Sons (estb 1770). Just down the road from Kennan's is number 26, a four storey building, which is believed to be the oldest house in Dublin dating from around the 17th century. It is still lived in although it has had to be propped up since its neighbour was demolished in 1986.

ST. MICHAN'S CHURCH, CHURCH STREET

St. Michan's Church was founded in 1096 and named in honour of a Danish bishop. For 600 years it remained the only parish church on the north side of the Liffey. During the resurgence of the area, under the guiding hand of the Duke of Ormonde, the rector of St. Michan's, Dr. John Pooley, decided in 1686 to substantially reconstruct the building.

The church is steeped in history. Edmund Burke was baptised here, Handel reputedly played the Cuvillie organ in 1742 (the original keyboard is on display in the porch entrance), and Charles Stewart Parnell was a regular worshipper. The rector of the time attended the execution of Robert Emmet in 1803 and the churchyard is one of the claimants as the ill-fated patriot's burial place.

A highlight of a visit to the church — which itself displays some fine carvings and a magnificent organ — must be the rather macabre tour of the vaults. Here the combination of constant temperature, dry air, limestone walls and the chemical properties released from the ancient subterranean remains of an oak forest has naturally mummified bodies and preserved coffins. The effect is not uniform, as some bodies have crumbled into dust and their caskets have disintegrated.

One vault contains the remains of the Sheares brothers, put to death for their part in the 1798 Rising. Their Execution Order is displayed alongside. In addition to the various family vaults there is another that rivets the attention. Four mummified corpses lie in uncovered coffins waiting to greet visitors. They are over 300 years old and features such as skin, fingernails, teeth and veins can be plainly ascertained. Records show one to be a nun and another is claimed to be a crusader. Whatever he really was in life, he was too tall in death for the coffin and his legs had to be broken to make him fit. A few moments spent here is a sobering experience.

The Church and vaults are open to the public.

ST. MICHAN'S CHURCH

ST. MARY'S ABBEY

ST. MARY'S ABBEY CHAPTER HOUSE, MEETINGHOUSE LANE

St. Mary's Abbey first began under the Benedictine rule in 1139, but 12 years later it submitted to the Cistercians. In time the Abbey became one of the largest and wealthiest in the country and served as an important ecclesiastical and lay power-centre.

The Chapter House (built 1190 and so called because a chapter of the rules was read here every day) was one of Medieval Dublin's very few permanent buildings spacious enough to accommodate large meetings, and was often let out for such purposes. It was to here in 1534 that 20-year-old Lord Thomas Fitzgerald came to take up his position as acting President of the Privy Council. Silken Thomas, as he was known on account of his sartorial tastes, had just heard the rumour of his father's execution in London by Henry VIII. To the astonishment of the gathered councillors the enraged youth flung down his Sword of State, swept off his ceremonial robes of office, declared himself henceforth an enemy of the King and galloped away with his contingent of armed men to start an abortive rebellion. Three years later he and his five uncles swung from the gallows at Tyburn.

Surviving Silken Thomas by only four years, the Abbey succumbed to the edicts of Henry VIII. It was then used as an artillery arsenal and 40 years later the land and buildings were granted to developers. The Church itself was demolished in 1676 to provide stones for Essex Bridge. Over the next century all traces of the monastery vanished.

It was not till the 1880s that an exciting archaeological discovery was made underneath the then Capel Street premises of Boland's Bakery. Standing eight feet below the present street level the almost intact Chapter House had been rescued from the grave.

ST. CATHERINE'S, THOMAS STREET

St. Catherine's long history was inaugurated in the 1180s by the monks of St. Thomas' Abbey. Their medieval church was demolished in 1765 to make way for the present Roman doric-fronted building, designed by John Smith and completed four years later. An ambitious spire was intended to cap the tower but due to a lack of finance the idea was scrapped.

The most famous event associated with St. Catherine's, or rather with the street outside, was the hanging in September 1803 of Robert Emmet. Fellow insurrectionists who also paid the price of treason are commemorated on a wall tablet, and it is interesting to note their stations in life. A preponderance, seven in all, were carpenters; a trade which undoubtedly supervised the impeccable construction of their scaffolds.

In the early 19th century the vicar, the Reverend Whitelaw, undertook trojan work to bring relief to the unfortunates made destitute after the collapse of the weaving industry. His plaque is voluminous in praise and is rendered in a flowery verbiage also to be found on William Mylne's tablet, which "informs posterity of the uncommon zeal, integrity and skill with which he formed, enlarged and established on a perfect system the waterworks of Dublin".

A decline in the contregation due to the population shifts caused the Church of Ireland to abandon the building in 1967. It was taken over by the Bell Tower Trust who, assisted from time to time by the Corporation, undertook a programme of restoration. The South Inner City Community Development Association, a cataclystic organisation ably tackling many problems in the Liberties, joined the trust in 1982 and has been responsible for maintaining the tempo of refurbishment.

The old church will now fulfill a worthwhile role as a community focal point and as a centre for the performing arts.

(See illustration page 13.)

ST. NICHOLAS WITHOUT AND ST. LUKE'S, THE COOMBE

When the medieval parish of St. Nicholas Within was extended outside the city walls (St. Nicholas Without) no separate church was built. Instead the north transept of St. Patrick's Cathedral was allocated to the new parish. In 1666 a congregation of refugee French Huguenots were given use of the Lady Chapel at St. Patrick's and it was they who built, in 1707, the church of St. Luke which was then combined with the parish of St. Nicholas Without.

In the grounds of the church and fronting onto the Coombe stands the now empty "Widows' House". Originally a school house the Church of Ireland converted the building in the middle of the last century into a refuge for widows. Without the benefit of social welfare the plight of this vulnerable sector of society was harrowing to say the least. Their numbers were unusually high due to an above average rate in Dublin of adult male deaths as a consequence of rampant tuberculosis.

The Widows' House closed about four years ago and the building and the church have in the meantime been totally abandoned. Gradually falling prey to the mindlessness of vandals the church suffered extensive fire damage in 1986.

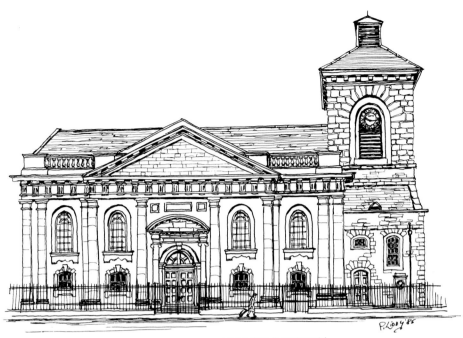

ST. CATHERINE'S, THOMAS STREET

TAILORS' HALL, BACK LANE

Tailors' Hall was built along the narrow and cobbled Back Lane for the Guild of Tailors in 1706. The entrance is through a quaint stone archway dating from 1714.

This Queen Anne building is the last surviving guild hall in Dublin. The two dozen or so guilds were medieval organisations representing the interests of trades and craftsmen. First formed in 1418 the Guild of Tailors commissioned the hall for their own gatherings but were prepared to share it with other groups.

Catholic Emancipation was debated here in 1792 by the Catholic Committee which earned it the name of the "Back Lane Parliament".

In 1983 Tailors' Hall became the headquarters of An Taisce, the National Trust for Ireland, The Liberties Association and the South Inner City Development Association. They have, subject to manifold financial constraints, carried out much needed refurbishment and rebuilt the boundary walls.

The derelict sites on either side of the Hall are also due for a sensitive Inner-City Renewal development. *(See page 169.)*

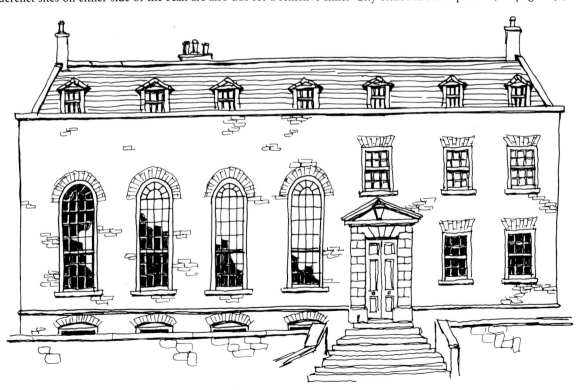

HIBERNIA

SHORT HISTORY OF THE POSTAL SERVICE IN IRELAND

1562   Nicholas Fitzsymon appointed first Postmaster for the city.

1599   Regular sea services between Dublin and London established.

1635   King Charles I appointed Thomas Witherings as Chief Postmaster of England and Foreign Parts.

1638   Evan Vaughan sent to Ireland to set up post stages and employ foot and horse posts along main roads. Dublin's Letter Office situated in Castle Street.

1657   Act of Parliament set up Government monopoly of the postal services which has lasted to this day.

1668   Letter Office moved to High Street, then Fishamble Street (1680) and Sycamore Alley (1709).

1711   Queen Anne passed a Bill making the Letter Offices around the Empire subject to the Postmaster General in London.

1755   G.P.O. moved to Fownes Court.

1760   Daily posts to various parts of the country.

1765   First attempt at a Penny Post by Dublin Post Office. For an extra penny the post was delivered to the door. The scheme was not successful as the rich preferred to use private messengers.

1771   G.P.O. moved to College Green.

1784   Irish Post Office separated from London control.

1789   First Dublin to Cork mail coach, followed two years later by the Limerick mail. Speed averaged four to seven miles an hour. Journey time London to Dublin reduced to three days.

1810   Revised Penny Post but only operated locally within urban areas.

1814   Foundation stone for G.P.O. in Sackville Street laid.

1818   New G.P.O. opened for business.

1830   Bianconi granted contracts to carry mail in his coaches.

1831   Irish Post Office remerged with British Post Office. Reforms carried out and Irish roads measured for the first time in English miles to bring postal charges in line with those in Britain.

1840   National Penny Post inaugurated by Rowland Hill. Postage stamps introduced. Letters up to a half ounce for one penny (Penny Black) could be posted to anywhere in Britain and Ireland. Post Offices established in many towns by now. Railways help the development of postal services.

MERCURY

| 1855 | Letters posted annually had grown from 9 million in 1839 to 42 millon this year. In the same period Post Offices had grown from 732 to 1,378. Journey time London to Dublin reduced to 11 hours with two daily deliveries. Pillar boxes introduced about this time. |

1855   Letters posted annually had grown from 9 million in 1839 to 42 millon this year. In the same period Post Offices had grown from 732 to 1,378. Journey time London to Dublin reduced to 11 hours with two daily deliveries. Pillar boxes introduced about this time.

1861   Savings Bank started.

1883   Parcel Post introduced.

1904   Post Office empowered to licence transmitting and receiving radio apparatus.

1909   Payment of old age pensions commenced.

1912   Post Office took over National Telephone Company. First exchange opened in 1880 by United Telephone Company on top floor of the Commercial Buildings in Dame Street with five subscribers. By 1900 there were 56 telephone exchanges around the country. (Incidentally, the country's last manually-operated exchange was replaced by the latest in digital technology in May, 1987.)

1916   General Post Office in Dublin occupied by rebel forces and destroyed.

1922   Independence from British control. Until the first Irish definitive stamps were printed in December the current British stamps were overprinted with "Rialtas Sealadach na hÉireann, 1922" (Provisional Government of Ireland). Members of Westminster Parliament angry at the defacing of their monarch's head. All pillar boxes prior to 1922 bear the royal insignia of the era. "V.R." represents Queen Victoria up to 1901. "E.R." is King Edward VII, who ruled from 1901 to 1910 and finally "G.R." for King George V, 1910 to Independence in 1921. After 1922 the royal red colour of the pillars changed to green.

1929   Reconstructed G.P.O. opened.

1935   Widows' and Orphans' pensions commenced.

1936   Air Mail introduced with the foundation of Aer Lingus.

1944   Children's Allowances introduced.

1982   Over 420 million items of mail now delivered annually by Post Office. There are 52 head post offices and 2,100 sub post offices as well as the G.P.O. and the Central Sorting Office.

1984   From the first of January, "An Post" was launched as a semi-state organisation. As a direct result a whole range of innovative marketing incentives and initiatives aided by new technology introduced.

FIDELITY

AN POST

The three statues which surmount the pediment of the General Post Office (see page 00) were sculptured by Edward Smyth. Hibernia is holding her spear and harp. Mercury, the messenger of the Gods, equipped with his caducues (wand), holds aloft a purse and Fidelity holds a key to her bosom.

SEAN O'CASEY'S HOUSE, 422 NORTH CIRCULAR ROAD

More than a few of Dublin's literary giants led an almost nomadic existence, when shifting family fortunes and paternal demise were often the influencing factors in decisions to uproot and move house. The constantly alternating panoramas, experiences and the sometimes unwelcome challenges which accompanied the changes enriched and developed these gifted minds.

James Joyce is credited with moving a minimum of 16 times in Dublin before he left for overseas in 1904. Patrick Pearse had eight addresses and creditors of George Russell (A.E.) would have had to cope with his nine changes of abode. George Bernard Shaw was modest by comparison with having to contend with only four furniture removals.

John Casey (he changed his name to Sean O'Casey in 1923 when "The Shadow of a Gunman" was first produced) was no exception to this pattern. Born in 1880 at 85 Upper Dorset Street the family shortly took leave for 9 Inisfallen Parade. After the death of his father poverty compelled the raising of the residential anchor on two more occasions. Two years after the death of his mother in 1918 Sean left home, first for Mountjoy Square, before settling down at 422 North Circular Road.

In 1926 Sean O'Casey left Dublin and Ireland altogether following the riots which attended the production of his unromantic view of the 1916 Rising — "The Plough and the Stars". The Abbey's rejection of "The Silver Tassie" confirmed him in his bodily but not his spiritual abandonment of his native city. (See illustration page 17.)

JAMES JOYCE'S HOUSE, BRIGHTON SQUARE

Street names in suburban Dublin are often amusingly inappropriate, and reveal a lazy convenience or a dearth of imagination on behalf of the site contractors, rather than an effort at accurate topographical description. Thus Crescents are straight, Groves are treeless, Lawns are grassless, Parks are concrete jungles and Rises are level.

Brighton Square was also misnamed as it is in essence not a square at all but a triangle. But it is nonetheless pleasant for the error, with its fine mature park, tennis courts and dignified, un-modernised lamp standards. It was in number 41 that James Joyce first saw the light of day 105 years ago on February 2nd, 1882.

James was the first child of five boys and six girls born to a Corkman, John Stanislaus Joyce, and his attractive Longford wife, Mary Jane Murray. Initially, John Joyce had an adequate income from some inherited property and his job in the office of the Collector-General of Rates and Taxes.

In 1891, John Joyce lost both his job and his sobriety, and financial crisis forced the family over the next twelve years to move house no less than nine times. Addresses included Blackrock, Drumcondra, Fairview, Cabra and the area around Mountjoy Square. Interrupted schooling and James' occasional truancy from Belvedere College afforded him the opportunities to explore the city.

The untypically long stay of four years in North Richmond Street provided fertile ground for the imagination of the eldest son, and the characters he observed in this working class neighbourhood people his novels.

If the Joyces had never moved from Brighton Square it is hard to imagine how Ulysses and the other Joyce classics would have been infused with such a complex and rich tapestry of life.

OSCAR WILDE'S HOUSE, 21 WESTLAND ROW

The house in which Oscar Wilde was born in 1854. A year later the family moved to number one, Merrion Square.

SEAN O'CASEY'S HOUSE

BRAM STOKER'S HOUSE, MARINO CRESCENT

It's a far cry from the chilling Transylvanian world of the tormented un-dead to the pleasant surrounding of Marino Crescent where probably not even a harmless bat ever bothered to venture. Yet number 15 is where, in 1847, the author of one of literature's most blood-curdling and macabre tales of all time, Dracula, was born.

Abraham (Bram) Stoker was the the third of seven children. After university he followed his father's footsteps and entered the civil service. He loved the theatre, became a drama critic and attracted the attention of Henry Irving. Stoker agreed to join Irving at the London Lyceum Theatre and thus ensued a successful business partnership which was to last for nearly 30 years.

After Irving's death in 1905 Bram Stoker gradually succumbed to increasing ill-health brought on by years of overwork and finally seven years later, he died. "Exhaustion" was the cause noted on his death certificate.

It is hard to imagine that the writer of children's stories and a treatise called "The Duties of Clerks of Petty Sessions" could also be the master of terror whose books are awash with blood, shadowy tombs and the machinations of dark powers. One explanation may be that his imagination was fuelled by the stories his parents related about the horrors of the cholera epidemics and famines of the 1830s and '40s.

Marino Crescent was built in 1792 by a painter named Ffolliot who, bearing a grudge against Lord Charlemont, erected the curving terrace of houses to deny a view of the sea to the Earl from his Marino House.

17

GARDEN OF REMEMBRANCE, PARNELL SQUARE

On Easter Monday, 1966, the golden jubilee of the 1916 Rising, President de Valera officially opened the Garden of Remembrance, which was built to honour the memory of those who gave their lives for Irish freedom. The idea for the garden had been first suggested to the Government in 1935 by the Dublin Brigade Council of the old IRA. The chosen site, part of the once fashionable Rotunda Gardens, had special significance. It was here that Óglaigh na hÉireann was founded in 1913 and after the surrender on the Saturday of Easter week the rebel prisoners were stockaded overnight here in the open.

Daithí P. Hanly won the prize in a 1946 competition for a design for the garden and work began to his plans 15 years later.

The garden, with sunken pedestrian areas and a pool, is basically cruciform in shape with a curving 12-feet-high marble wall enclosing it from the rear. The floor of the pool displays a mosaic pattern of blue-green waves interspersed with weapons from Ireland's Heroic Age, 300 BC-300 AD. The spears are shown broken, following the Celtic custom of throwing weapons into lakes and rivers when hostilities ended, perhaps as votive offerings to the gods of the district.

The decorative railings protecting the lawns have features copied from the originals in the National Museum — the Brian Boru harp, the Loughnashade trumpet (100 BC) and the Ballinderry sword (200 BC), pointing downwards to indicate peace. *(See page 19)*.

The bronze central sculptural group, weighing eight tons and standing 25 feet high, is by the late Oisín Kelly, and was cast in the Marinelli Foundry in Florence. The design was largely inspired by William Butler Yeats's poem "Easter 1916". To embody the concept that at certain moments of history men are "transformed utterly", Kelly decided on the theme of four human figures being transformed into swans, symbolising rebirth, victory and elegance underscored with a hint of pathos. This obviously echoes our mythological story of the Children of Lir.

The garden is beautifully maintained by the Commissioners of Public Works.

CHILDREN OF LIR

ST. MARY'S HOSPITAL, PHOENIX PARK

In the grounds of St. Mary's Hospital stands a curious monument dedicated to the "memory of the old boys of the Royal Hibernian Military School who laid down their lives for King and Country in the Great War of 1914-1918". Of the 1,250 "Hibs" who went into the trenches 80 perished.

The present St. Mary's was originally the Royal Hibernian Military School which had been founded in 1764 and granted a Royal charter and a site in the Phoenix Park five years later by George III. Although organisationally run on army lines the school was not a military academy as such but was primarily intended as a boarding school for orphaned children of deceased British Army soldiers.

With the withdrawal of the British Forces in 1922 the "Hibernian" was transferred to Shorncliffe and two years later absorbed into the Duke of York's Royal Military School near Dover.

ġaıRóın cuımneacaın

cuıreamar ar n-aıslınʒ aʒ snámh mar eala ar an abhaınn

Rınneaóh fírınne óen aıslınʒ.

Rınneaóh samhraóh óen ʒheımhreaóh

Rınneaóh saoırse óen óaoırse

aʒus óʼpháʒamar aʒaıbhse mar oıóhreachτ

a ʒhlúnτa na saoırse cuımhnıʒı oraınne, ʒlúnτa na haıslınʒe.
Uam mac uısτín

SA ROTUNDA
RINK A RAIBH
A SKUIMH SNA
CAIRÓEN TROBH
LEIS SEO A BUN
AIOÓH OÓLAICH
NA h ÉIREANN
25 SAMHAIN
1913

Details from the gates and the inscription panel of the Garden of Remembrance. The monument on the right commemorates the founding of the Volunteer Movement in 1913.

IRISH NATIONAL WAR MEMORIAL, ISLANDBRIDGE

When the senseless carnage that was the Somme, Verdun and the Marne was finally halted and the Irish nation counted the tragic toll of its dead sons, there was a groundswell of opinion that a suitable memorial should be erected. A committee was formed and, after its first meeting in the Viceregal Lodge in 1919, a fund was launched which raised £45,000 within a year.

The memorial record of the listed 49,400 Irishmen killed — the actual figure was incalculably very much higher — was compiled and a hundred copies published in 1923. The committee searched for a site and was offered the Longmeadows Estate, Islandbridge, by President W. T. Cosgrave in 1929.

Work commenced in late 1933 under the direction of the Board of Works and Sir Edwin Lutyens, R.A., famous for designing many stately gardens and responsible for the layout of New Delhi including the Viceroy's Palace. It was completed in 1939 and cost £56,000. Judging from old colour photographs the landscaping of the memorial was spectacular and incomparable with anything else in the city.

The Memorial is now being restored to its former glory by carrying out necessary repairs, replanting trees to replace the removed elms, and setting in roses, shrubs and flowers. The project will be carried out by the Board of Works in conjunction with the trustees of the Memorial Committee who are still responsible for the administration of the site.

The restoration should transform a relatively unknown and forgotten park into one of Dublin's most magnificent.

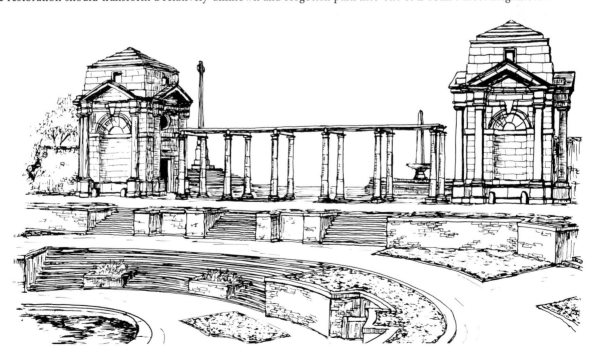

GOVERNMENT BUILDINGS

Designed by Sir Thomas Manly Deane and Sir Aston Webb work commenced on this group of buildings in 1904 and took 18 years to complete at a cost of £500,000. The Departments of the Taoiseach and Finance are among the occupants of this complex.

Chapter Two

The Powers That Be

Government

The Treaty was signed with Britain in December 1921 and after the Civil War ended in May 1923 the government of the new Irish Free State was able to concentrate on the business of reorganisation and reconstruction. The General Post Office, Custom House, Four Courts and O'Connell Street were rebuilt with great integrity. Government departments moved into the grandiose and recently finished complex on Upper Merrion Street and into countless other public buildings. Leinster House, built in 1745 for Lord Kildare and up to 1922 occupied by the Royal Dublin Society, was purchased to house the Oireachtas (upper and lower houses of Parliament).

The economy from the 1930s to the 1960s provided very little cash for ongoing maintenance so when the boom of the mid-sixties arrived the growing number of government employees were anxious to move to more modern premises. A rash of uninspiring office blocks appeared everywhere and many of the former public buildings sank into further deterioration.

Economic restrictions and public service cutbacks brought in following the oil crises of the 1970s and a worsening national debt situation put an effective brake on further inane office development. Attention was again drawn to the condition and environmental value of the still existing stock of old buildings and a programme of necessary, but by now very expensive, restoration was initiated on many fronts.

In March 1987 there were 15 Government Departments (which is the maximum number fixed by the Constitution) led, of course, by 15 Ministers and an equal number of Ministers of State. Every department is a separate legal entity. Of the country's 30,200 civil servants 22,000 are located in Dublin administering public expenditure programmes which in 1986 amounted to £8.1 billion representing 49% of G.N.P. and collecting revenue of £6.7 billion or some 41% of G.N.P. The civil servants are also assisted by 300,000 Public Service employees of whom the majority are based in Dublin. Government office space in the capital occupies a total acreage of 4.8 million square feet or about 100 acres (40 hectares).

In 1987 the country faced a crippling and massive public debt — total income tax receipts were being swallowed up in merely servicing the interest on this debt.

In an effort to achieve unprecedented cutbacks in all areas of Government spending no institution, no matter how traditional or sacrosanct, was to be immune from possible elimination or reduction. A time of radical change had arrived.

Dublin Corporation

In 1172 King Henry II granted by charter the city of Dublin to his men of Bristol, and by this and the charter of 1192 Dublin Corporation came into being. In 1215 a Provost was appointed as the principal civic officer and feudal overlord of the city.

The office of Mayor dates from 1229 and the first holder of the title was Richard Muton. Although the Mayor was granted the title of Lord Mayor in 1641 it was not until 1665 that the Corporation availed itself of this right and elected Sir Daniel Bellingham as the first Lord Mayor.

By the passing of the "Municipal Corporation Act 1840", the original Charters (102 of them dating from 1172 to 1727) and Grants were in some respects altered or completely annulled. The first person to be elected as Lord Mayor by the Reformed Corporation, as it was styled, was Daniel O'Connell.

Today Dublin Corporation handles an annual budget of £331 million and employs 8,200 staff. The City Council consists of 52 Councillors of whom 12 are Aldermen (those who receive the highest vote in each of the 12 electoral districts). The present area of the city (i.e. excluding the suburban County Council territories) is 28,400 acres and the population in 1986 stood at 502,337. The population of the City and County exceeds one million.

CITY HALL

Thomas Cooley designed the City Hall which was built between 1769 and 1779. It was commissioned as an exchange for the Society of Merchants and became known as the Royal Exchange.

During the 1798 Rising the Exchange was converted into a military interrogation centre. Daniel O'Connell made his maiden public speech here in 1800.

In 1851 the building was handed over to Dublin Corporation by the Merchant Guild of the Holy Trinity. Since then the city council has met here in the converted coffee room of the old guild.

Lined by sculptures and decorated by mosaics and frescoes the centre rotunda is certainly worthy of a visit.

GENERAL POST OFFICE, O'CONNELL STREET

FUSILIERS' ARCH, ST. STEPHEN'S GREEN

MANSION HOUSE

ÁRAS AN UACHTARÁIN

GENERAL POST OFFICE, O'CONNELL STREET

The G.P.O. was erected between 1814 and 1818 and it extended at that time for only 120 feet down Henry Street. The architect was Francis Johnston.

In March 1916 the public office was reopened after extensive modernisation. One month later it and the whole building except the facade lay in rubble. The G.P.O. had been occupied as the virtual headquarters of the Rebels during the 1916 Rising and it had been set ablaze by the British artillery.

In 1929 a reconstructed G.P.O. opened again for business. Advantage had been taken of the destruction in Henry Street and the length of the building on that side was extended to 330 feet. A further extensive renovation was carried out in 1984 to mark the occasion of the creation of An Post, a semi-state company which had been formed from the old Department of Posts and Telegraphs. *(See illustration page 23.)*

FUSILIERS' ARCH

The first battle of the Boer War started at 2.30 p.m. on the 20th October 1899 when the Royal Dublin Fusiliers clashed with Luke Meyer's scouts at Smith's Nek Pass, east of Dundee.

In 1907 the Duke of Connaught opened the triumphal arch, erected at the Grafton Street end of St. Stephen's Green, as a memorial to the officers and men of the five battalions of the Royal Dublin Fusiliers who fell in the war. The names of some of the battlefields are carved around the arch and those of the dead are inscribed in panels over the gates. *(See illustration page 23.)*

MANSION HOUSE

Dublin had a residence for its Lord Mayor some 15 years before London when in 1715 the Corporation purchased Joshua Dawson's town mansion.

It is essentially a red bricked Georgian house now rendered with cement and embellished with Victorian trappings. The Round Room beside the Mansion House was built in 1821 for a visit of King George IV and it was here that the adoption of the Declaration of Independence in 1919 and the signing of the 1921 Treaty took place. The Mansion House is open to group visits by prior arrangement. *(See illustration page 24.)*

ÁRAS AN UACHTARÁIN

The only glimpse the public usually gets of Áras an Uachtaráin is through a formal break in the shrubbery along the main road of the Phoenix Park. This view is not unimpressive, but the overall size of the building including the east and west wings and adjoining outhouses is far larger than anticipated.

The original house was only the size of that section visible to passersby but without the columns. It was designed and built in 1751 for Nathaniel Clements the deputy Vice-Treasurer of Ireland, appointed in that year as Park Ranger and Master of the Game.

In 1782 Clements' house was purchased by the English Government and an attempt was made to induce the co-operation of Henry Grattan, the leader of the opposition in the Irish Parliament, by offering the house to him. He refused the overture. From 1787 an ambitious programme of renovation, expansion and enhancement was then carried out on the house to make it a suitable summer residence for the Lord Lieutenant. Known as the Viceregal Lodge it became a popular retreat for the Viceroys and their court followers.

Additions carried out to Clements' house included a north Doric portico and a south-facing Ionic portico, the latter designed by Francis Johnston. He also built extra wings which were further extended in 1848 and in 1911 the bedroom wing (now the President's private quarters) was completed.

The visits of various monarchs was often the spur for such improvements. George IV came in 1821, Victoria visited on four occasions (an evergreen tree she planted on the lawn is now a towering specimen), Edward VII was thrice greeted here and the last royal welcome was for George V in 1911.

After independence the Viceregal Lodge was handed over and from 1922 it was the residence for a while of the Governors General. In 1938 it became Áras an Uachtaráin with the arrival of our first President, Dr. Douglas Hyde.

Since then beautiful stucco work to ceilings and wall panels has been executed with even complete ceilings being transferred from houses threatened with demolition. *(See illustration page 24.)*

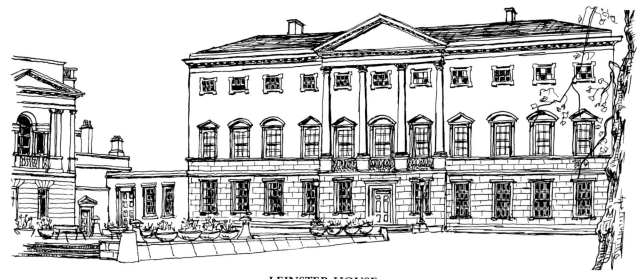

LEINSTER HOUSE

Built in 1745 by Richard Cassels for Lord Kildare, Duke of Leinster. It was the largest private mansion in the city. The Royal Dublin Society purchased the property in 1815 and over a period of time the Society added various other commendable buildings which have since evolved into the National Gallery, Natural History Museum, National Library and National Museum.

Leinster House was purchased for £68,000 from the R.D.S. in 1922 to accommodate Dáil and Seanad Éireann.

A number of improvements, additions and conversions have since been carried out and a significant restoration to the Seanad Chamber is next on the list.

IVEAGH HOUSE

Built in 1736 for Dr. Robert Clayton, the Protestant Bishop of Cork and Ross, the house passed through a parade of owners until Benjamin Lee Guinness purchased the property in 1856. He bought next door and the two houses were remodelled as we see them now.

In 1939 Rupert, the second Earl of Iveagh, presented the house to the Irish nation and ever since it has been the headquarters of the Department of Foreign Affairs.

Iveagh House, which for obvious reasons is not open to the general public, has one of the most sumptuous interiors in the whole of Dublin. The city and country has indeed been fortunate to inherit this and some other fine properties which have been made available through the generosity of various people.

26

THE CUSTOM HOUSE

The Custom House is the masterpiece of James Gandon, the greatest architect in the history of Dublin. The design was commissioned by John Beresford, Revenue Commissioner, who induced Gandon to forsake Catherine the Great's invitation to design new public buildings in St. Petersburg. Russia's loss was certainly Dublin's gain.

Building commenced in 1781 and it took ten years to complete at a cost of £210,000. The architecture of the Custom House was without precedence in Ireland and it is believed to have influenced Edwin Lutyens' famous Viceroy's Palace in New Delhi.

The Custom House Docks, now the site for Dublin's most ambitious renewal project to date, was laid out at the same time.

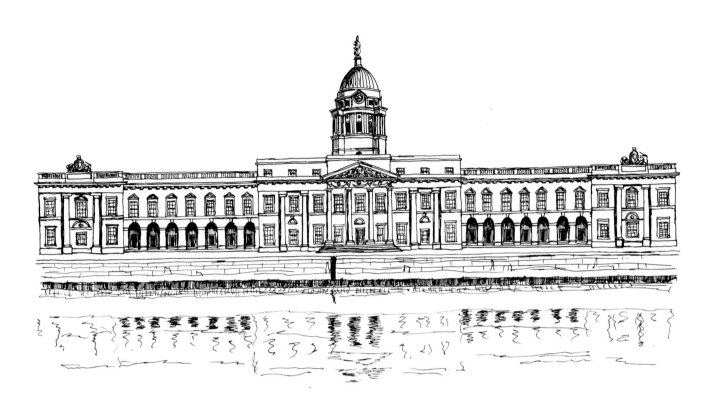

CUSTOM HOUSE RESTORATION

The Custom House has suffered many travails since its foundation stone was laid in 1781. Protesting mobs continuously harassed the initial construction phase and in 1789 a fire took place in the partially completed building. Another blaze nearly consumed the edifice in 1833 but fortunately it was reconstructed although the original interior was largely altered.

By far the greatest disaster to befall the stricken Custom House occurred after a fire started in May, 1921, during an engagement between the authorities and the IRA. Fuelled by tons of furniture and paper files the conflagration raged for days and from the evidence of molten brass the heat must at least have reached an awesome 1,850 degrees Fahrenheit, the temperature at which brass melts. The cracking of stonework due to cooling — some of the cracks were an inch wide — continued for six months afterwards.

The damage was so extensive that many thought that the gutted building would have to be demolished and others pressed that as it had represented British imperialism no effort should be made to save it anyway.

However, the basic fabric still appeared sound and good counsel prevailed. Dublin's main architectural glory was saved and at a cost of £300,000 the necessary reconstruction was carried out in 1926.

After the deterioration of some stonework became apparent in 1979 a detailed examination was ordered. Damage from the fires had been more deep-seated than was earlier understood, which may have been just as well or the 1926 reconstruction might have been aborted altogether. Also the stonework had become affected by atmospheric pollution and chemical interactions. Additionally the metal bands surrounding the building behind the facades had lost their lead casings in the 1921 fire and the resultant expansion from rusting was shattering the Portland, limestone and granite facings.

Since 1984 painstakingly slow, complex and detailed repairs have been carried out by the main contractor, John Sisk Ltd., under the direction of architects from the Office of Public Works. But even at a cost of millions of pounds their efforts will be well worthwhile as the Custom House is recognised to be one of the most notable buildings of its era, not just in Dublin but in the world.

CUSTOM HOUSE SCULPTURES

The sculptures were executed by Dubliner Edward Smyth. He fashioned the statue of Commerce on the dome, the Riverine Heads, the figures in the tympanum and the Arms of Ireland.

The Riverine Heads
These superbly carved heads are emblematic of 14 main rivers of Ireland. Dublin is represented by Anna Livia which is the only female head in the group. She is crowned with fruit and flowers and with a trident symbolising her importance as a seagoing port. The heads form keystones at various points throughout the ground floor.

The Arms of Ireland
These Arms differ from the more usual Royal Arms showing the Union of England, Scotland and Ireland through the Rose, Thistle and Shamrock. Here the Kingdom of Ireland is represented by the Shield and Harp surmounted by the Crown. The Lion and Unicorn are common to both types of Arms.

THE OFFICE OF PUBLIC WORKS

The Office of Public Works (O.P.W.) is responsible for the construction and maintenance of government and public buildings, for the upkeep and protection of national monuments and parks, arterial drainage, harbours, and our embassies abroad.

It was founded in 1831 and is supervised by a Board of Commissioners under the direction of the Minister of State at the Department of Finance.

Recently, the O.P.W. has skilfully and magnificently restored many fine buildings including the Casino at Marino and the Royal Hospital at Kilmainham and is currently working on Dublin Castle, the Custom House, the King's Inns, and the Phoenix Park among others.

Its headquarters is situated at 51 St. Stephen's Green.

THE ORDNANCE SURVEY OF IRELAND

Luke Gardiner was appointed Keeper of the Castleknock Gate, Phoenix Park, in 1728 and he built the house that was to become from 1825 the headquarters of the Irish Ordnance Survey.

Ireland has the distinction of being the first country in the world to be entirely surveyed on a scale sufficiently large to show all property boundaries. This Trigonometrical Survey, as it was termed, was carried out between 1825-1846 to calculate more equitable land valuation and taxation.

DUBLIN CITY COAT OF ARMS

The Coat of arms was first granted officially to Dublin Corporation in 1607 by Daniel Molyneux, Ulster King of Arms and Principal Herald of All Ireland. The Three Castle symbol of the city, however, is a much more ancient device and goes back to the Middle Ages.

The City Seal (opposite) is 13th century and is the earliest item in the City Regalia. Showing the city under siege, two sentries on the central watch tower are sounding the alarm, two heralds on the walls are doing likewise and on top of the gate towers two archers are aiming their crossbows. The decapitated heads of three transgressors are impaled over the gate as a grisly warning. On the second bronze seal (not illustrated) — two moulds were used to make the double sided wax impression — the scene depicts the city at peace as signified by a merchant ship at sea. Stamped around the rim of both seals are the words "Sigillum Commune Civium Dublinie" or "The Common Seal of the City of Dublin".

Over time the three watchtowers became separate castles and the soldiers were replaced by leaping flames symbolising the zeal of the citizens to defend Dublin. The City Coat of Arms (the example below right is taken from the mosaic on the floor of the City Hall Rotunda) displays the Three Castles on a shield flanked by two figures holding olive branches. Law also grips a sword and Justice holds out a scales. Groups of flowers represent Hope and Joy. The city's motto "Obedentia Civium Urbis Felicitas" roughly means "Obedient citizens make for a happy city".

The Lord Mayor's Coat-of-Arms features the City Sword, the City Mace and the Cap of Maintenance. The example below is copied from the front of the Mansion House.

CITY SEAL

LORD MAYOR'S COAT-OF-ARMS

CITY COAT-OF-ARMS

CITY REGALIA AND ROYAL CHARTERS

The city regalia is the name given to the unique collection of ancient artefacts which form the insignia of the office of Lord Mayor. Dublin saw the election of its first Mayor in 1229 and in 1665 the title was enhanced to Lord Mayor.

The City Sword is late 14th century and is believed to have been given to the city by Henry IV who laid down in his Charter that a Sword Bearer was to carry the implement before the Mayor in procession. It is fifty-four and a half inches in length.

In 1665 Sir Daniel Bellingham, the first Lord Mayor, provided himself with a Great Mace which, with the City Sword, was to be carried before him on formal occasions. Made of silver gilt and measuring sixty and three quarter inches in length the mace is identical in size to that of London.

The original Great Chain of Office was a gift from Charles II but it disappeared after the Battle of the Boyne. In 1698 King William of Orange issued the replacement that is still being worn almost 300 years later. Each alternate link consists of the letter "S" standing for "Sovereign". Other links represent a harp, a portcullis, the Tudor Rose and the Trefoil-shaped Knot which is the floral device of Ireland. The large gold medal is stamped with the bust of William.

King Henry II granted his first Charter in 1172 (illustrated) and between then and 1727 one hundred and two Royal Charters were bestowed on the city. They were granted to convey certain rights and privileges on the citizens and thus secure their continued loyalty. The Charters form the basis of our municipal legislation.

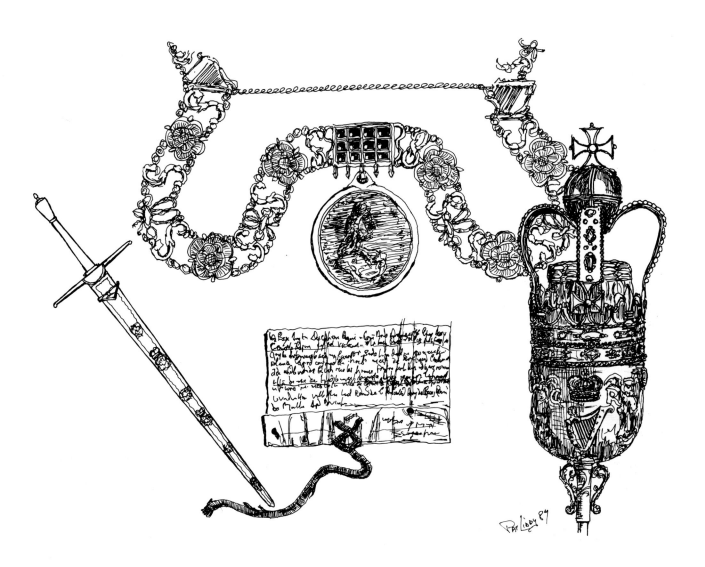

An example of the new Inner City Housing in Sean McDermott Street.

CORPORATION HOUSING

At the beginning of this century the near intact Georgian and Victorian architecture and streetscapes of Dublin seemed to reflect charm, character and a slightly faded magnificence but behind the veneers of past glories lay some of the worst slums in Europe. After 1922 it became an urgent national policy to ensure, as far as the limited resources of the economy would permit, that every family would obtain a dwelling of good standard at an affordable rent.

Families were relocated to such places as empty army billets while the tenements in "obsolete areas" were demolished. New flat complexes were built on the cleared sites but as these alone could never have accommodated the vast numbers displaced new municipal housing estates were developed in such suburbs as Crumlin, Cabra, Marino and Whitehall in the 1930s and Ballyfermot, Ballymun, Finglas and Coolock in the 50s and 60s.

Major building programmes were undertaken between the years 1932-38, 1948-56 and 1967-84. Altogether over 76,000 dwellings have been provided. Initially they were rented to tenants but under a purchase arrangement introduced in 1968 about 37,000 of these units are now owner-occupied.

Building of large estates has virtually ceased now with supply nearly balancing demand due to the advent of smaller family sizes and the vacating of Corporation houses by tenants who had availed of the £5,000 Surrender Grants Scheme.

From the mid 1970s there has been a switch in the inner city from the building of flats to the provision of single family houses two or three storeys high. These award-winning houses have been deservedly praised and have added a new vitality to areas such as Ringsend, Summerhill, City Quay and the Liberties. Nearly 2,500 of these dwellings have been constructed in the last 10 years.

The elderly have been especially catered for in two storey blocks of flats which are equipped with common rooms, communal kitchen facilities and a round-the-clock warden service. Senior citizens are now also being accommodated in delightful little brick bungalows grouped around landscaped gardens.

The Corporation housing record is one of the country's greatest achievements since Independence, and in conjunction with private developments it has been claimed the Dublin probably has the best housed population of any major European city.

PUMPING STATION, PIGEON HOUSE ROAD

The city's 19th century main sewers, most of which are still in use, were very solidly constructed in brick, sometimes two layers thick. They were formed into a clever ovoid shape so that their tapered bottoms provide sufficient depth and velocity of flow even when the volume of liquid is low.

Along the sewers are depressions called catch-pits where heavy foreign objects can fall and gather and these have to be cleared out by the resolute catch-pit gangs. So the next time you drop your false teeth, jewellery or money down the loo — all of these are amongst the lost items reported regularly to the Corporation — spare a thought for the searchers!

Initially disgorging their noxious contents directly into the unfortunate Liffey, the main sewers were linked, during a vast scheme undertaken by the Corporation in the 1890s, to interceptor pipes running parallel along both banks of the river. These two pipes join together under Hawkins Street where a massive eight feet diameter pipe propells the wastes by gravity fall to a sump underneath the Pumping Station at Pigeon House Road.

The pipe is by now several metres below sea level so that the task of the station's electric pumps is to raise the wastes to a higher main for transport to the treatment works.

Commissioned in 1906, the immaculately maintained pumping station has been replaced by a more modern facility built nearby, which has four times the previous capacity.

PIGEON HOUSE HARBOUR

Incongruous as it may seem at first, Dublin Corporation is actually the owner of two sea-going vessels. Their use is, however, very much in keeping with the management of an essential city service — sewage disposal.

The first boat, a steamship, christened Shamrock, was commissioned in 1906. She was replaced in 1958 by the twin diesel Seamróg II, built in the Liffey Dockyard to the specifications of the Corporation. Its 350 ton capacity is now no longer adequate, so an additional ship, at 293 feet twice the length of the Seamróg, was purchased from Thames Valley Water Authority. The name, Sir Joseph Bazalgetti, was retained in honour of this eminent British sewage system engineer who, coincidentally, was also associated with the 1906 construction of Dublin's pumping station. My drawing shows the Sir Joseph Bazalgetti passing the harbour mouth on its way to the purpose built jetty after the discharge (literally!) of its duty.

33

CLEANSING DEPARTMENT

Every year over 196,000 tons of refuse are collected in the Dublin City Area (excluding the County area). This includes more than 15,000 tons of litter and rubbish removed each year from streets and laneways.

MAIN DRAINAGE SCHEME

The Main Drainage Division is engaged in the maintenance of 2,000 km of sewers and 50, mostly culverted, rivers. It also operates 24 pumping stations including the newly commissioned main lift pumping station at Ringsend. This station has a capacity of 323 million gallons per day (17,000 litres per second) and is reputed to be Europe's largest.

The Greater Dublin Drainage Scheme was inaugurated in 1986 after 15 years' work and an expenditure of £60 million. As well as providing for the development of the new town areas it provides for the upgrading of the existing sewage system and gives a major improvement to water quality in both the Liffey and in Dublin Bay due to the elimination of untreated sewage discharges.

WATERWORKS DEPARTMENT

The rivers Liffey and Poddle provided the early needs of the citizens but not without attendant health hazards from waste pollution. In the 18th century the two canals supplemented the increasing need but again there were serious risks to wellbeing.

A proper water supply began to emerge from the new "City Basin" reserve, off Blessington Street, in 1722. It is now a duck pond and there are plans to stock it for fishing. The first real progress towards establishing an abundant flow of pure water for Dublin came through Sir John Gray who, as chairman of the Dublin Corporation Waterworks Committee from 1863 until his death, introduced the Vartry water supply to the city.

Today the three Water Treatment Works at Ballymore Eustace, Roundwood and Ballyboden produce 64 million gallons per day for the Greater Dublin area.

Examples of some older lamp standards which still grace many central city streets.

PUBLIC LIGHTING DEPARTMENT

During 1986 Dublin Corporation allocated over £5 million on public lighting maintenance and upkeep of 36,000 street lights in the city. In 1986 over 300 locations were upgraded which meant the replacement of older lighting with more efficient high pressure sodium fittings. The need to improve the daytime and nighttime appearance of the centre city streets has been recognised and more decorative columns are being used where possible.

34

ROADS AND TRAFFIC DEPARTMENT

This department is responsible for the construction and maintenance of the city's roads, footpaths and bridges.

A considerable achievement in 1986 and 1987 was the upgrading of the pedestrianised Henry Street and Mary Street. New environmental road and pavement surfaces were laid and decorative street lamps were erected.

Two new pedestrianised routes have been identified — one to link Grafton Street with Henry Street via the Halfpenny Bridge, the other to join Grafton Street with South Great George's Street. Work will continue in upgrading all these routes.

There are plans to reinstate the remaining locations where cobbles and setts still predominate and the endangered granite kerbstone will be retained in all city centre paving.

Some new routes exclusive to cyclists were opened but this programme is only in its infancy.

A view of the newly upgraded pedestrian route at the corner of Liffey Street and Henry Street.

WEIGHTS AND MEASURES DEPARTMENT, HARRY STREET

The Weights and Measures Department operates a consumer and legal metrology service and any member of the public is entitled to refer appropriate complaints to its inspectors. Their investigative processes fall into two categories; verification and inspection.

Verification involves the complete testing of new and repaired measuring equipment ranging from large industrial packaging machinery to the humble weighing scales in your local grocery. Inspectors check and seal meters such as on home heating oil road tankers and garage petrol pumps. The bagging and selling of coal, the grading of eggs, the capacity of pint glasses, the quantity in bottled gas cylinders, the deliveries of milk and grain, the alcohol percentage is bottled spirits and the pressure, purity and calorific value of gas supplies are some of the items that come under regular scrutiny. The correct pricing per weight and the authentic labelling of all prepackaged food also receives close attention.

The inspectors have to check off their everyday equipment against the Corporation's main collection of brass and stainless steel weights and measures. Although many of these latter high-precision instruments were manufactured over 100 years ago by Yeates of Dublin they are still lovingly kept in mint condition. At fixed intervals they have to be sent to the Institute for Industrial Research and Standards for verification with the State Standards.

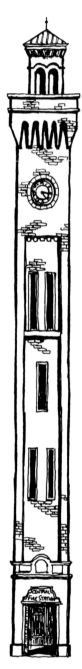

CENTRAL FIRE STATION TOWER, TARA STREET

THE FIRE SERVICES

The Dublin Corporation Fire Brigade Act of 1862 organised fire fighting in the city on a professional basis for the first time.

There are now 14 stations scattered throughout the city and the force of nearly 700 are equipped with 23 appliances and 11 ambulances. The number of fires attended to in 1986 amounted to 5,373 and ambulances were called out on 28,898 occasions.

The 125 feet high tower of the Central Fire Station in Tara Street. This station, which was erected in 1907, will soon be redundant but the tower with its replica Big Ben clock and lookout balcony is to be preserved.

36

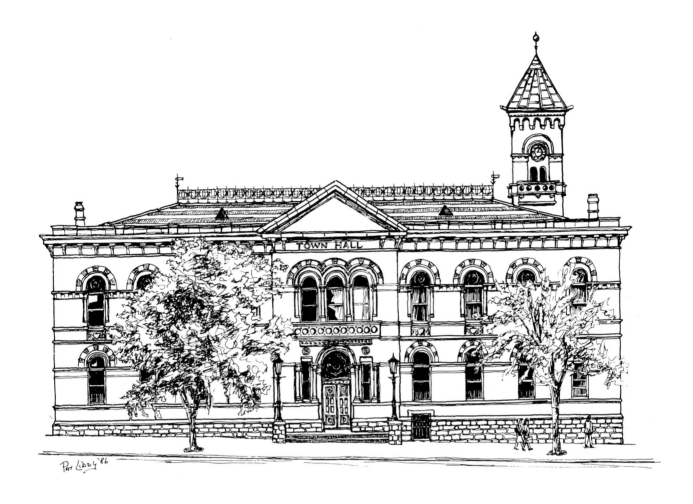

DUN LAOGHAIRE TOWN HALL

For a brief period in the 5th century Dun Laoghaire reached prominence as the site for the dún or fort of High King Laoghaire who occupied himself with hostile excursions against the western seaboard of England and Wales. However, the little fishing village soon reverted back to relative obscurity from which it did not emerge for close on another 1,400 years.

Previously anglicised to Dunleary, the town was rechristened Kingstown in 1821 to honour the visit of King George IV. The name reverted to Dun Laoghaire in 1921.

1834 was a milestone year for the growing town. A railway line — Ireland's first — was opened from Dublin and this venture coincided with the final closedown of Howth as a mail packet station in favour of Kingstown. The same year marked the constitution of Kingstown as a township and its eventual promotion to an urban district followed in 1899. An amalgamation in 1930 with the previously autonomous urban districts of Blackrock, Dalkey and Killiney/Ballybrack formed the present Borough of Dun Laoghaire.

The Town Hall, designed in a grand Venetian style by J. L. Robinson and costing £18,000 was opened in 1880. The extensive refurbishment carried out for its centenary celebrations included the restoration of some fine ceiling frescoes rediscovered under layers of paint.

The vestibule is impressive and is lit by a number of stained glass windows, some of which contain the borough's crest depicting a mitre, crown, tower and Viking ship.

Chapter Three

Courts and Castles

For many centuries the question of Law and Order employed the minds and energies of the Dublin authorities mainly in how to deal with the resentful native Irish who regarded them as the unwelcome representatives of an occupying power.

Throughout the Middle Ages and indeed down to the 18th century law enforcement was more concerned with putting down rebellion than in ensuring and protecting the rights of all the citizens.

Places of detention were grim to say the least. In converted towers, castles and purpose-built prisons like the infamous Newgate Jail prisoners were tortured, flogged, executed or prepared for deportation. The physical and mental health of the inmates was of no concern to their jailers unless a generous bribe was proffered.

Courts initially were under the jurisdiction of the Church and the Corporation and in time they became independent and respected law-giving institutions. But they could be still biased towards the British point of view.

The Victorian era brought a more enlightened approach to the treatment of convicted criminals where the process of rehabilitation replaced draconian and counter-productive punishments. Deportation or execution still awaited treasonable acts but commutations were now more freely applied. Older gaols were closed down (although Kilmainham remained to haunt Irish nationalism until Independence) and more humane establishments like Mountjoy Jail were opened.

Unfortunately, as with most Western democracies, the late 20th century has brought an upsurge in litigation which has swamped the courts and an increase in crime which has overcrowded the prisons.

Castles have always had a significant place in the topography of Dublin. The Anglo-Normans built them to defend newly conquered territories and until the English exerted firmer control outside of the greater Dublin area (known as the Pale) they had to ring the county with an extensive series of fortifications. Many of these still remain, some in ruin while others are in an excellent state of preservation.

Of the extensive system of walls and towers which once surrounded the core of the medieval town some sections as in Cook Street, High Street, Ship Street and inside Dublin Castle itself can still be seen.

Once the city expanded beyond the walls little need was seen for their retention and they decayed or were dismantled to re-use their stone.

Dublin was not a wealthy city, a fact reflected in the building of Dublin Castle. It was never a pretentious or large castle in the accepted sense and it was barely adequate for the job as Ireland's administrative centre. Except for some towers and a series of important excavations little remains to remind one of a castle but these medieval remnants and the splendid 18th and 19th century additions are now being refurbished as part of a multi-million pound restoration programme.

DRIMNAGH CASTLE

Drimnagh Castle is unique for Dublin in that it is still surrounded by a water-filled moat. The structure is now being restored by An Taisce and AnCO.

38

SHIP STREET ENTRANCE TO DUBLIN CASTLE

Turning in off Upper Stephen Street into the gently sloping and narrow Great Ship Street you are at once aware of the cobbled roadway and the brooding but richly atmospheric hulk of the former Ship Street Barracks. Further down, the road bends sharply to the left where it becomes Little Ship Street.

Located at this point is a rear entrance to Dublin Castle. The old gatehouse is still perched over one of the arches. Immediately inside this gateway is where the EEC Conference Centre is being built.

Ship Street derives its named from "Sheep" rather than from any sailing vessel, although the now enclosed Poddle River flows directly underneath. In medieval days the Poddle was used to fill the moat surrounding Dublin Castle.

It is a great loss that within the city today we cannot see even a small portion of this historic river, whose waters were once the life blood of the old town.

One of the very few serious assaults on the Crown's bastion took place in 1534 from Ship Street. Lord "Silken" Thomas Fitzgerald attacked the castle walls but was driven off by superior cannon fire. Part of Stanihurst's Tower, one of the city's 32 towers and gates, which must have borne the brunt of Fitzgerald's foray, still stands, as do sections of the wall on either side.

On the rising ground behind Stanihurst's Tower lies Hoey's Court, the birthplace of Jonathan Swift in 1667. The original Dutch-styled house has long vanished and the site is now occupied by an employment exchange.

RECORD TOWER

39

RECORD TOWER, DUBLIN CASTLE

The longest surviving near-intact structure of Dublin Castle is the massive 16-feet thick south-eastern corner tower now known as the Record Tower. Erected around 1205 it is probably the oldest secular building still standing in the city. It received its present title in the early 19th century when it became the repository for historical and state papers. This conversion included the punching of windows through the walls and the addition of a top storey and battlements. An unsightly concrete hut on the roof is a reminder that the tower served as a gun platform during the Emergency.

Before it became known as the Record Tower it was variously called the Black Tower, the Gunners' Tower and the Wardrobe Tower, the latter originating from the 18th century when it contained the Royal Robe and the other trappings of official ceremony.

The tower was also used as a state prison up to the 1700s and many believe that it was from here that Red Hugh O'Donnell made his two famous daring escapes in the bleak winters of 1591 and 1592.

Now one of the most important links with the castle's historic past, the tower was almost demolished 200 years ago but was sensibly saved to be included in Francis Johnston's plans for a new Royal Chapel.

Replacing a succession of churches going back to the foundation of the castle, Johnston's Chapel Royal was a rich example of the emerging Gothic Revival style and was built between 1807 and 1814 at a cost of £42,000. The church is noted for the internal plasterwork, the oak wood carvings, the coat-of-arms of all the Viceroys and especially for the 90-odd heads carved in limestone by Edward Smyth and his son John. Mostly representing English monarchs, the heads also include St. Peter, Dean Swift (the north door), Brian Boru and St. Patrick (the east door).

Renamed the Church of the Most Holy Trinity, it was adapted for the Roman Catholic services in 1943 and is presently closed for renovation. *(See illustration page 39.)*

POWDER TOWER, DUBLIN CASTLE

After the fire of 1684 destroyed the viceregal quarters in Dublin Castle the medieval fortress, never popular anyway with resident Lord Deputies, was largely dismantled and more stately accommodations were constructed. Except for the Record Tower, part of the Birmingham Tower and some adjoining wall the fortifications were either destroyed or swallowed up inside new buildings. The western turret of the gateway was used to support the present Bedford Tower and the Powder Tower at the north-eastern end of the Castle (behind City Hall) was buried beneath the Chief Secretary's offices.

An extension to this latter building was later erected over the old moat. However as the contractor was unable to strike bedrock even at 33 feet below ground level he constructed the extension over a foundation of granite lintels and wooden beams. The wood eventually rotted causing irreparable structural damage. The recent demolition of this block has again revealed the impressive remains of the Powder Tower with its widening base batter and the excavations are adding much additional information to our knowledge of the medieval castle.

An important section of curtain wall and a substantial part of the old city wall joining onto the Powder Tower have also come to light. The city wall at this point is supported by an archway which presumably allowed the moat to be filled with water. This archway was blocked up sometime in the 14th or 15th centuries.

The moat itself, which protected the western and northern walls (the River Poddle served this purpose on the other two sides) was considerably larger than earlier thought. It was 60 feet wide and over 30 feet deep. This mammoth ditch also conveniently supplied the kalp limestone and black mudstone used in the construction of the castle.

The exciting rediscovery of the Powder Tower is being taken into account by the Office of Public Works in their major reconstruction programme for Dublin Castle and the plans for the lower levels of the new building are being amended to ensure that the walls and the tower base will be preserved and exposed for public appreciation. *(Not illustrated.)*

FOUR COURTS

In 1785 James Gandon took over Thomas Cooley's design for the Four Courts when the latter died. The new building was designed to replace the old laws courts near Christ Church Cathedral.

It is one of Dublin's finest buildings and it richly counterbalances the Custom House further down the quays.

The "Four Courts" were actually five in number and they were the Courts of Chancery, King's Bench, Judicature, Exchequer and Common Pleas. *(See illustration page 41.)*

BEDFORD TOWER, DUBLIN CASTLE

The building known until recently as the Genealogical Office is being restored to its original status as a two-storey structure. The third storey had been added in the last century.

Designed by Thomas Ivory as apartments for the Master of Ceremonies, the building was erected between 1750-1760. The first-floor balcony was provided for the State Musicians who performed before the assembled officials and the garrison cavalry on special occasions such as royal birthdays.

It later became the Office of Arms and it was from here in 1907 that the so-called Irish "Crown Jewels" were mysteriously filched under the very noses of armed sentries. They have never been recovered. The Genealogical Office and the unique Heraldic Museum were the last occupants before structural faults forced the building's evacuation in the early 1980s.

Over the two gateways stand the statues by John Van Nost. "Fortune" guards the western gateway which had always been a blind gate but is now being opened to lead to a bridge over a symbolic moat to Castle Street. "Justice" bestrides the eastern entrance. Because she faces inwards Dublin cynics used to bemoan that Justice had turned her back on the city. Further caustic comments were engendered when her scales used to dip unevenly. It seems rainwater used to fill one of the trays (the other was protected by the outstretched arm). A solution was found by boring holes in both trays.

The Bedford Clock Tower, named after the Lord Lieutenant, John Russell, Duke of Bedford, was constructed over the base of the original western gate tower of the medieval castle. *(See illustration page 41.)*

FOUR COURTS

BEDFORD TOWER

O'CONNELL MONUMENT

The monument, sculptured by Dubliner John Henry Foley and finished after his death by his assistant Brock, was unveiled in 1882.

Erin holds up a copy of the 1829 Act of Emancipation to Daniel O'Connell. About 30 more figures represent the church, the professions, the arts and the working classes.

The four winged victories, some displaying neat bullet holes from the 1916 Rising, symbolise the virtues of Courage, Fidelity, Eloquence and Patriotism, said to be the hallmarks of O'Connell's career.

THE STATE APARTMENTS, DUBLIN CASTLE

In 1684, when fire suddenly broke out in the viceregal quarters of Dublin Castle, the Lord Deputy, the Earl of Arran, barely escaped with his life. Clad only in his night shirt he directed operations and to prevent the fire from spreading to the gunpowder store in the Powder Tower and to the State Records repository in the Birmingham Tower, he ordered the blowing up of the connecting buildings and walls. This action marked the end of the medieval fortress and introduced the changeover to a more fashionable palace.

Designed by the Surveyor-General, Sir William Robinson, the Lord Deputy's new apartments were ready by 1688. Throughout the next century the Upper Yard (roughly the area of the old castle enclosure) took on the form we know today. In 1779 it was said that "this castle is far superior to the palace of St. James as well as in the exterior, as the size and the elegance of the apartments within".

Shielded from the sights of oppression, hunger and poverty outside the castle walls, the administration led a fanciful existence. The authorities and the upper classes amused themselves with a busy round of splendid state and ceremonial events, occasional visits from royalty and the balls, receptions and levees of the "Castle Season" which lasted from February until St. Patrick's Day.

This fantasy-land was finally dispelled in 1922 when the last viceroy, Lord Fitzalan, handed over the castle to the Provisional Government. Such were the pent-up feelings towards the previous incumbents that the State Apartments' rich collection of furnishings, works of art and the trappings of colonial power were in danger of being removed. Only the wise and provident council of Eamon de Valera saved them, when he insisted that they were now part of our heritage.

Today the State Apartments are a major attraction and a fitting location for formal state occasions such as Presidential inaugurations and during the periodic presidency of the EEC.

HOWTH CASTLE

Howth Castle owes its origins to the Norman knight, Sir Almeric Tristam, who wrested the peninsula from the Norsemen in 1177. Sir Almeric assumed the name St. Lawrence (possibly after St. Laurent in France) and his direct line of succession ruled across the vicissitudes of Irish history without interruption until 1909. The ultimate earl's nephew, Julian Gaisford, then came into the inheritance and his family still own the castle.

Nothing remains of the original fortifications, but the square gate tower is probably mid-15th century. Additions and embellishments were commissioned at various times including some work carried out this century by the eminent architect Sir Edwin Lutyens.

Famous sea-borne visitors to the castle included Lord Mountjoy in 1600, the Duke of Ormond on his return as viceroy in 1662 and Queen Victoria and Prince Albert in 1853. Grainne Uaille (Grace O'Malley), the pirate queen, was denied hospitality in 1575 and, taking umbrage, she kidnapped the young heir apparent. The young lad was returned when his father promised never to close the gate again at dinner time.

The deformed skeleton of a 400-year-old elm tree, opposite the gate tower, is regarded with some respect. Legend has it that if a limb should fall off then surely a member of the St. Lawrence family will die.

Christopher Gaisford-St. Lawrence, the present owner, has been responsible for making the castle demesne so much part of the Howth social and cultural life.

SWORDS CASTLE

Swords was an important village long before the Norsemen first established their base or longphort at Dublin in 841. In the mid 6th century St. Columcille placed St. Finian as the first abbot of his monastery at Swords of which the 75 feet round tower is the sole surviving structure. The lure of the monastery (where, incidentally, the bodies of Brian Boru and his son Murrough were rested overnight after the Battle of Clontarf in 1014) proved too much for the rampaging Vikings who plundered it no less than six times between 1012 and 1166. Even the King of Meath, not to be upstaged by mere foreigners, sacked the village in 1185.

In 1200, Swords passed under the rule of the Normans and John Comyn, the first Norman Archbishop of Dublin, built, in the style of a strong castle, his archiepiscopal palace here. In times of turmoil the local population sought refuge behind the protective walls of the castle until the defences crumbled under the onslaught of Edward Bruce in 1316. Judging his palace now untenable the archbishop moved residence to Tallaght in 1327.

The early abandonment of the castle probably saved it from further destruction and today it survives in remarkable condition. The outer curtain wall, or baun, survives almost intact as do large portions of the watch towers. Sections of the chapel and the Constable's residence remain but the soldiers' quarters, stables, kitchens, dairy, granary, workshops and great hall have long since disappeared.

Formerly under guardianship of the Office of Public Works the castle has been acquired by Dublin County Council who are now undertaking feasibility studies with regard to a possible restoration programme and its future use as a local community and tourist centre.

CLONTARF CASTLE

The first castle was erected in Clontarf after the Norman invasion by one Adam de Phepoe. A commandery of the Knights Templars was later established on the grounds and after their suppression it passed to the Knights Hospitallers.

Another invasion in 1649 brought an imposed new owner to Clontarf Castle. He was John Vernon, Quartermaster General to Oliver Cromwell's army and he began the long succession of his family's tenancy which only ceased in the middle of the present century.

The old castle fell into decay and was totally reconstructed by architect William Morrison in 1835. An attempt had been made to preserve the Norman tower but faulty foundations frustrated this endeavour. In any event the 70 feet high tower was rebuilt in the fashion of the original keep and the rest took the form of Tudor revival (described by the *Penny Journal* of 1840 as "perhaps the purest specimen of Tudor architecture to be found in Ireland").

Fixed over the main entrance is the heraldic badge of the Vernons featuring the bear and accompanying family motto: *Vernon semper viret* — Vernon always flourishes.

After the Vernons departed in the 1950s the castle lay empty and was in danger of being demolished only to be saved when a new use was found for it as an entertainment centre. However, it was not until the present owner took possession around 1973 that a systematic lengthy and costly programme of refurbishment was undertaken and is still continuing. Restoration of the previously neglected tower, reroofing of the entire complex, remoulding of decorative timber beams, the addition of stained glass windows, tapestries, period pieces (some salvaged from the condemned or remodelled buildings) more than compensated for having to partition off part of an open gallery over the Great Hall and its sweeping staircase.

Clontarf Castle is a good example of the difficulties and compromises that must be faced up to when adapting an old building to a purpose never originally envisaged for it but now necessary for its survival.

RATHFARNHAM CASTLE

Rathfarnham Castle (not illustrated) was purchased by the state in February 1987. It dates from Elizabeth I and was continuously occupied from 1585 until vacated by the Jesuits in 1985. It was redecorated with fine Georgian style interiors in the 18th century.

BULLOCK HARBOUR

Before the development of Dublin Port many of the small inlets skirting the bay served as landing places for city-bound traffic. Bullock Harbour, more important than its size might suggest, was used both as a passenger and as a fishing port. In the 16th century, records show at least two Lord Lieutenants among its prestigious arrivals.

The small walled town of Bullock (from the Norse, "Bloyke") was administered from the 12th century by the powerful Cistercian Abbey of St. Mary whose religious and temporal rule mainly extended over much of the city north of the Liffey. The Abbey maintained their own fishing fleet and also exacted a toll of one fish from every fishing boat using Bullock.

The Norman castle dates from either 1132 or 1170 — sources on the exact date vary. After the suppression of the monasteries in 1537 the castle was granted to a Peter Talbot. It was garrisoned again with the outbreak of the Royalist wars with the Parliamentarians in the 1640s. During this period over 50 men, women and children were drowned by Parliamentarian troops off Bullock while attempting to flee the pogroms in the city.

In the 1920s the castle was bought by the Maguire family, direct descendants of Cuconnacht Maguire, the Gaelic chieftain who helped procure the ship for the Flight of the Earls from Lough Swilly in 1607. The Maguires reroofed the castle and in 1947 repointed the stonework.

Bullock Castle and grounds were sold in 1961 to the Carmelite nuns, who subsequently built a home there for the elderly, while preserving the fortress and the adjoining house.

MALAHIDE CASTLE, CO. DUBLIN

Malahide Castle was not merely a castellated residence but was built as a genuine fortress in more troubled times. The Knight, Sir Richard Talbot, arrived from Shrewsbury with King Henry II in 1177. Prince John granted the lands of Malahide to Sir Richard who then took up residence on the present site in 1185.

Down through the centuries the castle was extended and strengthened, and in the 14th century it formed part of the perimeter defences of the Pale. One of the present castle's towers dates from that period.

In 1649 the Talbots fell foul of the Cromwellians and lost the castle and lands. In 1665, following the restoration of the Monarchy, the property was returned to the Talbots. In 1690 the family backed another loser, James II, and fourteen Talbot cousins died at the Battle of the Boyne.

Sadly, when Milo Talbot died in 1973, his sister had to sell the castle to pay the death duties. At this time the house contained a remarkable collection of 17th and 18th century paintings, furniture, manuscripts, silver, armoury and other artefacts which were internationally sought after. The loss of these items to the country would have been a cruel blow so several interested bodies came together as a matter of urgency and a plan was formulated.

Dublin County Council bought the castle and the 268 acres of land as a public amenity. They in turn leased the castle to Dublin Tourism who, with a subvention from Bord Fáilte, bought much of the furniture at the public auction. Most of the art collection was, however, lost to overseas buyers. The National Gallery then stepped in and granted the National Portrait Collection on indefinite loan. Since then many other acquisitions have been made by purchase, gift or loan.

The castle is open to the public all year round.

ROUND TOWER, LUSK

St. MacCuillinn was appointed first bishop of Lusk in 497 and he is credited with founding the abbey there. The peaceful and scholarly pursuits of the monks and the surrounding community lasted over 300 years before they were shattered by a series of destructive raids.

Being situated near the coast Lusk was easy prey to the Vikings who pillaged the abbey in 827 and again in 856. Next it was the turn of the Irish themselves who were often more vengeful and merciless than the Norse. On no less than four occasions marauding Irish war lords sacked Lusk. In the 1089 assault 180 people, who had taken refuge in the abbey church, perished.

A remarkable survivor of all these attacks and the subsequent passage of the centuries is the round tower, the only remnant of the early monastery. Ninety-five feet high with walls four feet thick the structure is an excellent example of an Irish round tower. It has a single entrance doorway facing east, little apertures which light the landings and four small windows at the top, each facing a cardinal point. These towers were unique to Ireland and were no mean achievement for their builders as the use of stone and mortar had only been introduced into the country around the time of the early Viking incursions. Usually resorted to for protection during a raid, the towers by their very design, acted as giant chimneys when a determined enemy lit a fire at their base thus smothering or burning the trapped and terrified refugees.

All that remains of the Anglo-Norman church, built to replace the original abbey, is a square battlemented tower rounded on three corners with the fourth corner linked to the old round tower. The present church attached to the east side is comparatively recent, dating from 1847. It contains an interesting folk museum.

MARTELLO TOWERS

Blunting a massive attack by sea and land in 1794, the little round defensive tower at Cape Mortella, on the Corsican coast, finally capitulated only after the wooden roof went up in flames. So impressed was the British Admiralty with the firepower potential and virtual impregnability of this tower that it ordered similar structures to be built to guard its strategic colonial harbours.

In the shadow of a Napoleonic invasion threat, 74 such towers were erected in Ireland between 1804 and 1815, mainly along the east and south coasts. They were almost forty feet high, the walls eight feet thick and, averaging £1,800 in cost, they each took six months to build. A single or brace of 18-to-24-pounder guns was mounted on a traversing roof platform. Built into the parapet was a shot furnace which could re-heat the iron cannon balls for the purpose of setting ships alight.

The doubtful effectiveness of the towers in the Irish context was never battle-tested. With the passage of time most of them fell into disuse, while some were garrisoned into this century. In 1904, Oliver St. John Gogarty rented the Sandycove Tower from the British War Office, but had to wait until the military vacated it before he could move in with James Joyce as co-tenant.

Most of the 28 towers in a line from Balbriggan to Bray Head have survived and are variously used as residences, shops, cafes, a Joycean museum or lie empty and forlorn.

On Tuesday 27th June, 1922, while the opera Samson and Delilah was playing to a packed audience in the Gaiety Theatre the Provisional Government was planning an assault on the Four Courts. Two months earlier anti-Treaty forces had commandeered Gandon's masterpiece and now, in the early hours of Wednesday morning, columns of nationalist troops were fanning out to surround them. The Civil War was imminent.

At the first light of dawn hostilities commenced and a battery of four 18-pounder field guns began to shell the defences. At 12.30 on Friday a devastating explosion, set off by an Irregulars mine, wrecked the central area of the Four Courts and shattered windows as far away as Grafton Street. Dense, billowing clouds of black smoke gushed from the ruins and the spreading conflagration triggered off more detonations from ammunition caches. Occupation became untenable and the defenders surrendered.

The explosions had ripped through the Record Office and huge quantities of charred and tattered pieces of paper showered down on streets and back gardens all over the city, even as far away as Ballsbridge. These remnants were all that remained of the vast collection of the country's public records dating back to 1174. The Government quickly issued urgent appeals to the public to return any rescued fragments. The loss of deeds, leases, parish registers (ironically deposited for safety), ecclesiastical records, wills, legal cases, bills of exchange etc. has left us with a great void in our historical records.

At least the restoration of the building was a crowning achievement as only the solid granite walls had been left standing. The reconstruction was completed in one year less than the ten years it first took to build the Four Courts. The official opening took place on the 12th October, 1931 and once more wigs and ermine graced the walnut and oak panelled courtrooms. (See also page 41.)

KING'S INNS

This was Gandon's last great public building. The foundation stone was laid in 1795 but the building was not finally finished until 1827. It is shared by the Honourable Society of the Benchers of the Inns (the organisation for barristers) and the Registry of Deeds.

The King's Inns gets its title from the days when barristers lived as well as studied here. An age old custom still survives where barristers-to-be must eat a certain number of dinners at the Inns before qualifying.

Now undergoing a massive restoration the King's Inns is unique in that it contains the only interior of Gandon to survive in a major public building i.e. the dining room. All of the great architect's other interiors have been radically altered, bombed or burnt.

KILMAINHAM JAIL

The Paris mob made its legendary assault on that symbol of repression and tyranny, the Bastille, on 14th July, 1789. Such was the popular hatred towards the Bastille and all it had stood for, that within a few years it had been totally dismantled. Yet, barely two years before the Paris uprising, the foundations for an equally grim institution were being laid in Kilmainham. Indeed the Dublin authorities, fearing a spread of the French revolutionary ideals to these shores, carried out further expansions to the original plans for the jail and thus delayed the official opening until 1796.

The dark corridors, punishment cells and dungeons were soon filled with a succession of political prisoners that was to last for nearly 130 years. Among the first to arrive

were Henry Joy McCracken and many of his United Irishmen associates. The insurgents of 1798 were soon followed by the supporters of Robert Emmet's abortive revolt of 1803. Emmet himself spent a few hours in the jail before his hanging in Thomas Street.

The jailers were provided with a plentiful supply of "guests" resulting from the Young Irelanders' Rising of 1848, the Fenian Rising of 1867 and the activities of the Land League in the 1880s. Executions carried out included the five Invincibles found guilty of the murder of Cavendish and Burke in the Phoenix Park. The signatories of the 1916 Proclamation and most of the other leaders of the Easter Rising were shot by firing squad in the stone-breaking yard.

The War of Independence brought in fresh captives, and the final chapter was opened during the Civil War when the Free State incarcerated and executed Anti-Treaty soldiers here. The last prisoner to be held in Kilmainham Jail was Eamon de Valera, who was released on 16th July, 1924.

The fortress-like prison rapidly fell into serious decay and the roofs caved in. Nothing was done until an enthusiastic committee, inspired by Lorcan Leonard and P. J. Stephenson, delivered a set of proposals. The Office of Public Works granted a lease to a Board of Trustees and in May, 1960, the task of restoration commenced. The result today is truly astonishing, considering that most of the work was carried out through voluntary effort.

In 1986 the OPW took over the management of the jail and the museum is presently being upgraded.

KILMAINHAM JAIL INTERIOR

Interior view which has remained mostly unaltered since the jail was last used. The dark and dank corridors, thick iron doors, punishment cells, the chapel, the hanging room and the execution yard can still be seen in their original condition.

A significant museum, with items relating to the 1916 Rising as its core collection, is currently being enhanced and expanded.

The jail is open from 2 p.m. to 6 p.m. on Wednesdays and Sundays.

KILMAINHAM JAIL Rear view of the fortress-like structure.

MOUNTJOY JAIL

Lord Mountjoy (Luke Gardiner) had planned an ambitious scheme which he named the "Royal Circus". He had projected a majestic circle of stately mansions with several grand boulevards radiating out from the centre. Eccles Street was to have been one of these approaches but the whole development evaporated when Lord Mountjoy met his untimely death at the hands of the Wexford insurgents at New Ross in 1798. His dream is at least commemorated by the naming after him of an institution which today stands on the perimeter of his proposed project, Mountjoy Jail.

Victorian concern with the welfare of inmates, who were crowded into dark and grim prisons or deported on the dreaded convict ships, brought about some dramatic improvements. Pious aspirations that prisoners might now have a real opportunity to repent and offer penance for their injury to society led to the new generation of jails being called penitentiaries.

Known affectionately as "The 'Joy", Mountjoy Jail was built between 1847 and 1850. The prison initially housed 808 inmates and each was allocated an individual cell. The architectural arrangement was based on Pentonville Prison (considered the model prison of the time) with five main wings branching out from a central block.

The Hospital Building (1887), visible from the Royal Canal, was recently converted to house prisoners transferred from the Curragh Military Detention Camp in 1983. Facilities in the prison include a centre for AnCO training courses in metal work, carpentry, welding and such like, gyms, schools and a library.

The tall chimneys, so much part of the local topography, were designed to allow a complete change of air every eight minutes throughout the prison.

Many executions took place on the scaffold or in the Execution Chamber (which is still operational). The most famous was Kevin Barry, in 1920, and the last capital punishment was carried out in 1954.

Made famous by Brendan Behan in "The Quare Fella", "The Oul' Triangle" still goes "jingle jangle" to announce the "fall in" for work every morning and Mass on Sundays.

GREEN STREET COURTHOUSE

Protected behind ever-vigilant Garda barriers is one of the city's most historic buildings. Known today mainly for its role as the Special Criminal Court, Green Street Courthouse is also the seat of the Central Criminal Court and the Circuit Court.

In this drab but atmospheric building many revolutionary notables were tried for treason. Some of the leaders of 1798 and 1848 faced the justice of the Crown here and ironically a direct descendant of Charles Gavan Duffy later became a respected judge in the same chamber. Fenians and Invincibles sat in the identical dock that is still in use today. Robert Emmet delivered his famous "Speech from the Dock" on 19th September, 1803 and leaned on the bar that is now preserved in the hallway of the Halston Street entrance. In this hallway the original door knocker of the adjoining, but now demolished, Newgate Jail is mounted in a glass case.

The last public flogging in Dublin was ordered from the Green Street Sessions Court in 1815 when "Horish the Sweep" was whipped from outside the court all the way to the Royal Exchange (now the City Hall). He had probably risked the outlawed and cruel practice of tying goose feathers or branches to young boys and dispatching them to climb up the inside of large 18th century chimneys to dislodge the soot.

The courthouse, designed by Whitmore Davis, an associate of Thomas Cooley, the architect of Newgate Jail, was opened in 1797. It was renovated in 1894 and has substantially changed little since then. The courtroom is equipped with duplicate witness and jury boxes, a legacy of less complicated days when up to six cases a day were heard. As one jury retired to deliberate, another trial was immediately proceeded with.

BLUE COAT SCHOOL, BLACKHALL PLACE

Through the good offices of the Duke of Ormond a charter had been granted to Dublin Corporation in 1670 for the erection in Oxmantown Green of a school to cater for the care and education of families found to be in reduced circumstances.

It was officially known as the Hospital and Free School of King Charles II which was generally shortened to The King's Hospital or The Blue Coat School (because of the boys' military style blue uniform).

The early building became ruinous and the architect Thomas Ivory formulated an ambitious design for a replacement. The foundation stone was laid in 1773 and the work was completed ten years later.

Due to a shortfall in expected revenues the plans were modified during construction (causing Ivory's resignation) and the tall, elegant central tower was abandoned for the out-of-scale squat alternative of today.

Of topical interest, tickets for the first Irish State Lottery held in 1780 were drawn by two boys from the school.

The students of The King's Hospital moved out in 1970 to Palmerstown. The new owners, the Incorporated Law Society, have since carried out a major refurbishment of the building.

KEVIN STREET

KILMAINHAM

STORE STREET

ORIGINAL DMP STATION LAMPS STILL IN PLACE

Note that the Kevin Street lamp still says "Police" rather than "Garda Station".

Chapter Four

The Boys in Blue and Green

The Garda Síochána

For the first seven hundred years of Dublin's existence the maintenance of law and order was, in the main, left to the military occupation forces. The law enforcement agencies of the civil powers were represented by the baliffs, beagles and watchmen. This latter group supposedly guarded the city gates, patrolled the streets and called out the time of night. But the watchmen were mostly old and semi-invalided men who were poorly paid, received no training and when not drunk themselves had developed the convenient knack of being elsewhere when trouble broke out. Their complicity in violence, abductions and robbery was not always above suspicion either.

From 1778 the presence of uniformed Volunteers brought a veneer of civic discipline on to the streets but their dissolution five years later and the resultant depression following the Act of Union in 1800 lowered the city into a fresh spate of criminality. In deprived areas ruffians and robbers proliferated with begging and prostitution becoming growth industries.

The first regular police force was established in 1785 but it only survived ten years because citizens objected to paying taxes for its upkeep. Another attempt was made in 1808 which had more longlasting results. The city was divided into six divisional areas and permanent stations were opened. However, standards of recruitment were low, proper training was non existent and many of the 850 constables and watchmen were barely fit for duty.

It was time to start afresh and reorganise a highly trained, well structured and efficiently managed police force which had the confidence both of its members and of the public. An Act of Parliament in 1836, initiated by Under-Secretary Thomas Drummond, led to the formation of the unarmed but keenly disciplined Dublin Metropolitan Police more popularly known as the DMP.

Under the new legislation Lt. Col. Augustus Cuyler, late of the Coldstream Guards, vacating the office of Military Secretary in Ireland, and John Lewis More O'Ferrall, a barrister from Ballyna, near Enfield, Co. Kildare, were appointed Justices of the Peace "for improving the police in the district of the Dublin Metropolis". These two men set about their awesome task with flair and determination and virtually disbanded the old organisation. Recruitment to a high standard of physique and character was undertaken immediately and in a few years the new force had firmly grasped the nettle of lawlessness. In 1858 arrests numbered 42,509, of which 6,137 were for larcenies, 18,198 for drunkenness (females accounted for almost 7,000 in this category), 6,251 for disorderly conduct and 2,849 for prostitution.

Resented by many, this sudden upsurge in police activity was not without cost to the enforcers themselves as 4,183 of the apprehensions were for assault and obstruction of the officers. A journal of 1852 related that, despite the fact that the majority of the constables were at least six feet tall, 70 of their number were "grievously and seriously" injured in the previous year. The same publication reported that by then the force numbered 1,099 men of all ranks, including 103 sergeants and 12 detectives, spread over 16 station houses covering an area of 44 square miles.

Dogged dedication to duty and a firm but fair enforcement of the laws eventually won for the DMP the respect and admiration of the population. Because it remained unarmed and was not used as an oppressive force like the Royal Irish Constabulary the DMP retained public support even throughout the traumatic period 1916-22.

In 1925 the Dublin Metropolitan Police was amalgamated with the Garda Síochána.

It might be interesting to compare the Dublin Metropolitan Area (DMA) of the Garda Síochána today with that of the DMP for 1852 mentioned above. In 1986 the DMA consisted of 3,013 uniformed officers and 950 detectives spread over 5 divisions. Each division, controlled by a chief superintendent, is subdivided into a number of districts which are known by their alpha call signs e.g. "B" District for Pearse Street, "C" District for Store Street and so on. Nationwide there are almost 11,400 Gardaí operating from 701 stations.

In April 1987 the colour of the uniform was changed from a dark navy to a lighter blue.

The Permanent Defence Force

Preceding chapters have already accounted the tramping of several foreign armies — Viking, Anglo Norman, French, Spanish, Dutch, Scottish and English — over the soil of Ireland. From the late 17th century no Irish army was again to take the field for over another 200 years. True there were insurrections and popular uprisings but on the whole these were poorly organised and of brief duration. Even the 100,000 strong Volunteers, formed in 1778, engaged in little more than sabre rattling before voting themselves out of existence five years later.

We had to wait until the 25th November, 1913 when, with a great surge of national feeling, 8,000 men launched the Irish Volunteers at a public meeting in the Rotunda Rooms. The onset of the Great War sucked away many of these fervent early recruits when they answered the call of King and Country. Altogether 318,000 Irishmen are estimated to have left for the trenches of Europe. The depleted Irish Volunteers did, however, continue to drill and make threatening noises and hundreds of them joined combat with the British Army in the abortive Easter Rising of 1916. From 1918 the Volunteers, supporting the establishment of an independent Irish Parliament, became known as the Irish Republican Army.

The IRA possessed a sound military structure but avoided pitched formal battles preferring instead the hit and run tactics of guerilla warfare. After the Treaty with Britain in December 1921 the IRA, now

SENIOR ARMY OFFICER'S CAP BADGE

"FF" is the abbreviation of Fianna Fáil which, loosely translated, means Soldiers of Destiny.

53

numbering 114,000 combatants, began to organise itself into a regular army. The numbers needed for such a force were reckoned to be in the region of only 4,000 but the Civil War (1922-23) negated this calculation and by April 1923 the strength of the army stood at 55,000. (By 1927 this figure had been successfully reduced to a more manageable 11,000.)

The Civil War ended in April 1923 and an Act was passed to establish and maintain an armed force for the defence of the Free State. It was to be called Óglaigh na hÉireann. The foundation for the Permanent Defence Force had been laid.

In the Army today there are four territorial commands i.e. the Eastern, Western, Southern and Curragh and each is led by a Brigadier General.

Dublin falls within the Eastern Command whose headquarters is located in Collins (formerly Royal) Barracks. Other barracks in Dublin include Cathal Brugha (Portobello), McKee (Marlborough), Clancy (Islandbridge) and Griffith (Wellington). This compares with the British days when at the peak of their military presence there were seven major permanent barracks, eight semi-permanent posts and thirty-three other temporary installations. There were also several munition works.

MAGAZINE FORT, PHOENIX PARK

On St. Thomas's Hill, overlooking Islandbridge Gate, stands the grim-looking Magazine Fort. Originally the site of Phoenix House, the 17th century summer residence of the Viceroys, the fort was erected by the Duke of Wharton between 1732 and 1735.

It was built to supplement the munitions storage in Dublin Castle and it was also convenient to the artillery practice ranges in the vicinity of the Phoenix Park. By 1797, with the threat of French invasion a recurring menace, the capacity of the fort was considered inadequate and Islandbridge (Clancy) Barracks was built to accept the army's main supply of munitions. The fort, with some extra quarters being added, settled back to an uneventful existence, which was interrupted on only two occasions.

On Easter Monday, 1916, an insurgent raiding party posed as a group of footballers and lobbed their ball in the direction of the sentries. Taken off guard the sentries were quickly overpowered and the raiders gained forceful entry, burned 150 tons of ammunition and carried off a quantity of rifles to join the fighting at the Four Courts. The fort was handed over to the forces of the Free State on 17th December, 1922, when a Captain Byrne and 50 men took possession.

The second raid took place on the day before Christmas Eve, 1939, an IRA squad accompanied by 40 lorries took advantage of the festive mood and managed to take complete charge of the Fort. They captured rifles, machine-guns and over a million rounds of ammunition. Concealment of such a vast quantity of equipment proved impossible and it was all recaptured in one week. From then on no further munitions were stored there.

There have been suggestions to turn the fort into an army museum and this scheme should receive every encouragement. It is an excellent example of defensive architecture. With an unrestricted view for miles, the bastion is surrounded by three fences and a moat (once filled with water and crossed by a drawbridge). The thick walls, containing little recesses for holding powder and shot, are made of granite and are served by catwalks and five gun turrets. Set between the twisting cobbled paths are many buildings suitable for displaying garrison life down the centuries.

Dean Swift wrote of the Fort:
"Behold a proof of Irish sense;
here Irish wit is seen;
When nothing's left that's worth defence,
We build a magazine".

BEGGARS' BUSH BARRACKS

A main approach to the city once cut through the lands of the Earl of Pembroke with the sea on one side and the great estate on the other. It carried considerable traffic mainly comprising the well-to-do, business and officialdom. In the hope of receiving offerings, beggars and vagrants congregated in the wooded area, which eventually became known as Beggars' Bush.

The barracks was built in 1827 as a recruiting depot to train soldiers for service in Portobello, Richmond and Royal Barracks. It was used mainly by infantry although gun carriages for the Royal Artillery were also stationed here. During the "Troubles" the barracks contained a large force of troops and some dreaded auxiliaries also operated from it. Many executions were carried out within the walls including that of Erskine Childers.

In spite of the protection of thick, fortified walls, complete with rifle loopholes, the interior yards were very vulnerable to sniper fire from the high houses ranged along its outside streets. It was the first Dublin barracks to be taken over from the British Army when Commandant Paddy Daly occupied it on 31st January, 1922. It became a recruiting post again, this time for the National Army during the Civil War.

The barracks is now totally demilitarised. The Government Stationery Office has been in residence since 1922 although it is moving out for larger premises in the future. The large brick office block for the Department of Labour and the Geological Survey of Ireland now dominates the far end of the barracks. Several films were shot on location among the rambling and atmospheric old military quarters, including "Young Cassidy", "The Quare Fellow" and "Strumpet City". The Irish Labour History Society has been granted the lease of the main building (see illustration) for a permanent labour museum.

The strange-looking bollards lining the Haddington Road frontage of Beggars' Bush Barracks are actually real naval ordnance emplaced upright into the grass verge along the footpath over 150 years ago. The guns were once linked together by iron chains but these have since been removed.

With each weighing over half a ton, the cannon, according to P. D. O'Donnell in his "Barracks and Posts of Ireland", are believed to have at one time formed the complete heavy armament complement of a Royal Navy frigate which was refitted during a Dublin stopover. The eighteen and nine pounder guns have been dated back to 1760 and have an emblem of King George III struck into them.

A map of 1838 records 56 guns in situ but the collection now stands at only 43. Two others are being held in storage awaiting replacing when the temporary entrance to the Government Stationery Office is resealed. I have been unable to determine the whereabouts of the remaining 11 guns.

During the 18th and 19th centuries it was quite common in these islands to purchase redundant cannon — for about ten shillings each — and use them for fencing or as bollards to protect a building's corner or entrance from being damaged by cartwheels. A cannon ball was usually wedged halfway into the muzzle mouth. So popular did the practice become that, from the 1820s, iron foundries produced imitation cannon and examples of these can still be found around the city including Thomas Street, Smithfield and one in the Civic Museum.

Left as they are the cannon are now no more than a curiosity totally lacking visual impact. Perhaps those flanking the main entrance could be left upright but they need to be set into a paved or cobbled area for greater effect and linked again with chains. The remainder could then be lifted and mounted on simple carriages behind the two lines of upright guns. If they were then placed on two stepped-up levels, representing a tiered Man-of-War, Dublin would gain a unique and significant tourist attraction.

ARMY HEADQUARTERS, PARKGATE

Eighteenth century enlightenment made the not unsurprising discovery that soldiers, like the rest of men, benefitted from specialised care when they fell ill. To this end the Army rented the top floor of Dr. Steeven's Hospital at a cost of £500 per annum. With the posting to Dublin of an ever increasing number of regiments it was decided to build two hospitals for the exclusive use of the army. One was sited at Arbour Hill and the other, the Royal Military Infirmary, was built between Infirmary Road and the Phoenix Park.

The first patients arrived to the Royal Infirmary in 1790 and found an elegant building well equipped with modern plumbing. The rooms were large and airy and convalescents could take their constitutionals along the gravelled banks of a wooded valley situated immediately opposite the front of the infirmary.

By 1910 the building had become outdated and a new hospital was commissioned on the site of the old structure at Arbour Hill. This replacement was named the King George V Hospital (later to become the present day St. Bricin's) and it received the transfer of patients from the Royal Infirmary in 1913.

Almost immediately the empty infirmary was taken over by British Army Headquarters Irish Command who had just vacated the Royal Hospital, Kilmainham where it had been stationed for over 150 years. It was from Parkgate that operations were directed by the Commander-in-Chief, Major General Friend, against the insurgents of 1916. Patrick Pearse was taken there to sign the unconditional surrender on the 29th April.

In May, 1923 the General Headquarters of the Free State Army moved to the Royal Infirmary from Portobello Barracks and have remained there ever since.

1916 MEMORIAL, ARBOUR HILL

A memorial on the spot where the leaders of 1916 were buried in quicklime was first mooted in 1928. A stained glass window in memory of all who died from 1916 to 1923 had been erected in the nearby Church of the Sacred Heart four years earlier so this latest suggestion was turned down by the Chief of Staff.

However the graves were already a place of pilgrimage and in 1948 the idea of a suitable memorial was again raised, this time with success. Erected in 1956, the memorial comprises three paved terraces backdropped by a curved wall on which sculptor Michael Biggs inscribed the Proclamation of the Republic in Irish and English. The names of the leaders are carved on the curb surrounding the burial plot: Thomas J. Clarke, Thomas McDonagh, Patrick H. Pearse, Edward Daly, Michael O'Hanrahan, William Pearse, Joseph Plunkett, John McBride, Con Colbert, Eamonn Ceannt, Sean Heuston, Michael Mallin, James Connolly, Sean McDermott.

ARBOUR HILL

Arbour Hill, on a site now occupied by St. Bricin's Hospital, started life in 1797 as a military infirmary and provost's prison. Rows of army stables, some of which still stand today, extended from the infirmary to the rear of the Royal (Collins) Barracks. Conveniently built only a year before the 1798 Rebellion the prison received captured insurgents many of whom were brutally tortured and murdered. Wolfe Tone died in captivity in Arbour Hill.

The new detention barracks (now used as a civilian prison) and the adjoining church were opened in 1848 and the grim provost's prison was closed down. Primarily intended for military personnel the detention centre played unwelcome host to a succession of political prisoners from Fenians to Sinn Féiners. Patrick Pearse was incarcerated on the 30th April, 1916 and he and thirteen of his fellow rebel leaders, all shot in Kilmainham Jail, were buried under quicklime in a plot behind Arbour Hill Prison. The site of their burial was turned into a worthy memorial in 1956.

In 1922 the Irish Army took over the prison. During the Civil War more prisoners arrived including Eamon de Valera. Political internees, including Brendan Behan, were again detained during the 1940s but in 1964 Arbour Hill ceased as a military prison.

The garrison church, renamed the Church of the Sacred Heart, was consecrated to the Roman Catholic faith in 1927 and is frequently used for army ceremonial events. The repatriated body of Roger Casement lay in state here in 1965, a reminder that he was lodged in the adjacent prison before his deportation and execution in England.

Hanging from the galleries of the recently renovated church are some old Army and Brigade flags and the flags "laid up" from returned units serving abroad with the United Nations. A wooden altar in the church came from the chapel of Kilmainham Jail before which the leaders of 1916 heard their last Mass and Joseph Mary Plunkett married Grace Gifford on the 3rd May, 1916, the eve of his execution.

GRIFFITH BARRACKS

Griffith (Wellington) Barracks was not a purpose built military establishment but was initially constructed as a remand prison. Known as the Richmond Male Penitentiary — the female version was across the Liffey at Grangegorman — it once had Daniel O'Connell as a "guest".

In 1877 it was transferred to the War Department but it was not until fifteen years later that the first unit, the Royal Munster Fusiliers, arrived. This same regiment took part in the attack on the South Dublin Union in 1916.

The troops in Wellington had their share of ambushes, killings and misadventures during the War of Independence but they could still display a great sense of chivalry, decorum and discipline when they handed over the Barracks to Captain Jim Harpur and his four Irish Army platoons on the 11th April, 1922. After Beggars' Bush it was the second barracks to be taken over from the British.

Griffith Barracks, as it was now called, suffered a surprise attack on unarmed parading soldiers during the Civil War as a result one man was killed and twenty others were wounded. During the Second World War (the Emergency) the 14th Battalion stationed at Griffith had to provide garrison duties for Dublin. Every day squads of men were sent out to guard vital institutions and installations.

The Boxing Association obtained a 99 year lease in 1939 of about half the parade ground area to build a stadium.

COLLINS BARRACKS

Collins Barracks is believed to be the world's oldest purpose-built barracks in continuous occupation. At one time it was also the largest, capable of accommodating four battalions of foot and one of horse — a total of 5,000 men.

The Duke of Ormonde's son, Lord Ossory, sold his 14-acre site to the Government in 1701 and within three years the barracks, designed by the architect of Trinity College Library, Colonel Thomas Burgh, was ready to receive the first troops. Building a barracks was a new military departure, as up to then soldiers had been billeted in the cramped confines of forts and castles, or were lodged in scattered small groups throughout towns. In the new arrangement discipline was more effectively maintained, and a more massive mustering was achievable in the event of sedition or attack.

Visitors to the city felt compelled to view this vast complex which had a frontal length of almost a thousand feet. A report of 1735 describes the establishment as "the most magnificent, largest and most commodious of its kind in Europe". First called simply "The Barracks" and then known as Royal Barracks, it remained the capital's only barracks for decades, supplying troops for various guard duties around the city. It was heavily involved in crushing the rebellion of 1798.

On Sunday, 17th December, 1922, General Sir Neville Macready took the salute of the last remaining troops to leave Dublin as they marched out of Royal Barracks. They were replaced almost immediately by two companies of Irish Army soldiers led by Captain Peter Flood.

The public waiting room in the barracks is a real surprise, for here some years ago a very talented sergeant, Michael Clarke, painted a striking mural depicting military scenes on the walls.

The two guns in the drawing are beautifully restored artillery pieces originally captured from the Russians in the Crimean War.

CLANCY (ISLANDBRIDGE) BARRACKS

Built in 1797 by convicts from the Richmond Penitentiary. In the mid 19th century mounted units including the 5th Dragoon Guards (the Inniskillings) and the 10th Huzzars were billeted here. Taken over by National Army on the 15th December, 1922.

CATHAL BRUGHA (PORTOBELLO) BARRACKS

Built 1810-1815 and occupied by a cavalry unit 4th Royal Irish Dragoon Guards, Portobello was one of the largest barracks. In 1817 over 100,000 people attended William Sadlier's spectacular balloon ascent from the Barracks. The cavalry left for the newly erected Marlborough (McKee) Barracks in 1888 and were replaced by infantry regiments.

Portobello became GHQ for the National Army in 1922 and it was from here that General Michael Collins departed on that fateful trip in August 1922 which ended in an ambush and his death at Béal na Bláth, Co. Cork.

The pacifist Francis Sheehy-Skeffington was murdered here in 1916.

ROYAL HOSPITAL, KILMAINHAM

THE CASINO, MARINO

PEARSE STREET GARDA STATION

McKEE BARRACKS

PEARSE STREET GARDA STATION

Pearse Street Garda Station is an impressive granite stone building which exudes the hustle and bustle of a busy operation having the responsibility for the city's main commercial quarter. Built in 1910 it replaced the premises in College Street and is still often referred to as "College Street" by old timers.

"B" District, controlled from Pearse Street, stretches from O'Connell Bridge down the south quays and along the inner side of the Grand Canal until it swings back from Portobello Bridge, skirts Christ Church and returns again to the quays. As well as having a fairly substantial inner-city residential population supplemented by the huge numbers of daily commuters and the large Trinity College complex, the area also boasts a lively night life. Acre for acre "B" District has to supervise the greatest concentration of licensed premises in the country.

Inside the building at the commencement of each duty the Gardaí muster in the parade rooms to receive their work allocations. The so-called "regular" shifts start at 5.45 a.m., 1.45 p.m. and 9.45 p.m. In addition to normal policing the station has also to provide security for Leinster House, Government Buildings, the Department of Foreign Affairs and the communications centre in Dublin Castle.

The fact that Ireland has a single national police force is a position we usually accept without a second thought. However, compared to many European countries and to the USA this is a rather unique situation. In the UK alone there are 43 separate constabularies, each with its own management structure.

On either side of the station's two main entrances are a pair of carved busts. One set represents the rank of inspector of the old DMP and denotes the officers' entrance. The second couple depict rank and file constables. One from each pair is dressed in a great coat, the other in his tunic. *(See illustration page 60.)*

McKEE BARRACKS

Built between 1888 and 1892, Marlborough Cavalry Barracks was initially occupied by the 10th Huzzars. The glamour and pomp of the cavalry was well matched by the magnificence and flamboyance of the barracks' architecture. In a composite of styles the ornate red-bricked buildings, unique in Irish design, sprout a symphony of towers, turrets, spires, cupolas and tall chimneys.

On the north side of the 120-yard-long square stands the Officers' Mess. Its ample rooms contain a splendid collection of military objets d'art, historical artefacts and portraits. The drawing illustrates the NCO's Mess which, along with other parts of the establishment, is undergoing sensitive refurbishment.

Flanking both ends of the Officers' Mess are the stables, originally built to accommodate over 800 horses. The billets over the east stable block were once heated by the rising body warmth of the animals. The adjacent Phoenix Park provided all the space needed for training and exercising both men and horses. During the First World War it was said that the departing cavalry men never touched soil again from the moment they mounted their steeds in Marlborough Barracks, and rode them directly on to connecting trains and ships, until they finally arrived at the battlefields of France.

Handed over to the Irish Army in December 1922, the barracks was subsequently renamed after Brigadier Richard McKee, who was killed by the Auxiliaries on Bloody Sunday, 1920.

The longest serving unit in McKee is, fittingly, the Equestrian School. Set up in 1926 to promote the reputation of the Irish horse abroad, this unique group has and still continues to singularly fulfil its role. After 1945 the school expanded to include the Presidential Mounted Escort. Founded in 1931 this unit, resplendent with sealskin busbies with plumes, colourful uniforms, swords and accoutrements, first came to prominence during the 1932 Eucharistic Congress. Alas, for organisational and financial reasons, the Blue Huzzars, as they were popularly known, were disbanded in 1948.

Perhaps the authorities might consider reforming the mounted escort. It would restore some badly needed pageantry to State occasions, would be more impressive than motorcycles, and wouldn't do our hard-pressed tourist industry any harm either. *(See illustration page 60.)*

CASEMENT AERODROME, BALDONNELL

In its varied roles the value of the modern Air Corps to this country is incalculable. On rescue missions alone hundreds of lives have been saved, thousands of patients with spinal injuries have been carefully ferried to rehabilitation centres, and hardship following severe weather conditions relieved. Other functions include maritime patrol and fishery protection, VIP and ministerial transport, Army and Garda co-operation and pilot and apprentice training.

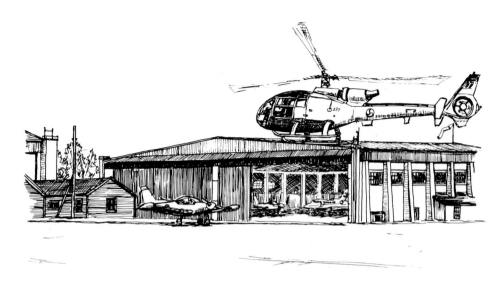

It all started in 1917 when a Captain Sholto Douglas was sent to Ireland to survey permanent sites for military airfields. He selected Gormanstown, Tallaght, Aldergrove, Collinstown and Baldonnell, the latter becoming the Royal Flying Corps headquarters in Ireland.

Immediately after the signing of the Anglo-Irish Treaty in December 1921 an Irish Aviation Department was set up at Beggars' Bush Barracks and six months later the first aircraft was delivered to the Irish Air Service, the forerunner of the Irish Air Corps. This was a Martinsyde A Mk 2 which, in fact, had been secretly purchased in November 1921 to fly out Michael Collins should the Treaty negotiations break down. By the end of 1922 the Air Corps had fourteen pilots, all Great War veterans, and as many planes.

The next two decades brought a succession of great events and famous names to Baldonnell. The German "Bremen" began the first successful east to west non-stop trans-Atlantic from here in 1928. Illustrating that, as in all armies, the paperwork must be completed, Commandant James Fitzmaurice, Baldonnell's commanding officer and one of "Breman's" pilots, had the £7.10s. cost of a sextant which he had lost on the historic flight deducted from his retirement gratuity.

In May 1936 Aer Lingus inaugurated the country's first scheduled air service when a DeHavilland 84 took off from Baldonnell to Bristol. In 1938 a puzzled "Wrongway Corrigan" arrived at the aerodrome instead of in California.

The stories and events at Baldonnell do not end here, of course, but it was from these early formative years that came the spirit of professionalism and dedication of a relatively small group with limited resources that serves us well today.

GRANGEGORMAN MILITARY CEMETERY, BLACKHORSE AVENUE

In excess of 300 people were killed as a result of the Easter Rising in Dublin. This figure included over 100 officers and men of the British Army. Many of these, including soldiers from several Irish regiments, were interred in Grangegorman Military Cemetery. The legends on some of the gravestones tell their own stories. The Irish Rugby Union Volunteer Corps erected their memorial to Reginald Francis Clery who "was shot during the Sinn Féin Rising on Easter Monday, 1916, while returning with the Corps to Beggars' Bush Barracks, aged 22".

These men rest alongside the remains of over 600 other servicemen from the First World War. The sinking of the RMS Leinster by German torpedoes when it was an hour out from Kingstown (Dun Laoghaire) on 10th October, 1918, accounts for the largest single group of burials. Only 270 of the 771 passengers — of whom 500 were soldiers returning from leave — survived. To add to the tragedy full armistice was barely one month away.

It is striking and poignant to note the extreme youth of many of the soldiers, whose ages often range from the late teens to the early twenties. Their equally young widows often lived for a further 50 or 60 years, as evidenced by several of the headstones.

Grangegorman was opened in 1878 as a family burial ground for members of the British forces and is laid out in well-ordered plots, one for each denomination. It had fallen into some neglect until the Office of Public Works took it in hand in the mid 1960s. Two years ago the OPW erected a memorial to commemorate the servicement of both world wars who are buried elsewhere in the country.

Grangegorman is now quite a pleasant and interesting place to visit, and you can ponder there on the adventurism of youth, the love of country and the futility of wars.

OLD POLICE OFFICE, DUBLIN CASTLE

A tradition spanning almost one and a half centuries was terminated when the Dublin Metropolitan Area Headquarters of the Garda Síochána finally vacated the Police Office in the Lower Castle Yard in favour of Harcourt Square. Now looking abandoned and forlorn this quaint old building was commissioned in the mid 19th century as the headquarters for the Dublin Metropolitan Police, replacing their temporary premises in Ship Street.

Every morning, in the days before telephone or radio communication, runners from each of the city's seven districts reported to the Police Office to transcribe the Orders of the Day. The police regulations provided that "the Order Books at the station houses should not be kept in a slovenly manner; the persons who take the orders at the castle must copy them into the books at the station houses and are responsible that there is no bad spelling and that the orders are copied correctly".

The drawing includes a constable of the 1850s period. His top hat, reinforced with whale bone, could be used as a platform to observe over crowds. The more familiar helmet is mentioned in the police regulations for 1889 but it had appeared at an earlier date possibly around 1870. After the Treaty in 1922 the British Crown insignia on plate badges of the helmets was changed to incorporate the Three Castles in the Arms of the City of Dublin. In 1925, with the amalgamation of the DMP and the Garda Síochána the helmet was now furnished with the latter's crest, in bright metal on the day helmet, in a dulled version on the night helmet. Helmets were discarded, and many would say for no good reason, in 1950.

GARDA HEADQUARTERS, PHOENIX PARK

Under the 1836 legislation introduced by Under-Secretary Thomas Drummond the various provincial police forces were amalgamated to form the Constabulary of Ireland. Local training depots at Phillipstown (Daingean), Armagh, Ballinrobe and Ballincollig were closed down and a new central depot was opened in the Phoenix Park. To a design by Jacob Owen, principal architect of the Office of Public Works, construction commenced in 1839 and was completed within three years.

A riding school (now the band room), a cavalry barracks, library and infirmary were soon added to the complex. As these were troubled times it had been felt necessary to throw a dry moat around the depot but this was replaced by the present railings in 1861.

In 1867 the name of the force was changed to the Royal Irish Constabulary as a mark of the British Government's appreciation of the role the police performed in helping suppress the Fenians.

After the Treaty the depot was transferred to the newly formed Civic Guard whose first units began to take up residence in December 1922. It remained the training centre for the Garda Síochána until this function was moved in 1963 to a former military barracks in Templemore.

Today the depot is the national headquarters of the Garda Síochána and houses the offices of the Commissioner and his staff. The forensic science laboratories, the new computer centre, the central stores and the very noteworthy Garda Museum and Archives are also located here.

The officers' club, formerly the officers' mess, was once a kind of international police college. Here were trained the cadre of several colonial police forces which were closely modelled on the RIC.

Exterior plastering stripped from the walls of the main building has revealed the visually more attractive granite stone masonry. Beside the main entrance gates stands the Garda Memorial which was erected in 1966 to commemorate the members who lost their lives in the performance of their duties.

KEVIN STREET GARDA STATION

Towards the end of the 12th century the first Anglo-Norman Archbishop of Dublin, John Comyn, determined to remove himself from the city's inhibiting jurisdiction. He chose a site beside his future cathedral of St. Patrick and built a palace which he named St. Sepulchre of Jerusalem.

The archbishop had been granted extensive lands around his new foundation by King John and which by royal charter later became the Liberty of St. Sepulchre. Comyn governed his territory from his episcopal palace and dispensed justice through his courts, prisons and even the gallows.

After the Reformation the palace was turned into the official residence of the Lord Deputy until the reign of Queen Elizabeth when the

restored Dublin Castle assumed this function. The Protestant archbishops returned to St. Sepulchre's until, in the face of encroaching slums, they finally relinquished it for the more salubrious surroundings of St. Stephen's Green.

Faintly echoing its medieval law-giving history St. Sepulchre's was taken over in the 1830s as the principal station and training depot for the newly formed Dublin Metropolitan Police. Kevin Street Depot, as it became known, housed the mounted troop who carried out patrols and crowd control. Dressed in splendid ceremonial uniforms they provided escort duties to dignitaries such as the Lord Mayor and the Lord Lieutenant.

The busy mounted constables were also responsible for operating a horse-drawn fire brigade whose pumps were manned by up to 20 recruits.

The dormitories accommodated over a hundred off-duty constables, a necessary requirement since members of the force were not allowed to marry until they had saved at least £40, no mean task on the wages of less than a pound a week.

Official appreciation of the historical significance of the station has ensured the survival of the remaining parts of the old episcopal palace. They include the high gate piers, a decorated internal door, a window surmounted by a coat-of-arms, the four feet thick walls, wooden beams and a very deep well.

CONSTABLE SHEAHAN MEMORIAL, BURGH QUAY

On 6th May, 1905, three workmen were overcome by deadly fumes in a sewer at the corner of Hawkins Street and Burgh Quay. A little boy saw what happened and alerted Constable Patrick Sheahan who was on duty near O'Connell Bridge.

Sheahan, aged 29 and attached to "B" Division in College Street was an impressive man who weighed 18 stones and stood six feet four inches tall. He managed to rescue two of the men before succumbing himself. So many people then became involved in rescuing one another that in the end the tragedy accounted for two deaths and twelve serious hospital cases. Medals for gallantry were presented to two firemen and thirty civilians.

The Lord Mayor opened an appeal to raise funds to erect a memorial to honour the memory of Constable Sheahan and the other rescuers. The monument was unveiled beside the scene of the incident in 1906.

Over the years the memorial had suffered from inevitable weathering and the inscriptions had become blurred but in 1985 a complete restoration was carried out.

STORE STREET GARDA STATION

A report of 1858 described police barracks as no better than the "tenements of the wretched poor".

In an effort to improve working conditions a programme for the construction of new stations was commenced in the late 19th century. One of the first to be built was Store Street, which opened for business in 1880. Erected on the site of a stablery known as the Queen's Mews, it housed a public office, charge rooms, administrative and dormitory facilities, a canteen and basement storage. Under an innocent-looking pitched roof was a massive 18-inch-thick concrete barrel vault which enclosed the eight single and three multiple cells.

The station figured prominently in the civil disturbances and the baton charges of the 1913 General Strike. Three years later it was caught up in the maelstrom of the Easter Rising. One officer was shot dead inside the building by a stray bullet. When news came through of the occupation of the GPO it is said that the station sergeant dispatched a sergeant and a couple of constables to evict the rebels.

The original Victorian exterior of the building was preserved when the interior was remodelled and a new block added between 1972 and 1975.

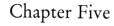Chapter Five

Street Craft

Streets can be considered as extensions to interior environments and as such consideration should be shown for the quality of their presentation.

They should complement and enhance the bordering buildings and offer a sense of enjoyment to their users. Elements which create ambience, atmosphere, character, respect for craftsmanship and historical perspective include decorative street lamps and iron work, paving and setts, monuments and carvings, shop fronts and signs, landscaping and colour.

Dublin is fortunate to still have a substantial stock of street furniture but misguided officials have in the past few decades ripped away irreplaceable items. There may now be a greater awareness of the city's individuality as expressed on its streets and this valuable heritage should now be jealously guarded or sensitively adapted to avoid any more shortsighted removal or replacement.

GEORGIAN DOORWAYS

Along the Georgian Terraces one doorway is hardly ever the same as any other. The differences, often small, sometimes dramatic, are part of the charm of these elegant houses. The doorway numbered "7" is that salvaged from number 7, Eccles Street, an address made famous in James Joyce's Ulysses. The doorway is on exhibit in the Bailey pub in Duke Street.

FORMER KILDARE STREET CLUB

Was snooker a monkey's game in the Dublin of the 1860s? These clever primates are in fact indulging in a sport more proper for Victorian gentlemen, a spot of billiards. This incongruous little scene is one of a collection of amusing stone carvings around the exterior of the former Kildare Street Club at the corner of Nassau and Kildare Streets. Other scenes include hounds chasing hares and bears playing violins.

The carvings are the work of Charles W. Harrison who worked closely with the architects of the building, Thomas Newenham Deane and Benjamin Woodward.

The Kildare Street Club was founded in 1782 to cater for Protestant landowners and the aristocracy. In time it became somewhat irrelevant to the evolving Irish world of the 19th and 20th centuries. The newly emerging Roman Catholic middle and well-to-do classes were not exactly encouraged to join the fraternity of aloof gentry, mustachioed bigwigs, retired colonels and returned expatriates.

When the original premises was burned down in 1860 the club had a new building constructed which turned out to be its greatest contribution to the city. The interior, which boasted a very striking carved stone staircase, was even more splendid than the outside. Sadly, however, 17 years after the Club sold off the house in 1954 the developers of the day ripped out much of the interior including the staircase.

Half of the building, that section nearest to Nassau Street, is now being used by the Cultural Institute of the French Embassy. The other part, since purchased by the State, has now been extensively refurbished and refitted. It will contain genealogical material, dating from 1552, and removed in 1981 from the Bedford Tower, Dublin Castle. The rooms will also hold an heraldic museum and a reading room for the manuscript department of the National Library.

FURTHER EMBELLISHMENTS TO GEORGIAN HOUSES WERE

decorative foot scrapers

balconies

and door knockers

DECORATIVE GATES

These three examples are among the best in the city and represent the high point in this art form. They are beautiful examples of the pattern work which made Irish iron works internationally famous.

Mansion House, Dawson Street (1929).

Leinster House, Kildare Street (circa 1900).

Ulster Bank, College Green (1891).

INDUSTRIAL CHIMNEYS

The lofty and gently tapering chimneys of a bygone age, although never great in number, offered a worthy contribution to the characteristic skyline of Dublin.

Their designs were usually pleasing and their construction called for the highest level of skill in bricklaying.

Every effort should be made to conserve the remaining stock of these elegant giants.

An example (in Thomas Street) of a cast-iron bollard.

Coal hole covers abound on many pavements and their designs are rich and varied.

Decorative public clocks are common-place except when you need one! The most decorative ones are often to be found on pubs.

THE SIGN OF THE THREE BALLS

Seventy years ago there were dozens of pawnbrokers in the centre city but today their ranks have been reduced to only four. Business is brisk for these survivors in a society that is again experiencing cash flow problems.

The sign of the three balls may have originated with a wealthy family of Lombardy merchants and money lenders. According to tradition, three sisters of the family were marrying simultaneously and each received a bag of gold as a dowry. The triple gift was immortalised when a symbol of three balls was inscribed into their family crest.

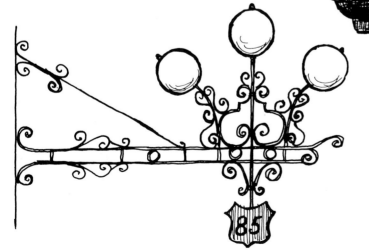

LIGHTING THE WAY

Street lighting has existed in Dublin since the early 17th century. The Candlelight Law, passed in 1616, decreed that every fifth house should display a light for the use of passers-by. The fine for every night's default was sixpence. Public lighting, fuelled by less than satisfactory fish-blubber, arrived in 1697. The lamps initially hung from wall brackets but were eventually placed on top of standards.

Lamplighters were employed to trim, light and clean the lamps and for the next 260 years they became an important institution of Dublin street life.

By 1825 piped gas lamps were appearing and the lamplighters discarded their rickety ladders for a long pole with which they turned the gas taps on or off. In 1884 the city had 3,750 gas lamps and some of these remained in use until they were finally snuffed out in 1957. The only present day survivors are in the Phoenix Park.

The quality of the light output from gas lamps gradually improved but, in spite of initial difficulties and scepticism, electric lighting started to make inroads. The first electric arc lamps appeared in 1860 outside the offices of *The Freeman's Journal* in Princes Street. More electric experiments appeared in 1880 along St. Stephen's Green and Nassau Street. This caused renewed tension and disputes with the Gas Company and territorial compromises were worked out.

The first electric lamps erected by the Corporation in 1892 stood in a loop from O'Connell Street to Henry Street via Grafton Street, Dame Street and Parliament Street. They were powered by the 900 Kilowatt generators in the newly opened Fleet Street station (the site of the present ESB offices). With the opening of the Pigeon House generating station in 1903 electric lighting extended right across the city.

Today we are fortunate in having such a diverse variety and quantity of standard and wall bracket lamps, which have survived over a period extending back 160 years.

THE FIVE LAMPS, NORTH STRAND

This highly decorative standard was intended both as a street light and a drinking fountain. It was erected around 1870 in memory of General Henry Hall who was born near Athenry, Co. Galway and went on to distinguish himself in the British Indian Army. Thousands of Irishmen, fleeing the famine at home, joined the army in India. For too many they had only swapped a lingering death from starvation in Ireland for brutal carnage in a far-away land.

The Five Lamps, once lit by gas, have recently been refurbished by Dublin Corporation.

Sea horses decorate the lamps on Capel Street Bridge.

One of the three-branched lamps on O'Connell Bridge.

70

BOTTLE TOWERS, CHURCHTOWN

I had always thought that those odd-shaped structures standing off Whitehall Road, Churchtown, were stalwart survivors from the era of the Industrial Revolution, possibly once serving as pottery kilns, drying sheds or windmills. Or could they have been a pointless architectural extravaganza or folly much in the same mould of Connolly's Folly in Maynooth or the obelisk on Killiney Hill? Such follies were often built by wealthy landowners merely to promote useful employment for the destitute of the district.

Erected in 1742 by Major Hall, on the grounds of his now demolished Whitehall House, the Bottle Towers were probably constructed to give employment to some local farmers who were hard hit by the great frost of 1741. These stone flights of fancy were, however, not follies but were, in fact, house and outhouse.

The larger tower, nicknamed Hall's Barn, had two main rooms which were furnished with fireplaces and windows. Tapering walls dramatically reduced the dimensions of the upper room so access was provided from an external winding staircase which still survives. Accommodation was probably quite cosy with the tower's thick stone walls and enormous oak beams and wooden floors. Unfortunately the interior was gutted when the building eventually fell into disuse.

The small replica tower was most likely a storeroom or even a pigeon loft, if we are to judge by the small upper door, but some believe that its cramped quarters also played host to human habitation.

Both towers are on the Corporation's Protected Buildings' List.

The cannon and sentry boxes at the Bank of Ireland, College Green date from the early 19th century when a militia was formed to guard the bank.

DRINKING FOUNTAINS

From late Georgian into Victorian times fresh water drinking fountains for man and beast were very common along the city's streets. As piped water became more commonly available the nuisance value of these fountains became more obvious. They were gathering points for layabouts and horses tended to foul up the surroundings. The streets were constantly wet around them and in winter they were like skid pans. Many were removed to obviate the problems.

They were very decorative and in retrospect their loss is to be regretted. Fortunately some do remain for our pleasure to behold.

Rutland Fountain, Merrion Square (1791).

Cavendish Row.

Lord Edward Street.

St. Patrick's Close.

St. Stephen's Green (1880).

TONGE & TAGGART IRON

Every day we walk on, over, under and past the multifarious products of this famous Dublin iron foundry. Established in 1869 in Bishop Street, the firm grew and prospered with the advancement of sewage, water and gas mains in the city. Besides meeting these functional requirements the foundry also exercised the artistry of its designers and craftsmen in supplying decorative iron work which was such a feature of the Victorian age. Thankfully, much of its work has survived to this day and considerably enhances our environment.

Many manhole, gully and coal-cellar covers, often bearing the inscription "cast in the South City Foundry" have been manufactured by Tonge & Taggart. Also cast were elaborately designed lamp standards, newels (corner posts) for railings and stairs, balconies, bollards, supporting columns, gates and railings.

Unseen by most of us is the labyrinth of underground municipal mains pipes, many of which are now over 100 years old and still perfectly serviceable. Cast iron is still popular for piping as it is far more resistant to corrosion than steel.

The manufacturing process is as old as the Industrial Revolution, and some of the techniques go back even further. A pattern is made in wood, plaster, metal or resin by highly-skilled pattern makers. The pattern is then placed in a moulding box which is filled with a chemically-treated sand. Once the sand has set, the pattern is removed leaving the impression in the hardened sand. Molten metal (the raw material is recycled scrap iron) is then poured from a ladle into the mould. When the metal has set the casting is separated from the burnt sand and further refinements are carried out.

Most of the patterns made since the foundation of the firm still exist, and this has allowed the recasting of such items as the lamp-posts in Trinity College and the Phoenix Park. Other re-castings include the decorative iron work on Sean Heuston Bridge (Kingsbridge), the railings on Bray Promenade and the bannisters in the Shelbourne Hotel.

The foundry moved to Windmill Lane in 1907, and in 1938 the present plant in East Wall was opened. Exports to the UK, Nigeria and the Middle East include great marine bollards, capable of holding ships of up to 40,000 tons.

W. B. YEATS

Henry Moore's best known work in Ireland is the bronze memorial to W. B. Yeats in St. Stephen's Green. It was unveiled in 1967. Moore, who died in 1986, also sculpted the "Reclining Connected Forms" in the grounds of Trinity College.

LA PIETA,
MARLBOROUGH STREET

THE THREE FATES FOUNTAIN,
ST. STEPHEN'S GREEN

This was a gift from the Italian Government in gratitude for the relief supplies sent to Italy during 1945-46. Executed in Carrara marble by Ermemegildo Luppi (died 1937) the group is nearly eight feet high and weighs sixteen tons. The Italian community living in Ireland paid for its transportation and it was formally unveiled in the Rotunda of the National Museum in 1948. It was later moved to its permanent site in the grounds of the Department of Education opposite to the Pro Cathedral in Marlborough Street.

In 1956 the fountain of the "Three Fates" was presented by the German Federal Republic to the people of Ireland in recognition of the contributions made by them towards the relief of distress in post-war Germany. It was erected at the Leeson Street entrance to St. Stephen's Green. The bronze monument was designed by the eminent Bavarian sculptor, Professor Josef Wackerle. His most famous work is the main fountain in Munich.

The nine foot high figures on the rocky limestone rockery are called Norenbrunnen, and portray the legendary fates from Nordic mythology as they spin and weave the thread of man's destiny.

THE PARKE MEMORIAL

Choking and filthy from the desert dust, the skirmish-weary British Nile Expedition of 1884-85 arrived at the gates of Khartoum too late to save the beleagured General Gordon. Among the relief columns was a young Irish surgeon major, Thomas Heazle Parke, who had already distinguished himself in the Tel-el-Kebir campaign of 1882, and during a devastating outbreak of cholera a year later in Egypt.

Parke was born in Drumsna, Co. Leitrim in 1857, qualified from the Royal College of Surgeons in 1878 and, after a brief spell of private practice, joined the Royal Army Medical Corps in 1881.

From Cairo in 1887, Parke volunteered to accompany Sir Henry Stanley on his famous expedition to the Upper Nile. Along the 3,000-mile journey into the very depths of Equatorial Africa over 500 men fell to the ravages of disease, starvation and attacks from hostile tribesmen. Parke saved the life of a Canadian engineer, William Grant Stairs, who had been struck near the heart by a poisoned arrow, by sucking out the venom. This incident is graphically depicted on the plaque fixed to the pedestal of the statue.

In April 1888 Parke (and not Stanley, who claimed the credit for himself) became the first European to discover the legendary Mountains of the Moon — the Ruwenzori Range. Stanley freely acknowledged that "without Parke, the cleverest of his profession, the expedition would have been a failure". A year later the Drumsna hero became the first Irishman to cross Africa from coast to coast.

These journeys undoubtedly took their toll and Parke died from a heart attack in 1893 at the age of only 36. A fund was organised for a statue in front of the Natural History Museum to which Stanley generously contributed. Sculptured by Percy Wood, it was unveiled in 1896.

DAVIS MEMORIAL, COLLEGE GREEN

The Thomas Davis Memorial commemorates the poet, leading Young Irelander and founder member of *The Nation* newspaper, the organ of the Repeal Movement. The Young Irelanders were an idealistic group of patriotic young people who sought to reverse the Act of Union but, unlike their contemporary Daniel O'Connell, were no pacifists. Their activities ended in 1848 following an abortive rebellion. Davis was spared any ignominy, having died three years earlier at the age of only 31.

The bronze statue stands on a nine-foot-high single block of granite quarried in the Dublin Mountains. The other bronze figures represent the Heralds of the Four Provinces standing on an ornamental framework and trumpeting water into the pool. Five of the six granite tablets surrounding the fountain group illustrate with bronze reliefs the poetry of Thomas Davis. The sixth graphically depicts the Famine.

Edward Delaney, who also was the sculptor of the Wolfe Tone memorial in St. Stephen's Green, modelled the statue, the Heralds and the fountain reliefs. The figure of Davis was cast in Milan, but the sculptor cast the remainder himself.

The architectural design of the memorial was worked out by the Office of Public Works in collaboration with the sculptor. The stylish lettering was carried out by Michael Biggs, who was also responsible for, among others, the inscriptions of the 1916 Proclamation at Arbour Hill and the Garda Memorial in the Phoenix Park.

PARNELL

This memorial to Charles Stewart Parnell was the work of Augustus St. Gaudens and was unveiled in 1911.

Two curiosities are worth noting, Parnell is wearing two overcoats and in the list of counties inscribed around the base two of them are written in the old usage: Queen's County (Laois) and King's County (Offaly).

CHARIOT OF LIFE, IRISH LIFE PLAZA

Oisín Kelly was commissioned by Irish Life in September 1976 to produce a sculpture which was to be a manifestation of the theme, Life, for the plaza of the Irish Life Centre. He worked on his vast creation for five years and completed it just a few weeks before his sudden death in October 1981.

The Chariot of Life represents Reason controlling the Emotions and not, as one Dublin wit put it, the state of the country being like two runaway horses with no one leading them. The human figure embodies the Intellect and the Will guiding and restraining the passions.

The steel reinforced bronze sculpture, the largest ever cast in Ireland, is 24 feet long, over 16 feet high and weighs nearly eight tons. The Dublin Art Foundry cast the 65 separate sections over a two year period. Other notable works from the foundry were Larkin's statue in O'Connell Street and the recasting of a bomb-damaged Victory from the O'Connell Monument some years ago.

The large scale undertaking of assembling the sculpture was entrusted to Daniel Miller and Company, Church Street. Millers handiwork ranges from the replaced roof for the Four Courts dome, shattered by a mine in 1922, to the refurbished weather clock on top of the Christ Church steeple.

The unveiling of the monument took place on 7th July, 1982, and now stands as a splendid epitaph to one of Ireland's most remarkable sculptors.

ALBERT MEMORIAL

Princess Victoria was only 18 years old when the throne was thrust upon her in 1837. During her long reign of 64 years Britain seethed with optimistic and aggressive vitality in the fields of industry, invention, discovery, art and imperialistic expansion. One of the most prominent patrons of this ceaseless and ambitious activity was Queen Victoria's German-born husband, Prince Albert.

He went everywhere, meeting and appreciating the work of that era's famous engineers, scientists, industrialists and artists. The Great London Exhibition of 1851, intended as Britain's shop window to the world, was mainly his brainchild.

In 1849 the royal couple came to Dublin and their visit, despite the distressful state of the city after the famine, was a triumph. They returned in 1853 to view Dargan's Great Exhibition in Leinster Lawn. A third visit was made eight years later. Then tragedy struck and a pining Victoria remained a widowed monarch for 40 years.

Memorials to the lamented Prince Consort sprang up all over the Kingdom and Dublin was no exception. The erection of the statue here, however, was objected to by Dublin Corporation and this rankled in the heart of Victoria. She excluded Dublin from her overseas itineraries until 1900 by which time the bronze of her late husband stood in the centre of Leinster Lawn.

John Henry Foley was the sculptor of this monument, which must rank among the best in the city. The prince, holding a book in one hand, is surrounded by four youths — a shepherd, an artist, a tradesman and an explorer/photographer. These figures symbolise the various interests of Albert.

The statue group, erected in 1871, was moved to its present secluded location beside the Natural History Museum in 1924 after an attempt was made to blow it up.

Foley also crafted the statue of the prince on the well-known Albert Memorial in London's Kensington Gardens. Another Dublin connection with Queen Victoria is the Royal Family's Irish State Coach, still much used on state occasions, weddings and funerals. This magnificent carriage was bought by the queen during one of her visits to Dublin from Hutton Coach-builders in Summerhill.

FARRELL GRANT SPARKS & CO., ANGLESEA STREET

Formerly the premises of stockbrokers Dillon and Waldron this exquisite shopfront won Dublin Corporation's Cultural and Environment Award in 1981.

ROYAL COLLEGE OF SURGEONS

ROYAL COLLEGE OF PHYSICIANS

Chapter Six

Bodyworks

In 1188, Ailred the Dane and his wife returned to Dublin after a pilgrimage to the Holy Land. Ailred, a wealthy land owner, carried palms on his way home and became known as Ailred le Palmer — Palmerstown is named after him. He was so impressed by the leper hospital of St. John the Baptist in Jerusalem that he immediately set about building Ireland's first hospital on the site of the present Augustinian Friary in Thomas Street.

Ailred, his wife and his subsequent followers adopted the rule of St. Augustine, and in 1260 the hospital was handed over to the Augustinian Hospitalers — the order distinguished by a red cross on a white robe, the forerunner of the Red Cross symbol. Ailred and his followers are buried in the graveyard now occupied by Joseph Kelly & Son, Timber Merchants, across the road from the present church.

The hospital and Friary were suppressed in 1540.

Another medieval hospital was dedicated in 1220 to St. Stephen on the site of the recently closed Mercer's Hospital. In 1394 St. Stephen's was endowed as a leprosy hospital but was later demolished. The next major hospital was the second of its kind in Europe after Les Invalides in Paris. It was the Royal Hospital in Kilmainham opened in 1684 for the reception of invalided and pensioned soldiers.

Epidemics, fevers and plain lack of care had for hundreds of years caused untold suffering and hardship and by the early 18th century concerned citizens and doctors began to organise and centralise the city's medical resources, such as they then were. Hospitals sprang up all over the city many of which have survived to this day, although their future is now being overshadowed by rationalisation programmes and health expenditure cutbacks. Jervis street began in 1721 as the Dublin Charitable Infirmary. Others included Dr. Steevens' (1733), Mercers (1734), Meath (1753), St. Patrick's (1757) and the Rotunda (1757).

Great progress was made throughout the rest of the 18th and into the 19th centuries and Irish medical procedures gained for the country an international reputation which has remained high ever since.

The 1980s saw the introduction of two new-generation private hospitals, the Mater and Blackrock Clinic, where patients are treated with the aid of ultra sophisticated equipment in luxurious surroundings.

The city currently has over seventy public, voluntary and private hospitals.

MID-TWENTIETH CENTURY SCALPEL

ROYAL VICTORIA EYE AND EAR HOSPITAL

A Bill was passed in 1897 to formalise the amalgamation of St. Mark's Ophthalmic Hospital (founded 1844 by Sir William Wilde) and the National Eye and Ear Infirmary (originally founded in 1814 by Naval Surgeon Commander Isaac Ryall). It was to be known as the Royal Victoria Eye and Ear Hospital in honour of the Queen's Diamond Jubilee.

The new hospital opened in Adelaide Road in 1904 and is presently one of the largest specialist centres in Europe for eye, ear, nose and throat illnesses.

During the Rising of 1916 the hospital was a first aid post for wounded British soldiers just as Baggot Street served the Irish casualties. *(See illustration page 81.)*

79

THE ROYAL COLLEGE OF SURGEONS, ST. STEPHEN'S GREEN

The statue of Lord Ardilaun, sitting in a relaxed pose, gazes on the comings and goings through the doorway of the Royal College of Surgeons. Granted a royal charter in 1784, the College first met in the board room of the Rotunda Hospital, and soon after inaugurated the Schools of Anatomy and Surgery in the Surgeons' Hall, a previously disused premises in Mercier Street.

Early success prompted the need for more space, so the college purchased an old Quaker cemetery at the corner of St. Stephen's Green and York Street and a new building, designed by Edward Parke, was opened there in 1810. By 1827 expansion was again considered necessary and the architect William Murray more than doubled the original width of the facade but retained Parke's design. The three Greek deities standing over the pediment were sculpted by John Smyth. Extensive restoration was carried out on the facade years ago.

During the Easter Rising a small group of rebels under Commandant Michael Mallin and Countess Markiewicz occupied the building for a week, and a bullet hole can still be seen in the boardroom door.

Built to accommodate lecture and conference halls, laboratories and offices, the modern wing to the rear was opened in 1977. Last year the former Mercer's Hospital was acquired and is currently being converted into a residence hall for students, as well as providing extra space for college facilities.

From the foundation of the College many illustrious and dedicated surgeons were responsible for enlightened surgical advances and the fame of the institution spread around the world. Today 840 students from up to 43 countries attend the various full-time courses. Governed by a council of 21 surgeons, the college is essentially a private organisation and receives no state funding.

All this is a far cry from the days of the barber-surgeon whose tonsorial expertise was far more trustworthy than his prowess with a scalpel. *(See illustration page 78.)*

COAT OF ARMS OF THE ROYAL COLLEGE OF SURGEONS OF IRELAND

ROYAL COLLEGE OF PHYSICIANS

The desire of King Charles I in 1626 to "erect in our Citty of Dublin a Colledge, Society and Corporation of Physicians" came to nought. Twenty-eight years passed before John Stearne, Professor of Physic and of Laws in Trinity, founded the Fraternity of Physicians and was granted a Royal Charter from Charles II in 1667. The original Grant of Arms is still scrupulously preserved by the college.

Sir Patrick Dun, personal physician to the Duke of Ormonde, became president of the fraternity in 1681 and eleven years later he widened the powers of the institution by gaining a new Charter and a new name — the King and Queen's College of Physicians in Ireland. In the same year the College abandoned Trinity Hall, its first home, and met in Dun's house. After his death in 1713 it had to wait a further ninety years before finding another permanent headquarters, this time in their new foundation, Sir Patrick Dun's Hospital.

A disastrous fire in the original Kildare Street Club in 1860 gave the college an opportunity to build its own premises. Designed by William Murray (whose father had been the architect for the facade of the Royal College of Surgeons) the classical building, which has some quite beautiful interiors, is far larger than one would expect from the outside.

Renamed in 1890 as the Royal College of Physicians of Ireland, the College today has five faculties for post-graduate specialisation; Community Medicine, Occupational Medicine, Pathology, Paediatrics, and the Institute of Obstetricians and Gynaecologists. It also performs many other roles including general post-graduate education and the maintenance of medical care standards. The college possesses possibly the finest medical library in Ireland and includes volumes dating back four centuries.

The advances in medical knowledge and practice in this country and our good standing abroad owe an incalculable amount to the college's founders, to famous presidents such as Robert Graves, William Stokes and Dominic Corrigan and to the generations of fellows and members. *(See illustration page 78.)*

DR. STEEVENS' HOSPITAL

Steevens' Lane is an unpretentious narrow road whose restrictive confines make it difficult to appreciate the facade of the hospital which gave it its name.

The hospital was founded in 1720 by Grizel Steevens with the estate left to her by her brother Richard, a medical professor at Trinity.

Colonel Thomas Burgh designed the building and, although early Georgian in character, it contained many features reminiscent of the previous century. The present site was chosen so as to be far enough away from the city and thus be isolated from the centres of fever and infection.

The hospital was opened in 1733, but some later additions were to follow, including the octagonal clocktower.

There are some examples of fine wrought-ironwork to be seen, especially at the main gates and inside the imposing arched main entrance. A curious and attractive feature are the supporting knobs for a number of hand-rails, which are fashioned into the shape of a clutching human hand.

The central cloistered courtyard is outstanding for its simplicity and charm. There is an atmosphere here more akin to a scholastic institution than to a busy hospital. But unfortunately, due to rationalisation, it may have to close.

ROYAL VICTORIA EYE AND EAR HOSPITAL

ST. PATRICK'S HOSPITAL

Jonathan Swift, a governor himself of a London mental hospital, especially pitied the mentally ill and resolved to ease their plight in his native city. He spent the last 14 years of his life in frenetic efforts to raise money and to prepare the way for the foundation of his menial institution.

It was Swift's intention that his establishment would be run with more enlightened procedures than were current at the time. Inmates were to be treated as patients and not as criminals. A board of governors, made up of his trusted friends, would administer the hospital, thus keeping control at a local level and avoiding state bureacracy. Today, it is still managed by a board of governors and run as a charitable institution, much as it was 230 years ago.

With the ample funds bequeathed in Swift's last will and testament, the hospital was founded in 1745. Designed by George Semple, the building was begun in 1749 on land donated by the governors of the nearby Dr. Steeven's Hospital. It opened in 1757. Curiously, while the official address is James's Street, it is actually situated at the corner of Bow Lane and Steeven's Lane.

Down the years many additions have been built onto the original structure. The long corridors of Semple's building whose lower-than-average doors once led to cell-like rooms, have been brightly painted to relieve the ponderous architecture and create a more relaxed and homely atmosphere.

St. Patrick's is one of the country's foremost (as well as being the oldest) psychiatric hospitals and is renowned for its treatment of alcoholism, fears, phobias and psycho-sexual disorders. It is a teaching centre for Trinity College and many of its professors and lecturers are on the hospital staff.

NATIONAL MATERNITY HOSPITAL, HOLLES STREET

While the Coombe and the Rotunda lying-in hospitals attempted to serve their own environs, up to the end of the 19th century infant and maternal mortality continued to ravage the densely populated poor areas of south-east Dublin. To help alleviate this tragic situation a number of concerned citizens led by Dr. William Roe bought the early 18th century town house of the notoriously extravagant Lord Llanduff in Holles Street and in 1884 founded the National Lying-in Hospital. In spite of obvious enthusiasm and self-sacrifice, financial difficulties forced closure in 1893.

The hospital was reopened on St. Patrick's Day, 1894, with a strong new Committee of Management under the patronage of Dr. Walsh, Archbishop of Dublin.

The first joint masters were Dr. Patrick Barry and Sir Andrew Horne, the latter immortalised by James Joyce in his reference to the hospital as the "House of Horne". Sanitary conditions, even among medical staff, were just beginning to be appreciated but even in Joyce's day childbirth was still a rough and risky experience. Joyce's arguably most brilliant but complex chapter in *Ulysses*, "Oxen of the Sun", concerned itself with the workings of the hospital, the ribaldry of the medical students and the contemporary burning questions of life and sexuality. Oliver St. John Gogarty, the great friend of Joyce, was a one-time medical student in Holles Street.

From 1934 to 1938 the present main structure was built — the construction being in two distinct phases so that the hospital could continue to function. By the terms of the lease only the residential Nurses' Home, with its neo-Georgian facade, was permitted to face onto Merrion Square.

From about 300 births in 1895 a record figure of 8,964 was reached in 1981, although the birthrate has since started to fall slightly. It is still the busiest maternity hospital in Europe and in conjunction with the Coombe and the Rotunda, has gained Ireland an enviable international reputation in obstetrics, gynacology and midwifery.

THE COOMBE HOSPITAL

The entrance to the now demolished old Coombe Maternity Hospital has been preserved as a memorial to the original charitable institution which was founded in 1826 for the relief of poor women in childbirth. On the steps at the rear of the monument are inscribed the nicknames of the Coombe's legendary street characters such as "Stab the Rasher", "Johnny Forty Coats" and "Shell Shock Joe".

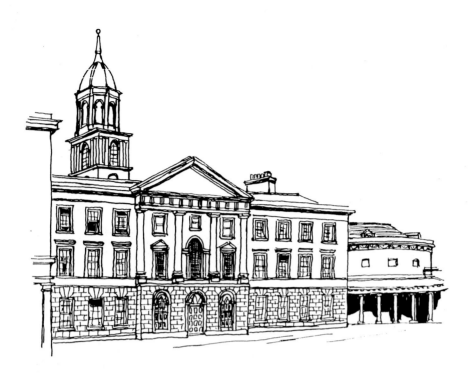

Justice could never be done in a short summary of this nature to one of Dublin's greatest gems both in the architectural and the social sense.

Poor women, living in appalling circumstances in 18th century Dublin, ran a high risk of losing not only their infants but also their own lives in childbirth. Dr. Bartholomew Mosse, a barber-surgeon who also practised the lowly-considered profession of midwifery, was moved to do something about their plight.

He first set up in 1745 a small hospital in a converted theatre in George's Lane, now Fade Street, which became "the first and only public one of its kind in his Majesty's Dominions" if not in the world. Another first was performed in the Music Hall in Fishamble Street in aid of the hospital. The Music Hall, where Handel had earlier conducted his first public performance of the "Messiah" in 1742, again resounded to the British Isles premiere of Handel's oratorio "Judas Maccabaeus" (this time without the personal appearance of its composer).

Mosse realised that he needed bigger premises and, with his architect Richard Cassels supplying a modified design based on Leinster House, four acres of land were bought on the north side of the Liffey. The foundation stone was laid in 1752 and it received its first patients in 1757.

To fund his venture Mosse opened pleasure gardens behind the hospital which became very fashionable for the upper classes. The Rotunda Room was built in 1764 (giving the hospital its familar name) and the Assembly Rooms between 1784 and 1786 and these entertainment centres gained further income for the hospital.

In 1987 the hospital refurbished, at a cost of £1 million, the Pillar Room, a highly decorative ballroom, which will now form part of a new medical teaching centre.

ROTUNDA HOSPITAL CHAPEL

Doctor Bartholomew Mosse died from all his exertions at the age of only 47 and was buried in an unmarked grave in Donnybrook. One of his greatest preoccupations before his untimely death was with the construction and ornamentation of the remarkable hospital chapel.

The chapel is, without doubt, one of the city's most unique places of worship and represents virtually the country's only excursion into the flamboyant rococo on such a scale. It is very reminiscent of Bavarian and Austrian baroque but stops short of their overwhelming flowing and cascading styles. In fact, the very restraint of the Rotunda rococo only serves to highlight its exquisitness and craftsmanship, which has gained it an international reputation.

The drawing shows the altar, lit by a Venetian window with relatively modern stained glass, surmounted by the Lamb of God sitting on a book with seven seals (Book of Revelations V. 1-7). Immediately overhead is the figure of Charity nursing her infant, with two children playing around her.

The plasterwork was carried out by a little known, stuccadore Bartholomew Cramillion, a Frenchman. For shaping his seven tons of plaster he was paid 500 guineas. The stucco work is finely complemented by the mahogany fluted columns, pews and panelling. A gallery, fronted with intricate iron-work, surrounds the 86 feet square chapel on three sides.

Mosse himself had planned a richer interior with more colour and gilding. For instance, the ceiling has large plain areas framed by plastered shields and a centre oval in which a famous Italian artist, Cipriani, should have painted scenes from the Nativity.

However, Mosse had died before a contract could be signed.

The chapel is open to the public at reasonable hours and helpful description leaflets are on display.

BAGGOT STREET HOSPITAL

In 1832, six eminent doctors founded the City of Dublin Hospital on a group of three upper Baggot Street houses, situated on land owned by Lord Pembroke. The infirmary was intended, to some degree, to serve as the teaching surgical hospital for the College of Surgeons.

Opening with only 52 beds it treated no less than 20,000 outpatients and 400 inpatients in the first year.

Various extensions and improvements were initiated over the next 50 years but it soon became clear that a new building was needed. In 1891, Lord Pembroke agreed to donate £6,000 towards the cost, provided that the public would also contribute a substantial sum. A bazaar, called the Kosmos Fete, was held over four days in Ballsbridge and raised the staggering sum of £12,000 towards the building fund.

The architect, Albert E. Murray, on instructions from Lord Pembroke, designed the outstanding structure that we see today. The gables facade, of ruabon brick and buff terracotta, nicely matched the existing buildings along this end of the street. The reconstruction was completed in 1898. When Queen Victoria visited Dublin in 1900 she commended that the hospital in future be known as the Royal City of Dublin Hospital. Royal patronage continued under the reigns of Edward VII and George V.

During the Great War up to 55 beds were given over to the War Office and nearly 900 sick and wounded soldiers were looked after. Over 200 casualties from the Easter Rebellion were also catered for.

Today the hospital specialises in Cardio Thoracic Surgery and Cardiological and Respiratory medicine. The services currently offered will eventually be moved to St. James's Hospital and, while the future use of the present building has yet to be decided, hopefully it will be preserved as a tribute to its countless generous benefactors and its exceptional medical traditions.

MERCER'S HOSPITAL

Mary Mercer built her house for the care of poor girls on this site in 1724 and ten years later it was converted into a 50 bed hospital. The oldest part of the present building dates from 1757 but the bulk of it is late Victorian.

Closed in 1983 Mercer's has since been bought by the Royal College of Surgeons and will be used for student accommodation and outpatient clinics.

SIR PATRICK DUN'S HOSPITAL

Opened in 1808 it was closed in 1986 as part of the Eastern Health Board's rationalisation plans. However, this much loved former hospital will still retain a connection with its past when it re-opens as a medical research establishment.

RICHMOND HOSPITAL

This red-bricked Elizabethan type building dates from 1900 and forms part of a trio which together make up St. Lawrence's Hospital. The three hospitals were built as the Hardwicke Fever Hospital (1803), the Richmond Surgical Hospital (1811) and the Whitworth Medical Hospital (1817).

KNIGHTS OF MALTA AND THE ST. JOHN AMBULANCE BRIGADE

When the Crusaders captured Jerusalem from the Saracens in 1099 two organisations were soon formed to safeguard the Christian shrines and the pilgrim routes. These were the Knights Templar or 'Templars' and the Order of the Hospital of St. John of Jerusalem or 'Hospitallers'. The latter adopted the eight-pointed white cross of their hospital sponsors, the Italian Amalfi Republic.

After the fall of Acre in 1291 both orders retreated to Cyprus where in 1312, the Templars fell politically foul of the Pope and were suppressed. The Hospitallers went on to suffer the vicissitudes of various wanderings, the great siege of Malta in 1565 and banishment by Napoleon and yet still clung on to survive and thrive to this day.

In 1174 Strongbow established Ireland's first priory of the Knights of the Hospital of St. John of Jerusalem on the site of the present Royal Hospital at Kilmainham. For hundreds of years the Order flourished but a decline had set in by the 16th century. By 1541 King Henry VIII's supression of monasteries had deprived the Order of all its possessions and, although it was not formally abolished, within a short time it virtually ceased to exist.

The appointment of a succession of titular priors preserved nominal continuity until 1862 but it was not until the 1930s that the Sovereign Military Order of St. John of Jerusalem, of Rhodes and of Malta (to give it its full title) was reformed here as an active association. In 1938 the Ambulance Corps was founded as the association's main instrument to care for the sick and needy. Operating as a 32-county institution the Corps now has over 5,000 members and 100 vehicles.

Activities consist of general ambulance duties and many specialist fields including first-aid and para-medical training, rehabilitation workshops, care of the sick during pilgrimages, lunches for the elderly, maintenance of a cancer research library and the provision of back-up services to Army contingents on peace-keeping missions.

The English Priory was dispossessed by both Henry VIII and Queen Elizabeth I and was not reconstituted until 1831, first as a Protestant and subsequently as a non-sectarian order. In 1877 a concern for those injured at work or by natural disasters led the General Assembly of the Order to form the St. John Ambulance Association.

The St. John Ambulance Brigade was founded in Dublin by Sir John Lumsden in 1903 and before long was called on to give heroic service during the Easter Rebellion, the 'Troubles' and the Civil War. The work it then carried out for impoverished families, including the kitchens set up to provide balanced meals to expectant and recent mothers and their families, was admired internationally. Today its members are engaged in many para-medical services and are also to be found at major sporting and cultural gatherings and one is present every night in each Dublin cinema.

KNIGHTS OF MALTA HEADQUARTERS

The headquarters on Clyde Road, acquired in the 1960s and since tastefully refurbished, is a fine example of this kind of suburban house. It had previously served as the rectory to adjacent St. Bartholomew's. The hall door, carved from an oak beam removed from St. Patrick's Cathedral, in 1898, maintains an ecclesiastical connection. In the front garden a stone basin removed in 1844 from St. John's Well in Kilmainham, a well famous for centuries for its curative powers, preserves a vital link with the Order's Irish origins.

ST. JOHN AMBULANCE FIRST AID POST

The first aid post in O'Connell Street was established after the street clashes of the 1913 General Strike on land provided by the Dublin United Tramway Company. The present recent replacement was donated by the Guinness's Brewery in James Street where the country's first division had been established.

THE SICK AND INDIGENT ROOMKEEPERS' SOCIETY

Once known by the grandiose title of "The Charitable Society for the Relief of the Sick and Indigent Roomkeepers of all Religious Persuasions in the City of Dublin", the society was formed by a group of five men in 1790. They had resolved to provide some measure of relief from the harrowing circumstances of Dublin's poor. Apart from the city's 2,000 or so beggars there were tens of thousands of forgotten wretches living in overcrowded rooms with only rags for clothes.

Up to 1840 the various committees met, as was the general custom, in public houses and taverns. This practice went out of fashion in the wake of Father Mathew's Temperance Crusade and the society was obliged to find permanent offices. The present house was acquired in 1851 and its central location is still a great convenience. It is Dublin's oldest existing charitable institution.

PRICE'S MEDICAL HALL

In the last century a medical hall was usually the building in which apothecaries carried out their dual profession of physician and chemist. Pharmacy as we know it today evolved after 1875 when the Pharmaceutical Society was formed.

John Price was an apothecary, and in 1867 he opened his Clare Street premises with a good business eye on the numerous physicians and consultants who lived in neighbouring Merrion and Fitzwilliam Squares. Patients of Oscar Wilde's father, Sir William Wilde, who lived in number 1, Merrion Square, must have presented their prescriptions for compounding at Price's.

In continued use, Price's possibly possesses the oldest surviving pharmacy frontage in Dublin. At night-time it is

unspoiled by ugly screening shutters — the security grill is placed internally.

The successful preservation of this Victorian shop front, which is not without its maintenance problems, should offer encouragement and example to shop owners generally.

DOGS' AND CATS' HOME, GRAND CANAL QUAY

It is probably not widely known that it was an Irishman, Richard Martin, MP for Galway, who founded the Royal Society for the Prevention of Cruelty to Animals in 1824, a movement that is now worldwide. Martin once owned a huge estate of 200,000 acres in Connemara and was highly respected for his kindness towards tenants and animals alike.

After a rather uncertain initial period the Dublin branch of the SPCA was reconstituted in 1875 and one hundred years ago the Dogs' and Cats' Home was opened at Grand Canal Quay. The premises had previously belonged to the Dublin Sugar Refinery Company which before that again had replaced a brewery. The attractive old house, still standing in the yard, once housed the brewery manager's personal groom and his family.

In 1906 an Act of Parliament decreed that the home should become the official dog pound for the city.

In a typical year the home will care for up to 18,000 stray, neglected or surrendered cats and dogs.

Chapter Seven

Soulworks

Concern for the hereafter was a preoccupation of the Celts and they readily embraced the Christian faith brought to Dublin by the monks of the 5th century. St. Patrick is reputed to have baptised local converts at a sacred well near the River Poddle (beside the present cathedral since named after him). A number of small religious communities sprang up in the region which were basically the only settlements when the Vikings first arrived in 841. These pagan marauders eventually settled down, built their town and, having embraced Christianity by the 11th century, erected their wooden cathedral of the Holy Trinity (later Christ Church).

The Anglo-Normans arrived in 1170 and in their train came the great religious orders; Augustinians, Carmelites, Dominicans and Franciscans. King Henry VIII's dissolution of the monasteries and the later Penal Laws against Catholics drove the Roman Catholic church underground. Protestantism became the official doctrine and during the 17th and 18th centuries Dublin welcomed other minority religions whose adherants sometimes came to escape persecution in their own countries. An Act was passed in 1662 to "Encourage Protestant Strangers to Settle in Ireland". Those who were to contribute so much to the life of the city began to arrive.

The French Huguenots poured in after the revocation of the Edict of Nantes in 1685. Dutch settlers were attracted in the 1690s by the military successes of King William of Orange.

The Religious Society of Friends was introduced into Ireland in 1654 by an Englishman, William Edmundson, and many others also came from Britain with the various waves of plantation settlers. These Quakers were mainly tradesmen, merchants and farmers.

Down the centuries the Friends took an active role in the commercial and philanthropic life of Ireland and some Quaker families, including those of Pim, Jacob, Bewley, Walpole, Webb and Haughton, became household names in Dublin. During the Great Hunger of 1846-47 a group of Quakers formed a Central Relief Committee and soup kitchens were opened throughout the country. To help the starving poor to become self-sufficient, the committee also distributed tons of seeds to farmers and grant-aid to fishermen.

The Dublin Meeting House moved in 1692 to Eustace Street. This building is now partially occupied by the Irish Film Institute.

A tradition claims that Dublin's earliest organised Jewish community, who were of Spanish, Portuguese and North European extraction, came over 300 years ago and worshipped in Crane Lane, off Dame Street. The first real evidence of their presence lies in the cemetery in Ballybough, Fairview, where the headstones date from 1777. Passersby may have wondered at the date inscribed on the adjoining house, i.e. 5618. This is the lunar calendar, and is the equivalent to 1857 AD.

The first group seems to have died out about 1790, but was replaced some thirty years later by a second influx of immigrants who opened

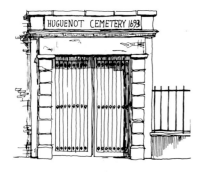

HUGUENOT CEMETERY

Situated beside the Shelbourne Hotel in St. Stephen's Green.

synagogues in Wolfe Tone Street and Mary's Abbey. However, their numbers never exceeded four hundred.

In the 1880s, large contingents of Russian Jews, fleeing the pogroms at home, arrived here. Little better than refugees, poor and uneducated in Western civilities, they were snubbed by their established middle-class co-religionists and so settled en masse around the South Circular Road. The area became known as "Little Jerusalem". By the mid 1940s, the number of Jews in Ireland exceeded 4,000, which had been mainly due to immigration but this figure has since diminished to the current level of around 1,800.

The Dublin Unitarians can trace back their origins to the arrival of non-Conformist Protestant settlers from Bristol and other parts of England during the reign of Elizabeth I. The earliest extant records tell us that they opened a Meeting House in Wood Street in 1673.

Reinforced by an amalgamation with the Protestant Dissenters in Mary's Abbey, the congregation moved in 1764 to a new Meeting House in Strand Street. Exactly when they began calling themselves Unitarians is not clear, but it was at least by 1843, as evidenced from inscriptions on communion plates still in the possession of the church.

Among other groups to follow, including some recent arrivals, were Methodists, Presbyterians, Lutherans, Moravians, Greek Orthodox, Mormons, Seventh Day Adventists and Moslems.

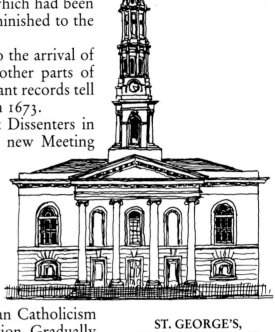

**ST. GEORGE'S,
HARDWICKE PLACE**

The spire of St. George's is sheer Georgian excellence and the whole church is a great tribute to its architect Francis Johnston. It was completed in 1814.

Lack of finance to remedy serious structural problems and an inadequate local population has left the future of this Church of Ireland building in some doubt.

It would be a tragedy and inexcusable negligence on everyone's part if at the end of the day Dublin was to lose this elegant landmark.

From the Reformation until the 18th century Roman Catholicism was met with various waves of persecution and prohibition. Gradually though, a measure of freedom to worship was gained culminating with the Act of Emancipation in 1829. Catholicism, which had always remained the dominant religion of the lower classes, was now also very strong among the newly emerging middle classes. On the other hand Protestant supremacy and control went into the first stages of decline. In 1869 the Church of Ireland was dis-established — it was no longer the official state religion. Over the next hundred years the number of Protestants living in the city sharply diminished, so much so in fact, that today several of their noteworthy centre city churches have already been vacated or are in danger of closing down.

The Roman Catholic Archdiocese of Dublin includes the City and County of Dublin, nearly all of Co. Wicklow and parts of Kildare, Carlow, Wexford and Laois. Of a total population of around 1,200,000 just under 90% is Roman Catholic. The Archdiocese is led by one Archbishop and six auxiliary Bishops. Since 1152 the See of Dublin has been occupied by 48 archbishops (up to June 1987) who were consecrated and recognised by Rome.

There are 194 parishes, 81 of which have been created in the last twenty years. Religious orders are in charge of 36 parishes. In the city centre the four mensal parishes — where the Archbishop is himself the parish priest — are, the Pro Cathedral, Westland Row, City Quay and Sean McDermott Street.

Assisting the secular clergy are 36 male religious orders, 73 different orders of nuns and 9 teaching and medical congregations of brothers.

ST. ANDREW'S CHURCH, SUFFOLK STREET

The original St. Andrew's was a medieval foundation and was situated close to Dublin Castle. In the 17th century it was decided to relocate it in one of the newly developing suburbs near Trinity College. An old bowling green was made available and another St. Andrew's was built. It became the parish church for the Irish Parliament until the latter's dissolution in 1800.

In 1860 a fire destroyed the second St. Andrew's so a new church was erected and opened for worship in 1873. Adroitly sited on its awkward location this fine Gothic building was designed by Charles Lanyon.

Behind the railings stands a marble column surmounted by a crown. It commemorates those who died serving with the 74th (Dublin) Company of the Imperial Yeomanry in the Boer War.

Across the road at the junction of Suffolk Street and Church Lane there once stood a formidable artificial mound called the Thingmote or Thingmount. This very substantial hillock was raised by the Norse, shovelful by shovelful, until it measured 40 feet in height and 240 in circumference. In common with similar mounds in other Scandinavian settlements the Thingmote was an important assembly point in Viking Dublin. Seated on the summit the King and his noblemen presided over a form of parliament, courts of justice and war councils.

In the Middle Ages it served as an outdoor amusement area and as a site for flogging criminals and burning heretics at the stake. King Henry II built a temporary palace here for the duration of his stay in 1172.

The sheer massiveness of the mound ensured its survival until 1681 when it was dismantled and carted over to what is now Nassau Street to raise that street eight feet above the previous level to protect it from flooding.

JOHN'S LANE, THOMAS STREET

The magnificent tower and spire of John's Lane, officially known as the Church of St. John and St. Augustine, is one of the great landmarks of Dublin.

It was built for the Augustinians between 1862 and 1911 and James Pearse, Patrick Pearse's father, was the sculptor of the twelve apostles in the niches of the spire. The architect was Edward Pugin.

ST. ANDREW'S CHURCH

92

JEWISH MUSEUM

In a pair of converted houses, the little Walworth Road Synagogue opened in 1918 and continued to serve the local community until the mid-70s, when the suburban migration of its congregation forced its closure. Now, thanks to the ardent efforts of some historically-minded Jews, the old synagogue has been restored as a museum. President Chaim Hertzog of Israel, who once lived in nearby Bloomfield Avenue, officially opened the museum.

In the foreground of the drawing, viewed from the Ladies' Gallery — the sexes have been separated in worship since at least the time of Moses — is the Bimah, or reading platform, beyond is the ornately-carved Ark, containing the Scrolls of the Torah or Law. Over the Ark is a replica of the twin tablets of the Ten Commandments.

This absorbing collection of Jewish — and, indeed, Dublin — memorabilia can be viewed on any Sunday between 10.30 and 12.30.

SAINT WERBURGH'S

Among their ecclesiastical foundations the Norsemen of Dublin included the church of St. Martin of Tours. This building was later replaced by the Anglo-Norman church of St. Werburgh's, dedicated to Werburgha, daughter of a Saxon king.

A chequered architectural history then ensued with a major reconstruction first in 1662 and again in 1715. Left ruinous after a disastrous fire in 1754 but, resilient as ever the church reopened for worship five years later.

This time it was decided to erect a tower whose spire soared to a height of 160 feet. Its elegant lines are portrayed in Malton's famous view of Dublin Castle. But it was the authorities in that same castle who ordered the spire to be dismantled in 1810. Edgy after the abortive Emmet Rising, they had feared that spies or snipers might have too good a panorama of the castle interior from such a convenient lofty perch.

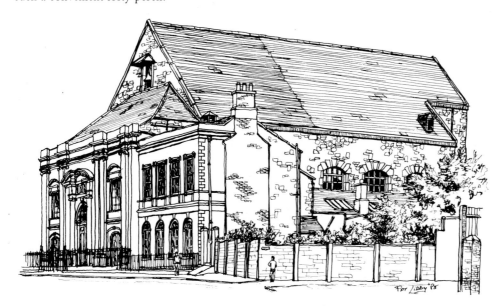

Until the erection of the Chapel Royal, St. Werburgh's was the parish church of Dublin Castle and the place where Viceroys were sworn in.

After his execution for his part in the Rising of 1798, Lord Edward Fitzgerald was surreptitiously laid to rest in the vaults while, ironically, his captor, the infamous Major Sirr, lies buried in the churchyard above.

The world-famous composer and pianist, John Field, creator of the nocturne, was baptised here in 1782.

Two old fire pumps, dating from the days when volunteer firemen operated from parish churches, are preserved within the buildings.

93

A City of Two Cathedrals

Dublin has the distinction of possessing two Protestant cathedrals whereas it lacks even one for the Roman Catholics. The Church of Ireland owes the existence of its twin Cathedrals to episcopal rivalries dating back to the Middle Ages.

Christ Church, the older of the two, was built around 1038 by the now Christianised Vikings under King Sitric Silkenbeard. The Normans replaced this wooden structure with a stone building in the 1170s. Until the Reformation Christ Church was attached to an Augustinian priory the remains of which can still be seen in the grounds of the cathedral.

In 1192 Archbishop John Comyn decided to place his jurisdiction away from the interference of the City Provosts and Christ Church Priory and so he converted the old Celtic chapel of St. Patrick, which was situated outside the city walls, into a collegiate church. Beside it he built his residential palace of St. Sepulchre which remained the seat of Dublin's archbishops until 1806 when it was sold off for use as a police barracks, a function it still performs. Later, in 1213, Comyn's successor, Henry de Loundres, raised St. Patrick's to the status of a cathedral.

For the next nine decades many heated and bitter quarrels broke out between the two cathedrals' opposing factions as to which church was the primary institution. A compromise was arrived at in 1300 whereby the precedence in age of Christ Church was recognised and it was agreed that future archbishops of Dublin should be consecrated there.

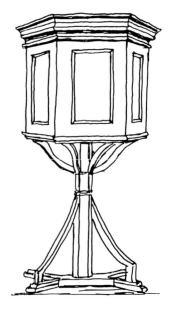

The wooden pulpit from which Dean Swift preached.

After the Reformation both cathedrals passed into Protestant hands and a new phase of their history began. State officialdom favoured the more central Christ Church but the influence of St. Patrick's remained considerable not least during the encumbency from 1713 to 1745 of Dean Jonathan Swift. The two buildings each suffered from major structural calamities arising from collapsing walls, military and civilian occupations, storm and fire damage and sheer neglect brought on by inadequate financial support. By the mid 19th century disrepair threatened irrevocable ruination which was only averted by the unlikely but not unholy alliance of religion and alcohol.

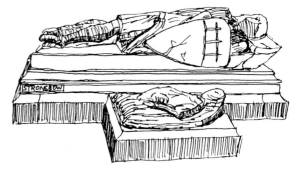

Henry Roe, a Dublin whiskey distiller, spent a fortune in the 1870s restoring Christ Church. He also cleared away the surrounding slums and erected the visually effective overhead bridge and the Synod Hall to which it is connected. The Synod Hall has recently been refurbished and is now being used as a community and tourist centre.

This monument stands close to the spot where Strongbow, the leader of the Anglo-Norman conquerors of Ireland, lies buried.

St. Patrick's was restored by a brewer, Benjamin Lee Guinness, who had large sections of the unstable cathedral rebuilt and strengthened. Successive members of his family continued the rehabilitation not only of the church itself but of virtually the whole neighbourhood.

Today Christ Church is the Cathedral of the Diocese of Dublin and the Metropolitan Cathedral of the Southern Province while St. Patrick's is the National Cathedral of the Church of Ireland.

CHRIST·CHURCH CATHEDRAL

ST. PATRICK'S CATHEDRAL

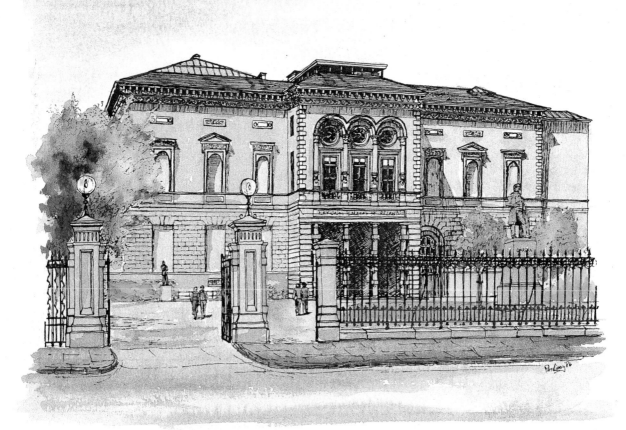

NATIONAL GALLERY

TRINITY COLLEGE

PRO CATHEDRAL, MARLBOROUGH STREET

The first St. Mary's was founded by St. Laurence O'Toole, 12th century Archbishop of Dublin. The second church of that name was the post-penal day mass house in Liffey Street. It was to continue this link with the past that the Pro-Cathedral, when it was opened in 1825, was also called St. Mary's.

The title "Pro-Cathedral" is applied because no Roman Catholic Archbishop of Dublin has asked the Pope to revoke the cathedral status granted to Christ Church (now belonging to the Church of Ireland) in the time of O'Toole.

A young unknown singer from Athlone applied in 1902 to join the Pro-Cathedral's Palestrina Choir. He was accepted and the career of John McCormack was launched.

Deceased Archbishops of Dublin are usually buried in the vaults beneath the church.

UNITARIAN CHURCH, ST. STEPHEN'S GREEN

A site was purchased by the Unitarians on the western side of St. Stephen's Green in 1857 and within six years the present Gothic-style church was erected. In 1867 the congregation was joined by the Protestant Dissenters from Eustace Street.

A special feature of the St. Stephen's Green building is its striking collection of French, Flemish, English and Irish stained glass. The latter is in the huge main window and is a splendid example of the work then coming from the revival of the Irish stained glass industry. Completed in 1917 this window, designed by Harold Child and executed by Sarah Purser, was the inspiration of the Rev. E. Savell Hicks, the incumbent minister for a remarkable 52 years (1910-1962).

The main body of the church is on first floor level, while underneath are various rooms. These include the old school which was closed in 1954 but is now in regular use as the Damer Hall (named after a wealthy 18th century merchant who bequeathed money to establish the church school).

PHIBSBORO

Phibsborough, now generally shortened to Phibsboro, is derived from Phippsborough which was named after the Phipps family who acquired land here in the late 18th century. Starting life as a quiet village its proximity to the centre of Dublin and the arrival of the canal, the railway and some light industry started a population explosion. Concern began to be expressed about the hundreds of families who were having to live in miserable conditions.

To provide an education for the local Roman Catholic children a committee was formed in 1826 which immediately set about constructing a school which also doubled as a church. Situated at the junction of the New Cabra Road and the North Circular Road this building was named St. Peter's and was the precursor of the present day magnificent structure.

The Vincentian Community took over St. Peter's in 1838 and the building was extended. Twenty-four years later the superior, Fr. McNamara, decided on a grander Gothic style church. However the central tower was the subject of controversy and it had to be eventually dismantled, the stone going into the construction of a nearby bank and public house. Work commenced again in 1902 adding further space, embellishments and an impressive new tower and spire. Soaring to more than 200 feet over what is already high ground the spire, to my knowledge, is the highest in Dublin.

MASONIC HALL, MOLESWORTH STREET

Erected in 1867 the Grand Lodge is the headquarters of the Irish Constitution. Freemasonry first arrived in Ireland in 1725 and Dublin, after London, is the second oldest lodge in the world.

SALVATION ARMY

The Salvation Army came to Dublin in 1884 and opened their Abbey Street chapel and administrative centre in 1913.

ST. ANN'S, DAWSON STREET

The parish of St. Ann was founded in 1707 and the building of the church commenced around 1720. The present Romanesque front by Deane and Woodward was grafted on in 1868. Both religious and cultural activities take place at lunch time on working days.

ST. STEPHEN'S, MOUNT STREET CRESCENT

Upper Mount Street, especially on an early car-empty Sunday morning, still presents an almost perfect view of a Georgian streetscape. Crowning the impressive vista and standing proudly on its solitary island in the centre of Mount Street Crescent is the neo-Georgian splendour of the Church of St. Stephen.

For many years the residents of the once populous Fitzwilliam Estate had clamoured for the erection of their own local church. However, it was not until 1821 that plans were prepared for a Chapel of Ease to the Mother Church of the vast parish of St. Peter which stretched from Sandyford down to Booterstown and across to Rathmines. Designed by John Bowden, renowned more for his courthouses and school buildings than for churches, St. Stephen's was consecrated in 1824. It cost £5,169 to build, £3,784 of which was donated by the Board of First Fruits, an organisation which was funded by taxing the first year's income of newly ordained clergymen.

The inside of the building, in contrast to the Greek-emulated exterior, is described as Victorian Renaissance and is noted for its fine furnishings and memorial windows. The organ case (the original organ was replaced in 1889) was constructed by the world famous organ builder and friend of Handel, John Snetzler. Edward Bunting, collector of Irish melodies, was organist here circa 1827. Another notable, Jack B. Yeats, was buried from St. Stephen's in 1957.

Fondly nicknamed "the Pepper Cannister", St. Stephen's, with its mixed cultural and spiritual programme of regular music recitals, afternoon retreats and special services, still plays an important role in the life of a community that is now commercial rather than residential.

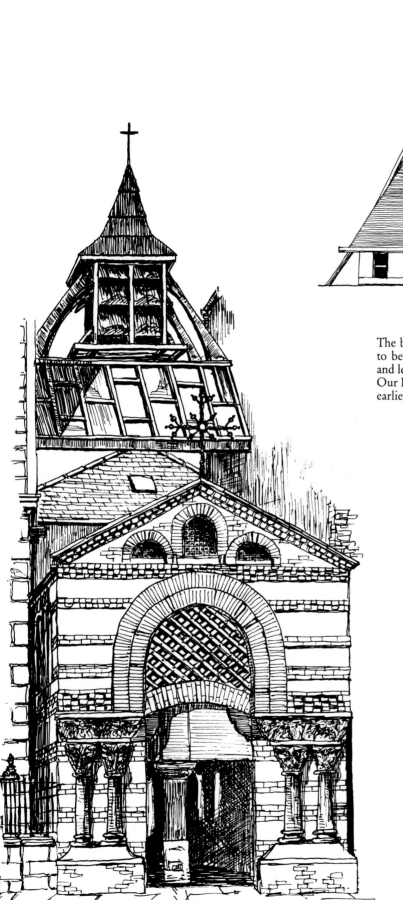

MODERN CHURCHES

The buildings of the last 15 years have tended to be smaller, more intimate and of a simpler and less expensive style. This pleasant example, Our Lady of Dolours at Glasnevin, replaced an earlier wooden structure.

UNIVERSITY CHURCH

This narrow entrance from St. Stephen's Green leads into the Collegiate Church of Ss. Peter and Paul — popularly called University Church. It was opened in 1856 and was attached to the fledgling Catholic University next door.

"AND INTO DUST THOU SHALT RETURN"

In Dublin about thirty funeral directors attend the arrangements necessitated by the city's annual 7,500 deaths. Rolls Royces and Mercedes hearses have long since replaced the more dignified carriage-hearses drawn by black-plumed horses. Traditional cemeteries like Glasnevin, Deansgrange and Mount Jerome are nearly full and several new plots have been pressed into service.

GLASNEVIN CEMETERY

Up to the 1820s Catholics could be buried only in Protestant graveyards, and priests were often restrained from reciting prayers at the gravesides. Daniel O'Connell and the Catholic Association campaigned for and achieved the right for Catholics to own their own cemeteries.

In 1828 the Catholic Association bought their first piece of land at Goldenbridge, beside Richmond Barracks, and three years later Prospect Cemetery at Glasnevin was opened. Both cemeteries permitted the burials of non-Catholics.

To avoid mourners having to pay tolls to pass the turnpikes on the old Glasnevin and Finglas Roads, O'Connell had a new road built which cut between the other two. O'Connell's success in outwitting the toll gatherers is said to have led to his famous promise that he would next "Drive a coach and six through an Act of Parliament".

Watchtowers were built around the perimeter wall of Glasnevin and the "dead watchers", assisted by their Cuban bloodhounds, had to ward off the "sack 'em ups" who robbed bodies in the interest of medical research. This unsavoury practice was made redundant in 1832 with the enactment of the Anatomy Act.

Over the next 50 years the size of the cemetery vastly increased and by 1878 nearly 300,000 interments had taken place. Many illustrious figures who had contributed to a resurgent Ireland — politicians, magistrates, clerics, poets, writers, industrialists, soldiers and rebels — undertook their final journey to Glasnevin, often accompanied by massive crowds.

Forgotten victims, numbered in their tens of thousands, of the several outbreaks of cholera, smallpox and famine were unceremoniously buried in mass graves. The underprivileged of Dublin, unable to buy plots of their own, were buried in the "poor ground".

To move with the times, a crematorium was opened in 1982. To date, the cemetery has received the remains of close on one and a half million people, giving its hundred or so acres a resident population greater than the living citizenry of the whole of Dublin.

The drawing features the round tower over Daniel O'Connell's vault and the mortuary chapel built in 1878, which was styled on Cormac's chapel on the Rock of Cashel.

MOUNT JEROME CEMETERY

Mount Jerome Cemetery received its first interment on the 14th September, 1836 when the tiny remains of the infant Pollack twins were lowered into their lonely grave. They have since been followed by close on 200,000 more burials.

The cemetery takes its name from the Rev. Stephen Jerome, vicar from 1639 of St. Kevin's parish, which encompassed the area of Harold's Cross. In the 18th century the lands of Mount Jerome were held by the Earl of Meath and a mansion was built on the site, which today survives as the administration offices for the cemetery.

One of the subsequent owners of the property was John Keogh, a leader in the movement for Catholic Emancipation. Keogh was also a firm friend of Wolfe Tone and later shared confidences and hospitality with Robert Emmet and John Philpot Curran.

It was from Keogh's descendants that the newly formed Dublin General Cemeteries Company purchased, in 1835, the 47-acre estate to open a non-denominational burial ground. The Cemeteries Company had originally hoped to purchase a section of the Phoenix Park but the Commissioners of His Majesty's Woods, Forests and Land Revenues replied that they "could not sanction the alienation of any part of the Phoenix Park".

A greenhouse was pressed into service as a mortuary chapel until the Gothic-style church was opened in 1847. Beside this building is a bush locally known as Christ's Thorn which is said to be similar to the one used for the "Crown of Thorns".

Along the paths, some bearing curious names such as Nunnery Walk, Orphan Walk, Catacomb Approach and Tenement Screen, the rich and famous mingle with the humble. In the older section you will encounter Thomas Davis, George Russell (AE), William Wilde (father of Oscar), poet George Petrie, some of the Guinness family and Thomas Kirk (sculptor of Dublin's late lamented Horatio Nelson).

There are some finely carved tombs, one of which the owner, possessing a dread of being buried alive, could open via chains and spring loaded locks from the inside of her coffin.

MOUNT ARGUS

St. Paul's Retreat, the Passionist church and monastery better known simply as Mount Argus, is an impressive structure. The scale of the building is further enhanced by its position on top of a small hill. Finely crafted sculpture and statuary enrich the facade and the massive, gold painted figure of St. Michael the Archangel surmounts the whole arrangement.

By 1856 the Passionists, who had originated in 18th century Italy, had arrived in Ireland and celebrated their first Mass in a Mount Argus farmhouse. The present church was opened in 1878 replacing an earlier one which had served for 22 years. One of the other men responsible for the foundation was Ignatius Spencer, a great-grand-uncle of Princess Diana.

While most religious orders centred their communities in the heart of cities it was a rule of the Passionists to seek places of solitude. In the last century Mount Argus, situated three miles from any urban development, was an ideal location. Despite its relative remoteness the reputation of the church as a spiritual centre soon drew regular crowds not the least to hear Father Charles (died 1893) whose case for beatification is now before the Vatican.

James Pearse, Patrick's father, was received into the Roman Catholic faith in Mount Argus in 1877 and his firm made and installed the present pulpit. Patrick himself came with his followers for spiritual assistance before Easter 1916. In the aftermath of the Rising, former Taoiseach Garret FitzGerald's father, Desmond, sought refuge from the military and was hidden in the monastery.

As with their forerunners, the Dublin Metropolitan Police, the Garda Síochána have Mount Argus as their special church and the Passionists provide a chaplain to the force in Dublin. Mount Argus became a parish church in 1974 and in the last few years a huge restoration programme was carried out on the monastery and the complete reroofing of the church was completed.

Chapter Eight

Entrances to Entertainment

Due to a variable and unreliable climate Dublin cannot support a society based on the passive recreation associated with pavement cafes or entertainment al-fresco. When chairs, tables and sunshade umbrellas do appear outdoors it is a spontaneous and almost urgent response to a spell of warm sunny weather.

Prominent among places of more predictable resort are the cinema, the theatre and the ubiquitous pub.

The cinema first became popular after 1910 and within a short few years the city went film mad. Large picture houses, many seating up to 3,000 patrons, were opened and the names of the latest Hollywood stars were on everyone's lips. The long queues which formed before every performance, especially at weekends, became attractions in themselves and lured all kinds of street entertainers to try their luck. From the 1960s television nearly killed off the cinema but the remaining survivors were revamped and divided into smaller, more luxurious and intimate auditoria and have thus managed to reverse the declining audience numbers.

Dublin's first professional theatre was opened in Werburgh Street in 1637 and was followed in 1662 by the famous Smock Alley Theatre in modern Lower Exchange Street and the Crow Street Theatre in 1758. In the middle of the last century there were three theatres — The Royal (later The Theatre Royal and demolished in 1962), The Queen's (closed 1966) and Dan Lowry's Music Hall (the present Olympia). The world famous Abbey Theatre opened in 1904 but the original building was replaced in 1966, after a fire, by an ultra-modern and rather plain structure.

Practically every street in the city centre boasts at least one pub if not several. During the 1960s pubs, in a hasty desire to modernise and throw off a dowdy image, threw out their Victorian legacy of mahogany and brass fittings and replaced them with cheap veneer and plastic. Ironically these same pubs are leading the way in restoring quality and craftsmanship to their premises.

It would be wrong to single out even a few dozen names among the ranks of over 600 pubs. Each has its own uniqueness and charm and awaits a personal discovery.

STREET ENTERTAINERS

A carnival atmosphere is created by the presence in the city centre of street entertainers and musicians. It must be said though that a surfeit of them can be annoying or can create bottlenecks on busy pedestrian streets. Designated sites at appropriate places, even to the extent of constructing pleasant little areas for them, would benefit both the genuine artistes and the passing public.

In 1930 the Gate Theatre took up residence in the former Great Supper Room of the Rotunda's Assembly Rooms and within a relatively short time it achieved international fame under the direction of Micheál MacLiammour and Hilton Edwards.

Orson Welles and James Mason began their acting careers at the Gate.

Brothers John and Michael Gunn erected the Gaiety Theatre in 1871, which has since played host to many famous Irish and overseas performers in comedy, revues, straight plays, musicals and opera. It was built in a remarkably short span of 28 weeks at a cost of £26,000 and interior furnishings included Burmese teak, Russian oak and British cast iron. Seating capacity is now just under 1,200.

The Gaiety has a special place in the hearts of Dubliners and the news of its closure in January 1984 was received with great dismay. However, the owners used the opportunity to reinvest in the theatre and carry out a much needed refurbishment and within the year the appreciative audiences were welcomed back again.

Crown Alley and the warren of narrow streets radiating out from it are fast becoming Dublin's Left Bank district. Restaurants, craft centres and theatre workshops are blossoming among the old buildings and the route through Crown Alley, under Merchants' Arch and across the Halfpenny Bridge is earmarked as part of an extended pedestrian link between the main northside and southside shopping precincts. *(See colour illustrations page 130.)*

SHELBOURNE HOTEL

Two Nubian Princesses guard the attractive entrance to the Shelbourne Hotel (erected 1867). On their outside stand a pair of slave girls — they are distinguishable by their fettered ankles.

THE GRESHAM HOTEL

Thomas Gresham started his hotel business in Sackville Street in 1817 and it quickly gained in reputation and size. Down the years various improvements were carried out but having survived the cataclysm of 1916 the hotel was destroyed during the 1922 Civil War.

The fine building we see today was rebuilt in 1927 and since then a number of redevelopments, mostly internal, have taken place. A procession of the rich and famous have stayed in the Gresham including Richard Burton, Elizabeth Taylor, Jimmy Stewart, General Eisenhower, Ronald Reagan, Bob Hope, Danny Kaye, Marlene Dietrich, Ingrid Bergman, Ray Milland, Bing Crosby and a host of others.

O'DONOGHUE'S

BRAZEN HEAD

KAVANAGH'S

A FEW DUBLIN PUBS

Mulligan's in Poolbeg Street, Kavanagh's of Aughrim Street, the Brazen Head in Bridge Street and O'Donoghue's of Merrion Row. "The Dubliners" ballad singing group and musicians extraordinaire commenced their career in O'Donoghue's, a career which has since brought them well-deserved world acclaim.

The Brazen Head has been one of Dublin's most popular watering holes since it was built in 1668. It is the city's oldest pub and there is a tradition which claims that the Inn has a history dating back to 1198.

It is a haunt of traditional musicians who like the atmosphere of the old interior which in years gone by saw the furtive hatching of several abortive insurrections.

The pub is now being revitalised in a very sensitive manner and there are hoped-for future plans to reopen the forty or so bedrooms and thus return the pub to its original function as an hotel.

MULLIGAN'S

AMBASSADOR CINEMA

Part of the original entertainment complex built to support the running of the adjoining maternity hospital (and incidentally giving the hospital its popular name) the Rotunda became a picture house around 1913 and later changed its name to the Ambassador. At one time there were 8 cinemas on or near O'Connell Street with some of them capable of seating nearly 3,000 patrons.

THE OLYMPIA THEATRE

The Olympia Theatre has also had its troubles in the 1980s and various schemes have had to be put forward to attract financial support. Deceptively small looking from the street the theatre has actually over a hundred seats more than the Gaiety.

The Olympia was built by Dan Lowry as the music hall, The Star of Erin, in 1879. It was renamed the Empire Theatre of Varieties in 1897 following a major reconstruction and the widening of the musical performances to include revue, plays and pantomimes.

BANDSTAND, PHOENIX PARK

This bandstand still provides opportunities for free entertainment in the natural amphitheatre of the Phoenix Park's Hollow. During the summer time band performances take place on the city's several Victorian bandstands including those at Blackrock Park, Dun Laoghaire Harbour and St. Stephen's Green.

Chapter Nine

Edifices of Edification

TRINITY CAMPANILE

TRINITY LAMP

Ireland's first formal schools were probably associated with the early Christian monastery settlements of which there were several in the Dublin region. It was not until 1320 that the city's first university was founded at St. Patrick's Cathedral. This institution had mixed success and an on-off existence and finally closed with the emergence of Trinity College. *(See illustration page 96.)*

Trinity College, founded by Queen Elizabeth I in 1592, is indisputably a part of Dublin's essence. For all that, it has retained a slightly forbidding mystique for most citizens and even for the 20,000 commuters who daily traverse the cobbled squares on their hurried shortcuts it has remained a place apart. Many probably at one time felt excluded for political, religious or class considerations but, once through any of the four main entrances, the modern visitor will find the college a surprisingly welcoming and open institution.

To appreciate the wealth and variety of the place a good guide book is essential, but even a casual walk around the 40 odd acres will fill a pleasurable morning or afternoon. Encompassing the central Parliament Square are the university's oldest buildings. They include the Rubrics, the Graduate Memorial Building, the Old Library, the exquisitely decorated Examination Hall and the Chapel, which ten years ago became probably the Republic's first fully multi-denominational church. Beside the church is the restored Dining Hall, which was severely damaged by fire on Friday, 13th July, 1984.

The sense of antiquity is heightened by the cobbles and the cast-iron bollards and lamps. Dominating the square is the Campanile occupying the spot where the medieval Augustinian Monastery of All Hallows had its bell tower. On the other side of the Campanile are the statues of Provost George Salmon and historian W. E. H. Lecky. Those dignitaries are comfortably seated, unlike erstwhile graduates Oliver Goldsmith and Edmund Burke, who have to be content to stand on their plinths outside the main entrance.

Contemporary artistic expression is found in the ultra-modern Arts Building, the Douglas Hyde Gallery, and in the open-air sculptures of Henry Moore and Alexander Calder.

The museum building has reconstructed fossil remains of the Giant Irish Deer on view and, further back into the hall are some interesting engineering models. Stroll around College Park for a spot of cricket or watch a game at the rugby ground or on the Botany Bay tennis courts.

The cultural and recreational activities of the 7,000 students can be best appreciated by studying the always-interesting posters at the Nassau Street and College Green entrances. Invitations to participate in some of these events are often extended to members of the public.

OLD LIBRARY, TRINITY COLLEGE

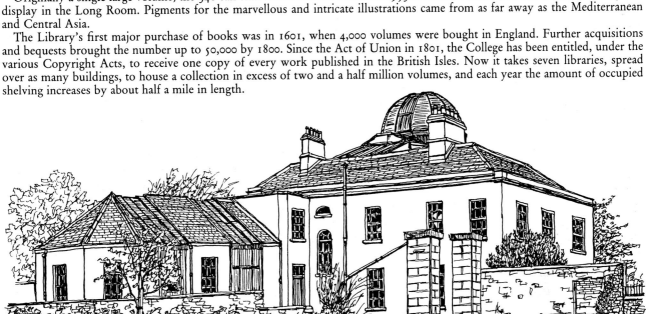

The Library of Trinity College is one of the world's greatest research libraries and holds Ireland's largest collection of manuscripts and books. The 200,000 volumes held in the Long Room of the Old Library (built between 1712 and 1732) are the College's oldest and most prized possessions. They include Greek and Latin manuscripts, Egyptian Papyri, 16th and 17th century Irish works and even a first folio of Shakespeare.

The crème de la crème must surely be, however, the Irish medieval manuscripts, which include the Book of Durrow and the Book of Armagh (containing the Life and Confessions of St. Patrick).

Outshining even these illustrious masterpieces is the world-famous Book of Kells. Produced about 800 AD in an unknown monastery, it was later brought to the great Columban Foundation at Kells, Co. Meath.

Stolen in 1007, it was recovered three months afterwards, shorn of its gold decorations. The Book remained at Kells until around 1653 when it was sent to Dublin for safekeeping from marauding Cromwellian soldiery. Subsequently, Henry Jones, Bishop of Meath, presented it to Trinity College.

Originally a single large volume, the 340 calf skin leaves were re-bound in 1953 into four volumes, two of which are always on display in the Long Room. Pigments for the marvellous and intricate illustrations came from as far away as the Mediterranean and Central Asia.

The Library's first major purchase of books was in 1601, when 4,000 volumes were bought in England. Further acquisitions and bequests brought the number up to 50,000 by 1800. Since the Act of Union in 1801, the College has been entitled, under the various Copyright Acts, to receive one copy of every work published in the British Isles. Now it takes seven libraries, spread over as many buildings, to house a collection in excess of two and a half million volumes, and each year the amount of occupied shelving increases by about half a mile in length.

DUNSINK OBSERVATORY

In 1785, at Dunsink, Co. Dublin, Trinity College opened its astronomical and meteorological observatory.

Until the invention of quartz clocks, the observatory provided a valuable time service. Highly accurate regulator clocks — still in perfect working order — were required to lose no more than one second in a week and these were connected by cables to the slave clocks at the Ballast Office, GPO, Bank of Ireland and Trinity College.

The observatory went into decline for a period after 1921 but, encouraged by Eamon de Valera, a former pupil of Sir Edmund Whittaker, director 1906-1912, it was reformed in 1947 as part of the School of Cosmic Physics, a constituent school of the Institute for Advanced Studies.

The following years have seen fruitful and important work in the study of solar activity, brightness measurement of the stars and the computation of the orbits of planetary bodies, asteroids and comets. Irish astronomers share facilities with other institutes in several countries including a ten per cent share in the one-metre telescope at the Spanish International Astrophysical Observatory 8,000 feet high on the island of La Palma in the Canaries. The first Irish space experiment, instruments for measuring cosmic rays, was included in a satellite launched in 1984 by the space shuttle, Challenger.

The main building, shown in the drawing, contains offices, storerooms and the residence of the director. On the left is the Meridian Room which once housed various instruments but was turned into a library in 1974. It was impeccably restored after a near disastrous fire in 1977. The roof dome houses a 28 inch reflector telescope which is no longer used.

THE RDS SHOWGROUNDS

On 14th June, 1731, 14 men met to form the Dublin Society to promote "husbandry, manufacturies and other useful arts and sciences". The venue for their first few meetings was a room belonging to the Philosophical Society of Trinity College. For the next 200 years the society was to lead a rather nomadic existence.

From October 1731 the meetings were accommodated in the Lord's Common Room at the Irish Parliament House in College Green where they were to be held for the next 26 years. Thence to Shaw's Court in 1757 and to Grafton Street ten years later. After a further span of 29 years Hawkins Street became the headquarters until the penultimate move to Leinster House in 1815.

When the Dublin Science and Art Museums Act of 1877 transferred control of the Library, Museum, Botanical Gardens and School of Art from the society to the Government, the council used the compensation money to lease 15 acres at Ballsbridge. From 1881 the Spring and Horse Shows were held here. That first site roughly corresponds to today's Jumping Enclosure.

The Agricultural Hall was removed from Kildare Street and re-erected in Ballsbridge to become known as the South Hall. Further building and land acquisition took place which reached a peak following the arrival of all the RDS departments after the Free State Government commandeered Leinster House in 1923.

The 1950s saw much needed expansion across the Simmonscourt Road which culminated in 1972 with the purchase of the Masonic Girls' School and its adjoining land. Daithi P. Hanly's gigantic 3½-acre Simmonscourt Pavilion was begun in 1974. This structure is surmounted by the 10×8 feet weathervane representing the legendary Arkle ridden by Pat Taaffe.

ROYAL IRISH ACADEMY, DAWSON STREET

The Royal Irish Academy is the country's principal learned society and was founded in 1785 to promote the "advancement of science, polite literature and antiquities". Treasures of the academy include the Ardagh Chalice, the Tara Brooch and the Cross of Cong (held in the National Museum) plus many rare books and manuscripts.

An important function of the Academy today is the publication of major works of reference of Irish interest.

THE NATIONAL MUSEUM

The Victorian legacy of laying out exhibitions in uninspired regimentation and unselective overcrowding is rapidly giving way at the National Museum to imaginative and modern display techniques such as the Treasury Gallery. Mounted here is the exhibition of Irish Treasures part of which formed the nucleus of the outstandingly successful touring exhibition which visited the USA and Europe from 1977 to 1984.

In turn the three rooms in the gallery illustrate the pagan Celtic backdrop to early Christian Irish Art, present an audio visual appreciation of the objects and finally contain the masterpieces dating from the 1st century AD to the 16th. Centrepieces of the display embrace the Ardagh Chalice, the Tara Brooch, St. Patrick's Bell, the Cross of Cong and several book shrines, croziers and crosses. Allied Irish Banks are patrons of this particular exhibition.

Some 70 musical instruments, mostly Irish made, grace the reopened Music Room. There are old Irish harps including one ascribed to Carolan, uilleann pipes, pianos, a barrel organ, harpsichords, a hurdy-gurdy, wind instruments, experimental stringed instruments and musical glasses. Other refurbished rooms include the Japanese Room and the Textile Room.

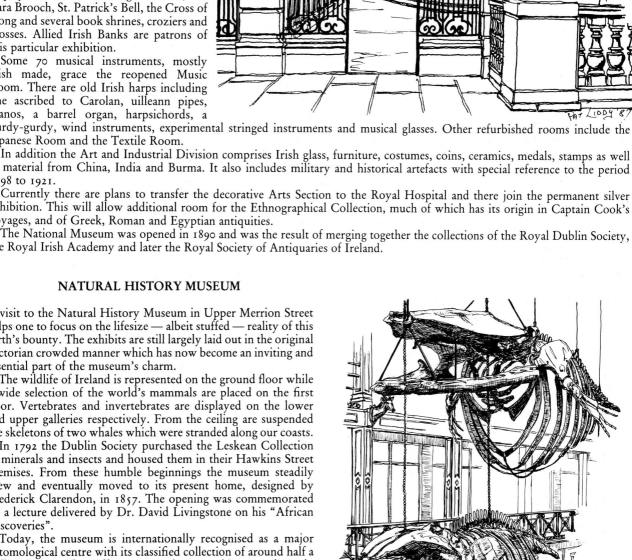

In addition the Art and Industrial Division comprises Irish glass, furniture, costumes, coins, ceramics, medals, stamps as well as material from China, India and Burma. It also includes military and historical artefacts with special reference to the period 1898 to 1921.

Currently there are plans to transfer the decorative Arts Section to the Royal Hospital and there join the permanent silver exhibition. This will allow additional room for the Ethnographical Collection, much of which has its origin in Captain Cook's voyages, and of Greek, Roman and Egyptian antiquities.

The National Museum was opened in 1890 and was the result of merging together the collections of the Royal Dublin Society, the Royal Irish Academy and later the Royal Society of Antiquaries of Ireland.

NATURAL HISTORY MUSEUM

A visit to the Natural History Museum in Upper Merrion Street helps one to focus on the lifesize — albeit stuffed — reality of this earth's bounty. The exhibits are still largely laid out in the original Victorian crowded manner which has now become an inviting and essential part of the museum's charm.

The wildlife of Ireland is represented on the ground floor while a wide selection of the world's mammals are placed on the first floor. Vertebrates and invertebrates are displayed on the lower and upper galleries respectively. From the ceiling are suspended the skeletons of two whales which were stranded along our coasts.

In 1792 the Dublin Society purchased the Leskean Collection of minerals and insects and housed them in their Hawkins Street premises. From these humble beginnings the museum steadily grew and eventually moved to its present home, designed by Frederick Clarendon, in 1857. The opening was commemorated by a lecture delivered by Dr. David Livingstone on his "African Discoveries".

Today, the museum is internationally recognised as a major entomological centre with its classified collection of around half a million insects. The staff are constantly engaged in research work, field studies, publishing papers on various aspects of Irish fauna and assisting many visiting specialists. Specimens for identification are received daily from health inspectors, the Departments of Fisheries and Agriculture, universities, industry and the general public. This is especially vital work in preventing the spread of imported pests.

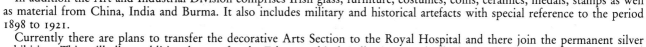

NATIONAL LIBRARY, KILDARE STREET

From its foundation in 1731 the Dublin (later to become the Royal Dublin) Society built up a library for the use of members. The books were transferred to Leinster House when this building became the headquarters of the RDS in 1815.

The library received a great boost in 1863 when it inherited the vast and varied collection of Dr. Jasper Joly. Joly had intimated in his will that his life's work should be made accessible to the general public and accordingly, after the submission of a special commission's report, the Dublin Science and Art Museums Act of 1877 was passed. Under the terms of this Act the library (except for certain specialised books), the museum, the School of Art, and the Botanic Gardens were transferred from the Society to the guardianship of the Government.

Some land on either side of Leinster House was also purchased by the Government and plans were drawn up in 1884 for the magnificent buildings which today house the National Library and the National Museum. On the official opening day, 29th August, 1890, the Lord Lieutenant, Earl Zetland, conferred the honour of knighthood on the senior architect, Thomas Newenham Deane.

Reference material in the library is mainly concerned with items of Irish origin or interest. It consists of books, newspapers, periodicals, maps, prints, photographs, manuscripts, topographical drawings and Government reports. There are collections of ballads and posters and copies of printed publications of Irish works where such originals are only held in foreign libraries.

The computer age has still to come to the library, but hopefully its introduction will only complement the scholarly ambience of elegant architectural surroundings, dark oak panels and carvings and old-fashioned desks complete with book stands and green-shaded lamps.

MUNICIPAL GALLERY, PARNELL SQUARE

James Caulfield, first Earl of Charlemont, commissioned Sir William Chambers to design what turned out to be one of the most splendid Georgian mansions in the city. Built between 1762 and 1765, the three storey house of Portland stone and rustic granite is beautifully set off by the flanking curved screen walls with niches and balustrades.

The Earl, founder member of the Royal Irish Academy, patron of the arts, member of Grattan's Irish Parliament and leader of the Irish Volunteers, died in 1799. Charlemont

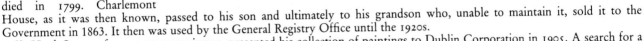

House, as it was then known, passed to his son and ultimately to his grandson who, unable to maintain it, sold it to the Government in 1863. It then was used by the General Registry Office until the 1920s.

Sir Hugh Lane, a famous art connoisseur, presented his collection of paintings to Dublin Corporation in 1905. A search for a suitable permanent gallery was undertaken and at one time it was seriously suggested to build a bridge gallery on the site of the Ha'penny Bridge. This idea was rejected due to the damaging humidity which would result from proximity to the Liffey.

The inability of the Corporation to settle quickly the question of a permanent home — a temporary gallery had been opened in 1908 in Harcourt Street — led Lane to withdraw his paintings and have them transferred to the National Gallery in London. Lane died aboard the ill-fated Lusitania in 1915 and in an unsigned codicil to his will he reversed his previous decision and bequested the collection to Dublin. After many years of debate and legal wranglings his 39 Continental paintings were eventually returned on a share basis with London, to hang in Charlemont House which had been purchased by the Corporation in 1927 to serve as the long-awaited Municipal Gallery of Modern Art. Caulfield, a renowned art lover himself, would have approved.

MARSH'S LIBRARY

This Library, the oldest public library in Ireland was opened by Archbishop Narcissus Marsh in 1701. The building, designed by Sir William Robinson, is much larger than it appears from the road. The inside has remained essentially unchanged since the 18th century and "cages" where readers used to be locked in with rare books are still in place. A major restoration, funded by the American Irish Foundation, was completed on the interior in 1986.

There are periodic exhibitions in the library based on the 25,000 plus volumes which date from the 15th century. Subjects include medicine, law, science, travel, navigation, music, mathematics, classical literature and liturgical works.

Until the 1860s, urban construction had by-passed the area immediately behind the southern side of St. Stephen's Green. However, the fields and gardens behind the elegant town mansions were soon to witness a massive but welcome development.

The second half of the Victorian era was the great age for publicly exhibiting the latest scientific and cultural achievements. To this end a classical edifice, fronting what is now Earlsfort Terrace, was commenced in 1863, and behind it, on the grounds of Coburg Gardens (part of which is now the Iveagh Gardens), rose the glass and iron magnificence of the Winter Gardens. Opened for the International Exhibition in May 1865, these buildings were hailed as "structures where the citizens might enjoy natural recreation combined with the elevating influence of the Arts" and the Winter Gardens were to allow "exercise and recreation during the severe and protracted winters of our climate".

Pre-dating the modern concept of large indoor leisure centres, Dublin's Crystal Palace did not survive the transfer of the main stone building to the Royal University of Ireland.

After University College Dublin took over in 1908, R. M. Butler, redesigned the college to what we see today.

When the majority of UCD's faculties moved out to Belfield, the Government decided in 1974 to convert the Great Hall into a Concert Hall which has been one of the great successes among recent arts ventures in the city.

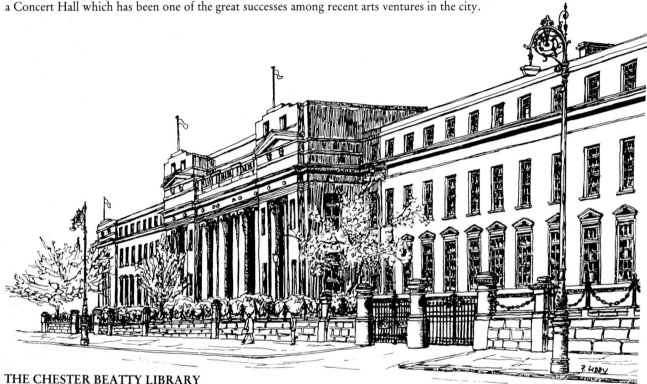

THE CHESTER BEATTY LIBRARY

Sir Alfred Chester Beatty's decision to move to Dublin in 1950 bestowed on the city an incalculable treasure of international significance. The Library and collection of Islamic and Far Eastern art which he had personally assembled is, without doubt, in terms of consistent quality one of the finest in the world. In countries from Egypt to India, Dublin is often synonymous with only one thing — the Chester Beatty Library. So who was this extraordinary man?

Born a New Yorker in 1875, he became the founder of an international mining corporation. His childhood interests in collecting mineral specimens found adult expression during his visits to Egypt when he commenced his serious hobby by purchasing Chinese snuff bottles, made largely from semi-precious stones. Almost up until he died in his 93rd year Sir Alfred painstakingly built up his supreme collection of manuscripts, minature paintings, scrolls, textiles, furniture, seals, prints, clay tablets, papyri and book bindings. Their origins stretched from Europe through the Middle East to India, China and Japan.

In 1954 Chester Beatty officially opened his new library and on his death in 1968, in accordance with his wishes, the collection passed to the Nation.

It is hard to appreciate fully the breadth and scale of Chester Beatty's legacy. For instance the library contains the oldest known New Testament papyri, one of the most comprehensive Japanese print collections, the world's largest compilation of Jade books and rhinoceros horn cups, the 1259 manuscript of the Omar Khayyam and one of the best collections of Ottoman paintings outside the libraries of Istanbul.

The Library and Gallery of Oriental Art is open Tuesday to Saturday, and guided tours and theme exhibitions are regularly organised.

THE ARTANE BOYS' BAND

Stone from Artane Castle (demolished 1825) was later reused in the building of the Christian Brothers Industrial School on the same land. Opened in 1870 the school, at its peak, housed 800 boys who, because of unfortunate family circumstances or as a result of disciplinary problems, were found to be unsuitable for regular schools.

The school band was formed in 1872 and due to the foresight and determination of its late director, Brother Joseph O'Connor, it survived the Industrial School's closure in 1969. He had obtained permission to keep the band going by enlisting new members from other schools on the city's northside.

The link with the GAA goes back to 1886 when the Artane Band played "A Nation Once Again" on the occasion of the first major field day organised in the city by the newly formed association.

However, the annual programme of the band goes far beyond the 16 or so appearances at Croke Park. In tours that take them all over the country and abroad to Britain and the USA its versatility finds expression in classical concerts, Strauss balls, choral works and even jazz sessions.

The 150 members are divided, depending on experience, between three band units, the First Band being the main performing group. The ages of the boys range between nine and sixteen and many of them go on to become professional musicians.

ST. ENDA'S, RATHFARNHAM

From their home in Ranelagh, Patrick and Willie Pearse launched a daring educational experiment in 1908. Their philosophy of Gaelic Ireland, first but not to the exclusion of other traditions, was alien and an anathema to the establishment of the time.

In an effort to expose their students to the wonders of nature the brothers purchased the lease of the Hermitage Rathfarnham which was ideally located in 25 acres of wild parkland. The Pearse family moved into the house and extensions were built to accommodate classrooms. The school was named Scoil Eanna or St. Enda's after the saint who taught his pupils amid the rugged splendour of the Aran Islands.

Mounting debts soon preoccupied the brothers, as did their increasing involvement in nationalist politics. Some of the guns landed from the Asgard in 1914 were hidden at St. Enda's and volunteers drilled in the grounds. In the Rising of 1916 pupils fought alongside their tutors and four of the latter, Patrick (Irish and History), Willie (Art and Drama), jovial Thomas McDonagh (English and French) and Con Colbert (Physical Education) were executed in Kilmainham Jail.

In 1919 the remaining members of the Pearse family were able to purchase the house and grounds with the proceeds from a special fund started in America, but dwindling attendances and increasing financial stress finally closed the school in 1935. When Senator Margaret Pearse died in 1968 the property passed to the nation to be kept, in accordance with the wishes of their mother, as a memorial to the Pearse brothers.

Totally refurbished by the Office of Public Works, the house now contains a very interesting collection of Pearse memorabilia, excellently supplemented by an audio-visual presentation. The original classrooms now incorporate a nature study centre freely available for schoolchildren.

The park and the house are well worth a family or school visit and are open everyday all year round.

NATIONAL MARITIME MUSEUM

An appropriate connection was struck in 1977 when the Maritime Institute of Ireland, a body devoted to the promotion of our seafaring heritage, opened the National Maritime Museum in the former Mariners' Church at Haigh Terrace, Dún Laoghaire. The church was built in 1837 for the benefit of visiting sailors and those from the Royal Navy guardships permanently stationed in the harbour. A notable curiosity of the building is the pair of detention boxes in the gallery, still to be seen, which were used to accommodate naval defaulters present under escort.

Dominated by the revolving lighting optic, which shone from the Baily Lighthouse up until 1972, is one of the most significant maritime collections in these islands. It includes curiosities such as an early 19th century model made by French prisoners-of-war, replicas of ships familiar around our coasts for centuries, muskets and cannonballs from the wrecks of the Spanish Armada and even a fully working model of the internationally-coded buoy system.

A contender for pride of place must surely be the 38 feet long French naval ship's boat normally used for ferrying senior officers. It was captured after the French invasion fleet, inspired by Wolfe Tone, turned back from Bantry Bay in 1796. Still displaying its untouched post-Revolution colours of red, white and blue, the craft is believed to be the oldest surviving ship's boat in the world.

There is also a model of the gunboat "Helga" which shelled rebel positions in Dublin during 1916 and ironically went on to become the "Murchu", the first vessel of the newly formed Irish Naval Service.

A much-envied working model of the Great Eastern, which was once owned by the master of the real life gargantuan, Wicklow born Captain Robert Hallin, is the focal point of a varied and impressive collection about the life and times of the great ship and its commanding officer. Five times larger than any ship of the day and only 12 feet shorter than the Titanic, Brunel's masterpiece was sold in 1888 for a mere £16,000 scrap money after only 30 years in service, mostly at cable laying.

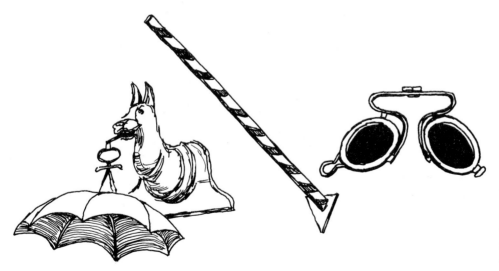

CIVIC MUSEUM

This old building in South William Street houses a collection of municipal artefacts and historical items relating to the city. It was originally built for the Society of Artists and in 1791 the Corporation moved in when the Tholsel was found to be unsafe. Council meetings took place here until 1852 when the Corporation moved to the newly acquired City Hall on Cork Hill.

The drawing illustrates the symbols once used by shopkeepers to indicate their line of business; an umbrella, a barber's pole and a pair of pincenez.

Three major newspapers dominate the Dublin scene. The oldest is *The Irish Times* which was first published in 1859. *The Irish Independent* and *Evening Herald* were being sold from 1891 while the youngest of the trio, *The Irish Press*, was launched in 1931. Almost a hundred newspapers have at one time or another been published in Dublin since. An Account of the Chief Occurances of Ireland was circulated in 1659.

MUNICIPAL LIBRARIES

Dublin Corporation opened its first two public libraries in 1884 in Capel and Thomas Streets. Today there are 21 libraries in the city and 15 in the county area supplemented by 12 mobile libraries. Each year there are two and a quarter million borrowings with an additional two million books lent through the special school service.

Library activities have now expanded to include such items as exhibitions, seminars, lectures, reference services, creative writing groups and local Community Information Services. The Central Library in the Irish Life Centre off Henry Street has an extensive music library, computer self-training courses, language laboratories and a large business reference section.

MALAHIDE LIBRARY

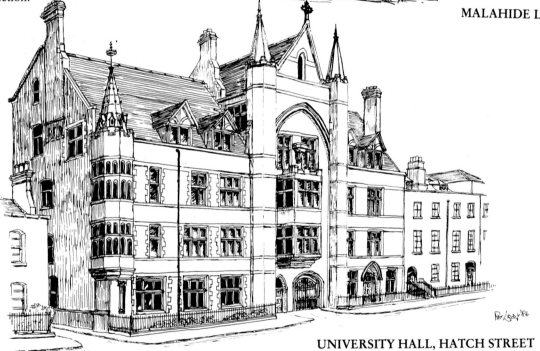

UNIVERSITY HALL, HATCH STREET

Too many city centre private institutions and colleges succumbed to the property boom of the 60s and 70s. These bodies, almost frantic in their efforts to relocate to the suburbs, left their original premises, often magnificent architectural specimens, prey to the demolition squads.

One worthy institution which resolutely clung on and now thrives (as all the others might have done if they could have stayed on) is the University Hall in Hatch Street. The Hall was founded by the Jesuits to provide hostel accommodation for students attending the National University.

No expense was spared in designing a very dignified building. The Hall was opened in 1913 when three priests and thirty students moved in.

The Jesuits have been associated with University life in Dublin since the foundation in 1854 of the Catholic University of Ireland.

During the academic year the Hall accommodates male students attending the city's third level colleges. In the summer months the doors are open to both sexes who come to Dublin, including many from abroad, to pursue various specialist courses.

"THE BAYNO", BULL ALLEY

The philanthrophy of Edward Cecil Guinness, as embodied in the Iveagh Trust, extended to erecting decent accommodation for the general poor of Dublin especially those who lived in the wretched slums between Christ Church and St. Patrick's. Capped by attractive mansard windows and roofs, the Iveagh Buildings were built to last, as evidenced by their 18-inch thick brick walls.

The families of the poor were large, uneducated and spent their lives on the streets. In order to provide useful alternatives for them the Iveagh Trust founded in 1909 a play centre, one of the first of its kind in these islands, in an old building in Francis Street. Two years later the children in the centre were treated to a royal visit by King George V and Queen Mary.

Such was the success of the play centre that Lord Iveagh donated £38,000 to build the impressive structure in Bull Alley. Opened in 1915 it had 11 classrooms, three large halls and an outdoor playground. Very advanced for its day, the curriculum included sewing, dancing, art, cookery, singing and swimming. From 1915 to 1959 a staggering total of 7,820,520 visits were made by the children of the inner city aged between three and fourteen.

The locals affectionately nicknamed the centre the Bayno — from beano, meaning feast — perhaps a reference to the cocoa and buns handed out to the little patrons.

The play centre, by now no longer functioning in its original role as a result of a declining local population, was partly occupied in 1968 by the Liberties Post Primary School. The building was bought outright in 1977 by the City of Dublin Vocational Education Committee and is now the home of the Liberties Vocational School.

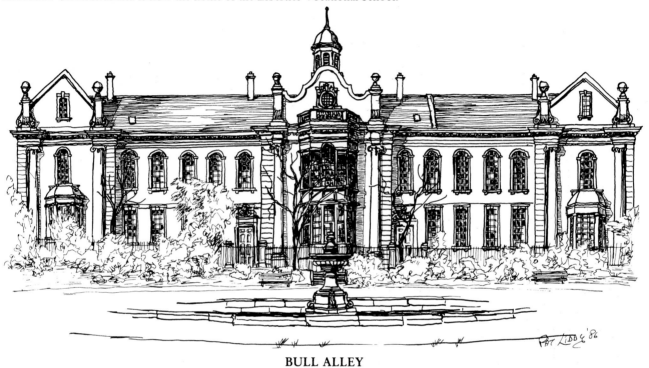

BULL ALLEY

NATIONAL GALLERY OF IRELAND

Inside a temporary Crystal Palace type structure erected on the lawn of Leinster House the country's greatest art collection up to then was assembled for showing at the 1853 Great Industrial Exhibition. This event inspired the foundation of the Irish Institution to promote the idea of a National Gallery. Public interest was generated by holding annual loan exhibitions of Old Masters and with subscriptions starting to come in a number of paintings were acquired.

At the same time a committee had been formed to commemorate in some permanent way the munificence of William Dargan, the outstanding inaugurator of many Irish railway companies who had almost single handedly financed the Great Exhibition. Agreeing that an Irish National Gallery would be a fitting testimonial for Dargan the committee donated £5,000 to the Irish Institution.

Built as a copy of the neighbouring Natural History Museum, the Gallery was opened in January 1864 — on the same day Dargan's statue in the front lawn sculptured by Thomas Farrell was unveiled. In 1903 the Gallery was enlarged and the present portico entrance was constructed. A further extension to the north wing was opened in 1968 and both these additions are very well matched with the original narrow south wing.

The success of the Gallery is in part due to the succession of gifted directors who arranged many shrewd acquisitions. Early directors such as George Mulvany Henry Doyle (the uncle of Sir Arthur Conan Doyle), Walter Armstrong and Sir Hugh Lane established the international reputation of the Gallery by purchasing important works of famous artists such as Fra Angelico, Titian, Reynolds, Rembrandt, El Greco, Rubens, Gainsborough and Goya. In subsequent years Irish artists were not neglected.

George Bernard Shaw spent many a youthful day appreciating these treasures and his bequests to the Gallery, principally the royalties from "Pygmalion" and "My Fair Lady", have helped to further enrich the collection and make the National Gallery one of the finest for its size in the world. *(See illustration page 96.)*

Chapter Ten

Bustling Business

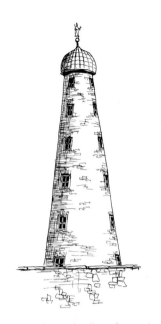

The old windmill at the Guinness plant actually dates from the time when George Roe and Company operated a whiskey distillery here. The windmill, now shorn of its giant vanes, is 70 feet in diameter at the base and 150 feet in height and is surmounted by an onion-shaped cupola.

·Although it never achieved the status of a great commercial centre Dublin was none the less established by the Vikings as a trading port of some importance. From excavations we can deduce that the import business thrived and one of the Norsemen's great foreign revenue earners was the export through Dublin to other Scandinavian colonies of Irish and British slaves. By the 12th century locally-made gold and silver ornaments, textiles, hides, live horses and dried fish comprised some of the cargoes that filled the holds of ships which plied between the ports of Dublin, Dalkey and Howth and places as far apart as Iceland and the Mediterranean.

The Middle Ages saw a rise in the wealth and prestige of the merchant classes and the organisation of the powerful trade guilds. While most trades were carried on indoors the sale of food items such as fish, meat, corn, vegetables and the like took place in outdoor markets, a practice which has survived to this day in Moore Street.

Religious refugees from Europe, who began to arrive in 1576 and throughout the next hundred years included Dutch Reformists, French Huguenots and Russian Jews of whom many were merchants or industrialists. They wasted little time in re-establishing their enterprises and linen, woollen and silk mills sprang up in places like the Liberties where the Huguenots first settled. British trade restrictions from 1699 impoverished many Huguenot families and after the collapse of the weaving industries the Liberties sank into a state of decay and despair from which they have never fully recovered.

However, there was modest success in other ventures and by the 19th century there was great activity in the export of agricultural goods and in the emerging brewing and distilling firms. The swelling ranks of the middle class created a huge demand for consumer products and their needs were supplied by local manufacturers and an increasing number of retail outlets. For all that Dublin never became a major industrial city and has been spared the worst excesses of environmental and atmospheric pollution associated with large plants. The majority of manufacturing is now grouped into industrial estate units located in the outer city.

PENNEYS, MARY STREET

The dome of Penneys in Mary Street is a well known Dublin landmark. Originally built between 1902 and 1906 for Todd Burns the store possesses one of the most dramatic facades in the city.

THE DUBLIN CHAMBER OF COMMERCE

Sailing from Ringsend in 1695, the armed merchant vessel, the Ouzel (old English name for a blackbird), set course for the Middle East. After three years without news of the ship it was presumed lost and the owners, Ferris, Twigg and Cash, claimed on the underwriters.

Then, remarkably, in 1700 the Ouzel limped back into Dublin, patched and bullet holed. The crew explained that they had been attacked and imprisoned by Algerian pirates but after a number of years they had succeeded in repossessing their ship while their captors were drunk. Their welcome return soon caused consternation as to the rightful ownership of the pirate booty which had filled the holds. Ferris, Twigg and Cash had already been paid in full and the insurers had claim only to the ship itself and the original cargo.

The courts of law haggled interminably for 5 years so the matter was submitted to and quickly settled by the arbitration of a group of merchants and traders who instructed that the pirate treasure was to be sold to alleviate poverty among the merchants of Dublin. From this success arose the Ouzel Galley Society, a permanent arbitration body which lingered on until 1888.

A committee of Merchants evolved from the Society in 1761 which in its turn instituted the Chamber of Commerce in 1783. Thus the Dublin Chamber shares with two other chambers in the United Kingdom the distinction of being the oldest in Britain and Ireland.

Number 7, Clare Street was bought by the Chamber in 1964 following their move from the Commercial Buildings in Dame Street.

121

CLERY'S

M. J. Clery bought the Dublin Drapery Warehouse Company in 1883 and gave his name to one of Ireland's most famous department stores. The shop was destroyed in 1916 and the present building, designed in a massive and pleasing classical style by Ashlin and Coleman, was opened in 1922. The legendary Denis Guiney acquired Clery's in 1940 and after his death in 1967 his wife Mary took over control.

Clery's famous ballroom has recently been restored so it may resound again to musical outpourings and shuffling feet.

ROCHES & ARNOTTS, flanking the newly pedestrianised Henry Street

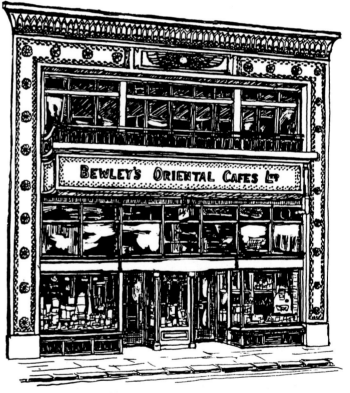

BEWLEY'S CAFES

The scent of Joshua Bewley's roasting coffee first began to waft through the air in the 1840s and since then his establishments have become part of the Dublin tradition. In late 1986 the company, which was facing financial difficulties, was taken over by Campbell Catering Limited.

SWITZERS, GRAFTON STREET

The coming of the railroads in the 1830s spurred on the exodus of the middle and the priviliged classes from the city centre to the new suburbs. Private homes were converted into retail outlets, warehouses and commercial institutions. This trend was particularly evident along Sackville, Dame, South Great Georges and Grafton Streets.

In 1838, a Swiss immigrant opened his shop at number 91, Grafton Street. In a short period this industrious and kindly man had solidly established his firm of woollen drapers, tailors and general clothiers. Switzers' 300 employees were busily engaged in turning out quality clothes which might include gowns for ladies and court dress for the gentlemen on the occasion of the Lord Lieutenant's Ball. In the 1850s knickerbockers were selling for one pound.

The time had come for significant expansion. Despite the famine disasters and the depression following in their wake, the retail business in the city was growing. Across the road from Switzers, Brown Thomas & Co. was flourishing, as also were shops such as Clerys, Arnotts and Pims. In 1859 a competition was held between four architects to design the new Commercial Hall for what was now to become Switzer, Ferguson & Co.

Rawson Carroll won the contract and his building is that part the large Switzer sign is presently attached to.

GARNETTS & KEEGAN'S, PARLIAMENT STREET

In 1860, Paddy Garnett first opened his shooting and fishing tackle shop in Bishop Street, later moving to Crampton Court and finally ending at No. 31, Parliament Street. From the turn of the century Larry Keegan ran a similar business at Inns Quay until he was bought over by Garnett in 1939. A year later, with revenues badly hit by the outbreak of war, the shops were sold to Frank Gordon. John Hanlon (his family gave us Hanlon's Pub and Hanlon's Corner on the North Circular Road) acquired the firm in 1949 and the business was then confined to Parliament Street.

Well known in the clothing trade and in sporting circles, John Hanlon died in 1981 and control has since passed to his son-in-law, Barry A. Mason.

Garnetts & Keegan's is famous for exquisite fishing flies, and countless British and Continental fishermen wait until they arrive in Dublin before procuring their baits.

123

BROWN THOMAS, GRAFTON STREET

John Brown opened his small Grafton Street haberdashery in 1848 and a year later he formed a partnership with James Thomas. Their firm became known as Brown, Thomas and Company and traded as linen drapers, silk mercers, costume and mantle makers, milliners, lacemen, hosiers, glovers and general outfitters.

Becoming famous for its policy of stocking only high quality and fashionable goods, the expanding enterprise soon swallowed up a number of neighbouring houses. By the 1890s over 300 staff were employed and the premises were described as "very extensive and forms one of the most striking architectural features of Grafton Street, the numerous plate-glass windows presenting, with their attractive exhibition of goods, a recherché appearance perfectly in harmony with the high-class character of the establishment".

The store was sold to Selfridges of London in 1928 but after the outbreak of the so-called Economic War with Britain it reverted back to Irish ownership in 1933. The purchaser was the legendary John F. McGuire who with his son, Edward, revitalised Brown Thomas. It was during their proprietorship that many physical improvements to the shop were carried out including the addition of an elegant marble staircase and pillars.

From the mid 1960s the company went public and within ten years it had been acquired by Galen Weston whose family also control Quinnsworth and Penneys.

Extensive restoration has already been carried out to the Victorian frontage which thankfully is not spoiled by ugly grilles at night time. A further programme of internal renovation will transform the first floor into a Colonial style revealing again the marble staircase and pillars in all their glory.

EASONS, O'CONNELL STREET

Charles Eason had been the enterprising manager for 30 years in W. H. Smiths bookselling business in Dublin when he bought the firm from the latter in 1886. The O'Connell Street premises was a victim of the 1916 Rising but phoenix-like another and more magnificant building rose quickly from the ashes and was open again for business in 1919.

Showing confidence again in the future of O'Connell Street and offering their own contribution to the improvement of the thoroughfare. Eason's undertook a number of enhancements to the front of their building in 1987. The plastic was removed to make way for quality old-style lettering and a huge chiming clock, made by Stokes of Cork, was erected. Next door, Clarks Shoes followed suit when they also revamped their ground floor with great taste.

This kind of sympathic treatment is not only agreeable to look at but is also good for business. When the untidy clutter of plastic signs is eliminated the whole impact or uniqueness of the building is brought into play and the individuality of the firm is stressed.

HANNAS, NASSAU STREET

Hannas Bookshops have played an important part in quenching our thirst for words and one of the foremost among these has been Hanna's of Nassau Street. From sometime in the mid 19th century William Magee ran a bookshop in Nassau Street and in the 1890s Fred Hanna joined the firm as a sales assistant. In 1907, on Magee's death, Hanna bought the business and 8 years later changed the name to Fred Hanna Ltd. Fred's brother Joseph was assistant librarian in Trinity which began the company's long association with that college.

Fred's sons Arthur and Walter were brought into the business and in 1926 a second shop, called the Dublin Book Shop, was opened at Batchelor's Walk. This shop, until it closed in 1976, became a browsers' paradise especially

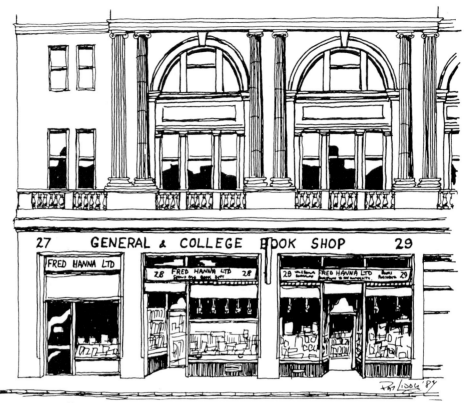

among the titles displayed on the pavement stalls.

Over the following years the business at Nassau Street expanded, the adjoining premises were purchased and Hanna's reputation has grown not only with regard to general bookselling but also in the areas of second-hand and antiquarian books. Children and third-level students are also catered for, the latter especially since 1979 when Hanna's took over the shop in UCD.

At any one time Hanna's has to cope with handling up to 70,000 different titles (including 300 on cookery alone) and annual sales of up to half a million items ranging from Irish interest books to Malay dictionaries and a volume dealing with trekking in the Himalayas.

WALTON'S, NORTH FREDERICK STREET

A Feis Ceoil violin gold medalist, Martin Walton, looked older than his 15 years when he was eagerly accepted as a courier between the beleaguered GPO and the Jacob's strongpoint during the Rebellion of 1916. With his knowledge of the back streets, he succeeded in exchanging messages and in spiriting rebels through the ever-tightening army cordons.

He escaped capture after the surrender but in November 1920 he was imprisoned in Ballykilnar Internment Camp for his activities during the War of Independence. It was here that he met Peadar Kearney, the composer of the National Anthem, and both of them helped to form the prison band.

After his release, Martin Walton devoted himself to teaching music and in 1924 he founded his music college at No. 2, North Frederick Street. He followed this successful move by opening a musical instrument shop and in later acquiring the three neighbouring premises.

The launching of the Glenside label in 1952 did much to promote Irish music and brought us many memorable tunes and performers. They included Noel Purcell and his "Dublin Saunter" and the "Whistling Gypsy" of Joe Lynch.

In Walton's you can select any instrument, from a tiny Jews Harp to a 300-year-old fiddle or a £10,000 grand piano. This many-faceted company has also gained an international reputation for manufacturing musical instruments, especially those of the Irish tradition. Recognition of this was evidenced recently in the purchase of a number of folk harps by the Frankfurt, Cologne and Stuttgart Opera Houses.

The early and continuing popularity of Irish music owes a great deal to the efforts of Martin Walton and his family.

125

BIRD MARKET, PETER STREET

Dublin's Bird Market is an ancient institution, being perhaps over 900 years in existence. This, if true, would make it second in age only to its counterpart in Moscow.

The long-established tradition almost came to an end, when the Society for the Prevention of Cruelty to Animals expressed understandable concern for the welfare of the birds in their small cages, often exposed to inclement weather along open streets. It was actually deemed illegal to sell birds in a public place under the 1965 Protection of Animals Act.

The organisers of the market, the Dublin Bird Market Association, frantically looked for a solution, which eventually came in 1969 from an unexpected source. Sam Stephenson, of architectural fame, offered the yard behind his headquarters, Molyneaux House, on Bride Street. With this move the bye-law conditions could now be satisfied, as admission was under private control, and there was a greater element of protection.

Every Sunday morning, between 10.30 and 12.30 the chirping of canaries, linnets, budgies, finches and mules (crossbreeds) echo across the yard.

FRUIT AND VEGETABLE MARKET

In 1892, the Fruit and Vegetable Market was erected by Dublin Corporation at a cost of £100,000, replacing the numerous individual markets operating unhygienically from various backyards around the locality.

The attractive red and yellow brick building, designed by Spencer Harty, was built adjacent to the site of the historic Abbey of St. Mary. In fact the Chancery Street car park is reputed to lie over the monks' graveyard. The varied herringbone designs of the brickwork, the food motif carvings, and the ornamental iron grilles and gates embellish the building. The main entrance of Mary's Lane is surmounted by a huge limestone representation of the City Arms.

Originally established to serve the Dublin area, the market has now become the national clearing centre for the 26 counties. About 50 merchants have stalls within the main hall, but many others trade outside from their own premises.

Enshrined in the bye-laws of the market are principals which maintain competition, oppose monopolies, and allow merchants to operate with manageable overheads, thus ensuring a constant supply of fresh food at reasonable prices.

During the morning peak hours the air of urgent hustle and bustle is augmented by the shouting of vendors, the jostling of buyers, the clanging of auctioneers' bells, and the continuous shunting of forklift trucks.

THE IVEAGH MARKET

Under the direction of the Iveagh Trust, established by the first Earl of Iveagh, Edward Cecil Guinness (1847-1927), houses and social services were provided for the poor in both Dublin and London. As one of its projects, the Trust financed the landscaping of St. Patrick's Park, an area left vacant after the slums beside the cathedral were cleared.

The demolitions had ousted the street vendors who for generations had plied their trades in the warren of alleyways, lanes and narrow roads. They had been promised accommodation in the proposed new Iveagh Market but the hardy clothes and fish dealers, preferring the outdoor life and fearing the imposition of rents, refused to move and became embroiled in lengthy litigation. In the end the matter was resolved and the market was opened in 1907.

The Edwardian brick building boasts some fine carved keystone heads, emblematic of the various nations around the world. It is well worth looking out for the extraordinary bearded, winking face with the impish grin — some say that it represents Lord Iveagh himself.

While business, especially in the old clothes department, may not be as good as it used to be, the dealers still carry on. To give up might otherwise bring social isolation and loneliness. So strong are family traditions in the market that many of the stall owners are still known by their mothers' maiden names.

SOUTH CITY MARKETS, GEORGE'S STREET

Replacing the grimy old Castle Market, the monumental structure of the South City Markets was opened as the city's first major shopping centre in 1881.

Then in the early hours of Saturday, 27th August, 1892, the city's biggest fire to date consumed the entire building. Only the unstinted efforts of the fire brigade over the next 24 hours prevented the bonded liquor in the cellar from igniting and perhaps devastating the surrounding blocks.

Miraculously, no one was killed but the shopkeepers lost their premises and overhead homes. The stall-holders suffered greater financial loss because, owing to the transient nature of the business, they had been unable to insure their merchandise. There was a flood of public sympathy for them and a subscription fund for their relief was organised.

The centre was restored in the same style, but without the four great pyramid towers, and was reopened in September, 1894. Further modifications were carried out in 1955, and ten years later the present owners, MEPC, acquired the property. In 1982 this company carried out the tasteful "Victorianisation" of the market arcade.

127

The tradcart was introduced in 1987 to help create a new standard of environmental improvement in Moore Street. The first four carts were sponsored by the Dublin City Centre Business Association. Moore Street needs to be upgraded and stalls based on the tradcart style, i.e. a crafted wooden stall with an awning, would contribute greatly to this end.

MOORE STREET MARKET

Decayed houses, stench-filled alleyways, putrid slaughter houses and hopeless living and working conditions were part and parcel of the scene around the teeming market areas of the 19th century Moore Street environs. From 1853 various attempts were made to improve the situation with abortive plans proposing projects ranging from a circular market hall, new abattoirs and a wide arcade from Moore Street to Sackville (O'Connell) Street.

After the 1962 Planning and Development Bill was passed, Dublin Corporation compulsorily purchased about seven acres to the west of Moore Street and resold them for £3 million to Irish Life in 1977. Thus the building of the ILAC Centre swept aside the dereliction that was once Horseman's Row, Riddle's Row, Cole's Lane and Sampson's Lane.

There are up to ninety casual traders who have Corporation permits to operate in Moore Street on fixed numbered pitches. They are mostly women and many of them have been there for over 60 years and their mothers before them.

They start work at 7.30 a.m. with a visit to the Fruit and Fish Markets, from where their loads are delivered by three quaint horse-drawn carts.

The sound of the friendly and colourful exchange of banter is one of the pleasures of a slow, appreciative stroll down Moore Street.

THE ADAM SHOWROOMS, ST. STEPHEN'S GREEN

Nineteenth century commercial life in Dublin was enriched by several immigrant businessmen from Scotland, including James Adam. He set up his famous fine art auctioneering firm in 1887 at No. 19, St. Stephen's Green. Acting for the leading people around the whole country, both he and his business prospered.

Auctions in Adam's include period furniture, paintings, glass, silver, porcelain, wine, china, books, manuscripts and the like. Occasional or unusual items such as model trains and toys are presented for sale, as were some model ships sold on the instructions of the liquidator of Irish Shipping. Every three or four months special sales of the works of Irish artists take place.

And is it worth rummaging around in the attic for a forgotten valuable heirloom? It was for one lady who discovered a damaged old painting which later fetched her a neat £77,000.

TRUSTEE SAVINGS BANK

The T.S.B. Head Office in Grafton Street was originally built for the Northern Bank in 1904.
The building was extensively refurbished in the 1980s by the T.S.B.

GATE THEATRE

GAIETY THEATRE

CROWN ALLEY

PALACE BAR

McDOWELL'S JEWELLERS

McDowell's, trading since 1870, moved to Sackville (O'Connell) Street in 1904. Destroyed in the Rising of 1916 the shop was rebuilt very quickly. An elegant refurbishment was undertaken in 1986.

WEIR'S, GRAFTON STREET

A Scotsman, John Boyd Dunlop, by now living in Dublin, pondered on ways to improve the bone-shaking bicycle ride over the rough roads for his ten-year-old son. In 1880, from his Stephen's Street premises, he submitted his revolutionary patent on a pneumatic tyre — although the actual principle of the inflatable tyre had been invented 43 years earlier.

One of his friends and collaborators in the project was a fellow-countryman, Thomas Weir. He was a Glasgow goldsmith and diamond setter, who came to Dublin in the mid 1800s and took up a position as foreman in the workshops of West's of Grafton Street. By 1869 Weir had opened his own shop down the street at No. 5.

Always an imaginative and innovative man, Weir's love of experimentation resulted in the submission of some patents of his own, including a design for the provision of mudflaps for spats! He soon moved premises to No. 3, Wicklow Street, nostalgically taking with him the original front door of No. 5, Grafton Street. This unique door, with its frosted glass lettering and decoration, can still be seen at the upper entrance on Wicklow Street.

The business flourished and, perhaps also because of his profitable association with Dunlop, Weir was able to expand into the adjoining premises. The firm has since extended around the corner and into Grafton Street again. Employing around one hundred staff, including silversmiths, valuers, engravers, watchmakers and other specialists, Weir's is now the fourth largest single unit jewellers in Europe. The silver department, to take one example, is famous for its work, which includes designs ranging from commemorative shields to Bishops' croziers and supplying the Royal Dublin Society's Aga Khan Cup.

One of the few major city-centre stores still remaining in family hands, the preservation of traditional values at Weirs is jealously guarded. Old fashioned sunblinds still protect the Victorian styled shop front. The elegant interior is dominated by the 1910 vintage tall curved glass and carved mahogany showcases.

131

GUINNESS, ST. JAMES'S GATE

Every year a sign writer passes under the keystone's head, aptly garlanded with hops, places his ladder against the front gate of Guinness's and record the start of another year in the life of a brewery which first commenced business in 1759.

Richard Guinness passed on his brewing expertise to his son, Arthur, who, at the age of only 34, bought an old disused brewery on a plot of land opposite the site of St. James Gate, once a part of the city's western defences. The lease, obtained from a Mark Rainsford, was for 9,000 years at an annual rent of £45. Occupying four acres, the brewery initially consisted of a copper, a kieve, one mill and two malthouses. In contrast, over 60 acres are now employed making it the largest brewery in Europe. Its modern central brewhouse can produce two and a half million pints per day.

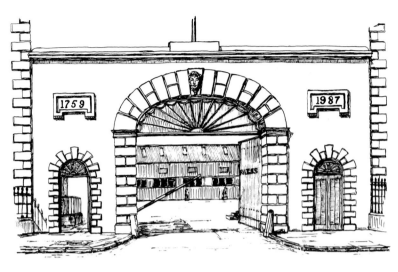

Ale was the first product but Arthur saw a better possibility in an English brew made dark in colour by the use of roasted barley. This beverage had been popular with the porters at Covent Garden and Billingsgate in London so hence the name "porter". Then a stronger brew was manufactured. It was called extra stout porter which was shortened to become "stout".

Soon, in the best tradition of "Coals to Newcastle", Dublin was exporting the Guinness porter to London. Admittedly, the first shipment in 1769 was only six and a half barrels. But today, James's Gate exports more beer than any other single brewery anywhere else in the world. Some 300 million pints a year are shipped abroad by the Guinness Brewing Group in Ireland.

The first Arthur Guinness, having made an extraordinary success of his firm at a time most Irish industries were collapsing, died at his home in Gardiner Street in 1803.

Guinness is transferred to Britain in two specially constructed company-owned tanker ships — m.v. Miranda Guinness and m.v. Lady Patricia. There is also a sister brewery at Park Royal in London, as well as others in Nigeria, Malaysia, Cameroon and Ghana and the "black stuff" is produced under licence in a further 16 countries.

NORTHERN BANK, COLLEGE GREEN

The Northern Bank, which first came to Dublin in 1888, purchased the former Hibernian Bank at the corner of Church Lane and College Green in 1979. There then followed an outstanding refurbishment which can be especially appreciated at night time when the plastered ceiling of the banking hall is wonderously illuminated by upward projecting lighting. In 1987 The National Australian Bank took over the Northern Bank chain.

THE STOCK EXCHANGE

Entrance to the Stock Exchange on Anglesea Street.

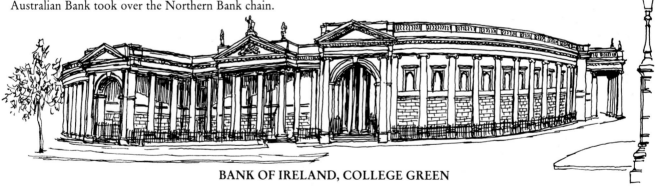

BANK OF IRELAND, COLLEGE GREEN

Because of its flat and enclosed situation it is hard to take in the full grandeur of the Bank of Ireland building in College Green. It would have to be set on a hill away from other buildings to appreciate the sweeping, curving magnificence of a building that, over a period of time, engaged the energies of at least four of Dublin's greatest architects; Edward Lovett Pearce (the central section started in 1729), James Gandon (the east portico in 1785), Robert Parke (the Foster Place portico in 1797, admittedly to Gandon's original design) and Francis Johnston (the curving screen wall and the armoury annexe in Foster Place in 1803). The Bank was originally built as the House of Parliament but after the Act of Union in 1800 the building was adapted by Johnston for the sole use of the Bank of Ireland.

The old House of Lords is still largely intact and has two large tapestries hanging from the wall. They illustrate the Battle of the Boyne and the Siege of Derry and were first hung in 1735. The mace of the Speaker of the House of Commons is also on display.

133

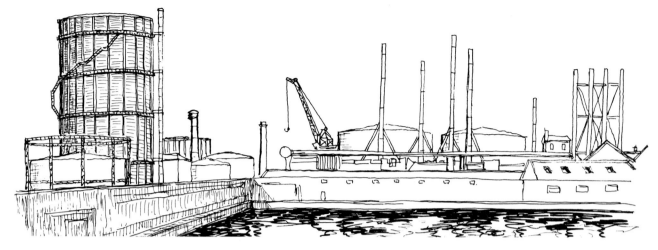

NEW DUBLIN GAS

The drawing shows the almost redundant works dating from the era before the advent of Kinsale natural gas. When gas was first manufactured in 1825 it brought the immediate benefit of superior street and home lighting.

The majority of the city's 2,500 kilometres of cast-iron pipeline was laid in the last century. Leaks were rare but the arrival of natural gas has caused problems to many of the 200,000 screwed land joints and a number of serious explosions took place in 1987. As a result remedial action had to be urgently undertaken leaving thousands of holes all over the city. They inspired frustrated Dubliners to fume and complain, to turn the gaping excavations into excuses for being late for appointments and to even write songs and ditties about them.

POOLBEG POWER STATION

Casting its reflections on the waters of Dublin Bay the rising bulk of Poolbeg Power Station, with its great soaring twin chimneys, does not altogether offend an environmentally sensitive location. Artists and photographers are drawn to the challenge of capturing or interpreting a massiveness that can be sometimes sheathed in delicate curtains of mist or clothed in the varying colours of its atmospheric moods. But hints of romanticism abruptly end outside the perimeter of the station, banished by the clinical manufacturing of raw power.

The first stage of Poolbeg was commissioned in early 1971 with the main power output supplied by two Swiss-made 120 megawatt, oil fuelled turbines. Despite the relative economy of scale compared to giant American and European installations. Poolbeg earned a place among the top five stations in the world for efficiency and availability.

By 1979 a second chimney and a 270 megawatt French-built turbine were added. Constructed extra high to keep the smoke clear of the city, the 680 feet stacks are known to Dubliners as the "candy sticks".

It takes maintenance men over an hour to climb their weary way to the top.

1984/85 saw the complex conversion to natural gas allowing the turbines to have the dual capability of switching between oil and gas. Operating by gas is cleaner and although it produces dense plumes from the chimneys these emissions are apparently nothing more harmful than plain water vapour.

Built partly on the site of the old Pigeon House station coal yard and partly on reclaimed land, Poolbeg was designed and engineered by the ESB's own Projects and Civil Works departments.

JOHNSTON, MOONEY AND O'BRIEN BUILDINGS

When Mr. T. O'Brien launched his bakery and confectionery business in 1835 at South Leinster Street he had to compete with 130 other similar firms operating in the Dublin catchment area. He must have been singularly successful as cakes were still being made there up to 1967. O'Brien's as such had meanwhile merged in 1889 with Johnston and Company of Ballsbridge (founded 1846) and John Mooney, Miller and Baker of Clonliffe Mills, Jones's Road. The amalgamation made the new bread bakery second in size only to Boland's.

Before expansion, the old bakery in Ballsbridge was powered by a mill stream from the nearby Dodder — the tunnel still conducts water which is linked to the fire sprinkler system. The high-wheeled horse-drawn breadvans of Johnston, Mooney and O'Brien soon became a familiar sight all over the streets of Dublin. The deliverymen became institutions in their own right.

In 1925 the stables housed 104 horses but these were to yield slowly to mechanisation in the form of electric vans. The last horse-drawn vehicle, which had been allowed to operate more for sentimental than for practical reasons, was finally and sadly withdrawn in 1969. As the bakery now delivers to a 50-mile radius of Dublin, even the electric van is being replaced by lorries but up to 60 of the former are being retained for the city centre deliveries.

While the city sleeps, the bakers, manning dough mixers, monstrous ovens, slicers and coolers, will be producing 90% of each full day's output. Salesmen start on their rounds at 5.45 a.m. to have the bread in the shops by 9 a.m.

MAGUIRE & PATERSON, HAMMOND LANE

Founded in 1882 this firm, producing over 28 million matches a day, still retains its inner city premises within a stone's throw of the Four Courts.

Chapter Eleven

Places and Spaces

Embraced by the sweeping protective arms of the bay the position of Dublin from a scenic, environmental and amenity aspect could hardly be more ideal. An ever-changing palette of atmospheric moods, especially in autumn and winter, washes over the capital's unmistakable skyline and settles on the placid waters of the Liffey. Sheathed in mist, elevated in haze or simply penetratingly clear the views to seaward or to the rising mass of the Wicklow Mountains reflect the city's variable tempers.

Nowhere is too far from a coastline of beaches and snug harbours. The lagoons at Malahide and Clontarf and the rivers Dodder and Tolka with the twin Royal and Grand canals are perfect for further development for water sports and as passive recreation areas. Dublin's outer ring encompasses attractive coastal and rural villages, the ruins of medieval castles and monastic settlements. Rich agricultural land in the north and west gives way to near wilderness in parts of the Wicklow Mountains. The five hundred feet high hills of Howth and Killiney afford stunning panoramas which stretch away to the horizon.

All the natural advantages are complemented by the many fine parks and estates managed by Dublin Corporation, Dublin County Council and the Office of Public Works.

GAS LAMPS

The lamps along the main roads of the Park are probably the last of their kind in Europe still to be lit by gas.

DEER HERD

Some of the 300 strong herd of fallow deer which are mostly to be seen around the fifteen acres.

THE PHOENIX PARK

The park covers an area of 1,752 acres and is the largest enclosed urban park in Europe. It was part of the Abbey of Kilmainham until the suppression of religious orders by Henry VIII. The Duke of Ormonde first enclosed the park in 1662 when he introduced a deer herd for the amusement of royalty. Further major improvements were carried out by the Earl of Chesterfield from 1745. The decades that followed saw the erection of monuments, mansions and lodges.

In times gone by, the Phoenix Park witnessed gentlemen's duels and bare knuckle boxing, armed raids and political assassination, monster protest meetings and religious gatherings. The Eucharistic Congress drew nearly 900,000 worshippers in 1932 and the occasion of Pope John Paul's visit in 1979 saw one and a quarter million people gather.

But it is in its everyday role of providing a vast arena for sporting activities and a close encounter with nature that the park is best appreciated.

In 1986 the park was classified as a National Historic Park and a management plan was prepared by the Commissioners of Public Works. This plan envisages cutting down on through traffic, introducing horsedrawn, and at some time in the future, electrified transport, re-erecting the main gates, planting 20,000 more trees, restoring Ashtown Castle and generally safeguarding the park from undesirable developments.

One of the many keeper's lodges scattered around the park.

THE PHOENIX MONUMENT

The thirty feet tall Phoenix Monument was erected by Lord Chesterfield in 1745. He probably chose the mythological bird in the mistaken belief that the park was named after it but in fact the title came from the corruption of the Gaelic term Fionn Uisce which means "Clear Water". The spring well which gave the park its name was probably located near the western boundary wall of Aras an Uachtarain.

The first known reference to the name "Phoenix" in connection with the park was "Phoenix Lodge", a residence built on the hill now occupied by the Magazine Fort.

DUBLIN ZOO

Dublin Zoo dates from 1831 and after Regent's Park is the oldest zoo in the world. It is beautifully laid out and has attracted world wide attention for its success in breeding certain animals in captivity including lions. The famous MGM lion was bred here in the Roberts House (shown in the drawing). A national aquarium is scheduled to be opened here in 1988.

137

WELLINGTON MEMORIAL, PHOENIX PARK

Variously called the Wellington Memorial Testimonial or Monument, the 205-feet-high structure, designed by Robert Smirke in an open competition, commemorates the Duke of Wellington's battle victories, including his triumph over Napoleon at Waterloo. While the Duke first saw the light of day in Ireland — he was born Arthur Wellesley, and lived at 24, Upper Merrion Street — he made his distaste for the land of his birth publicly known.

Overlooking or unaware of his castigations, the Irish nobility were proud of the Duke's achievements and a national collection to erect a monument in his honour raised £22,000. The site chosen was on the grounds of the old Salute Battery in the Phoenix Park. The foundation stone was laid on 17th June, 1817, by Lord Whitworth, the Lord Lieutenant.

The money ran out before the work was completed and the obelisk was topped off sixteen feet lower than was originally intended.

The bas-reliefs, commissioned with the aid of a Parliamentary grant in 1861, were cast in bronze from captured cannon guns. Two of them depict graphic war scenes and a third shows a debating Wellington being honoured for the civil and military reforms he carried through. Although not a supporter of it himself, the Catholic Emancipation Act was passed in 1829 while he was Prime Minister.

A close-up view of one of the panels showing a battle scene from the Indian Campaign. The other battle scene depicts Waterloo.

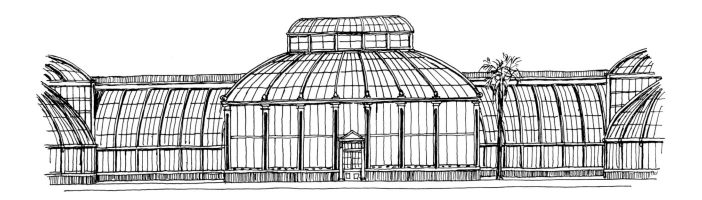

NATIONAL BOTANIC GARDENS, GLASNEVIN

Botanical gardens originally were cultivated on behalf of the medical profession, who recognised the curative properties of many plants. When the gardens of Trinity College were needed for new buildings, the Department of Medicine lobbied the Government, as also did the Royal College of Surgeons, for a new site. In the event, it was the Dublin Society that was nominated by the Irish Parliament in 1795 to establish the present gardens, for use in the study of the botanical, horticultural sciences.

Throughout the 19th century the gardens shared in the great discoveries brought back from the far-flung corners of the Empire, but they always lagged far behind those in Kew and Edinburgh in the financial support that they received, Nevertheless, Glasnevin became noted for some fine achievements, including the earliest reported attempt to raise orchids from seed.

The Botanic Gardens today contain over 20,000 species and varieties of plants. The oldest is nearly 400 years old and the tallest, at over one hundred feet, is the California Redwood, the same species as the four thousand-year-old giants in their native country.

The Great Palm House was built in 1884. The other main group of glasshouses, the Curvilinear Range, (seen in the drawing) was built between 1843 and 1869, mainly by Richard Turner, who also designed the houses of Kew and Belfast.

In 1877 the gardens were placed under direct Government control and today they are administered by the Department of Agriculture.

MERRION SQUARE PARK

A private park in the ownership of the Archbishop of Dublin it was handed over to the Corporation by Archbishop Ryan, after whom the park is now officially named, in 1974. It is beautifully laid out and the trees and shrubs form an extremely attractive perspective when viewing the magnificent Georgian square from inside the park.

139

DUBLIN CORPORATION PARKS DEPARTMENT

While we take them very much for granted nowadays, city parks are a relatively recent innovation. The crowded cities of industrial England lacked any decent recreational open spaces until the first park built at public expense was opened in 1843. During the next few decades major cities in Europe and America followed this example.

Victorian Dublin failed to make any significant contribution in this direction and continued to rely on the Phoenix Park and the green spaces in the centre of a couple of Georgian squares. Instead, the city between the canals was packed tighter with public and industrial buildings, houses, tenements and shops.

BEDFORD LODGE

Up to the 1940s the Dublin Corporation Parks Department was part of the section within the Engineering Department responsible for pavements, and several of its 50 or so staff were relegated here as convalescents from more active duties elsewhere. A reorganisation in 1949 changed all that and the modern Parks Department was born.

Today, about 500 staff tend to approximately 3,000 acres divided into 110 parks ranging in size from tiny St. Catherine's Park (0.4 acre) up to the broad expanses of Bull Island (over 700 acres). Active recreation is encouraged by the provision of hundreds of football pitches, tennis courts and playgrounds backed up by centres for swimming, golfing, fishing, basketball and athletics.

A more passive form of enjoyment can be found appreciating scenic landscapes, nature trails, riverside walks, flower gardens, historical sites, hand performances and wildlife habitats.

The drawing shows Bedford Lodge, St. Anne's Park, the nerve centre for the planning and control of the department's activities. From the adjacent nurseries 80,000 shrubs and 500,000 bedding plants are raised annually to adorn the city. Since an intensive planting programme began nearly 12 years ago, an average of 15,000 new trees are planted every year in parks and along roadways.

CITY HALL PARK

This little infill park, opened in 1987, is located next to the City Hall. The three statues, removed from the demolished International Exhibition Buildings on Earlsfort Terrace, represent the trades of stonework, ironwork and carpentry.

HERBERT PARK, BALLSBRIDGE

The famous Dublin International Exhibition of 1907 was opened on 4th May by Lord Aberdeen, the Lord Lieutenant, on the lands of the present Herbert Park. Trade exhibitors from all corners of the British Empire were represented, including a complete native village from Somalia. The various pavilions were dominated by the huge central building, constructed from glass in Crystal Palace fashion, with four protecting wings each signifying a province of Ireland.

The venture was a great success, but as soon as the turnstiles turned for the final time on 9th November the work of demolishing began and the park was relaid and replanted. Very little evidence of the exhibition now remains except for a couple of shelters, the pergola — originally the verandah of the Fine Arts Building — and the duck pond, the latter built as part of the popular Canadian waterchute.

The park was named after the Right Honourable Sidney Herbert (1810-61), Lord Herbert of Lea, owner of the Fitzwilliam Estate and father of the Earl of Pembroke. Comprising 32 acres, the park passed to Dublin Corporation in 1932.

The Dodder once overflowed onto this land, and at a point near the duck pond a bridge spanned the river beside the home of a Mr. Ball. The crossing became known as Ball's Bridge, later adapted to Ballsbridge.

ROADSIDE GARDEN

This charming example, hopefully the forerunner of many more, is situated in South Great George's Street.

141

CROPPIES MEMORIAL PARK

The Croppies Memorial Park is a half-acre site bordered by Wolfe Tone Quay, Temple Street West and Parkgate Street and offers a pleasant aspect when approached from Heuston Station. It originally formed part of the Military Recreation Grounds attached to the adjacent Royal, now Collins, Barracks.

Large Russian artillery pieces, captured by the British Army during the 1854-55 Crimean War, once stood on a stone platform in the park and the area became known as the Crimean Trophy Plot. The guns were removed some time ago and after restoration two of them were mounted around the flagpole in Collins Barracks. The park is named after the "Croppies" of the 1798 Rebellion who were captured, shot and buried in the vicinity. There is also the story that Little John, the right-hand man of Robin Hood, operated near the park collecting tolls from passing travellers and giving demonstrations of his archery prowess.

When the new Frank Sherwin Bridge was being built, the little park was used as a site depot which left it requiring substantial renewal. The project cost over £30,000 and was financed with funds associated with the bridge building and a Dublin Chamber of Commerce donation of £7,000 towards the fountain to commemorate its bicentenary.

The park received the 1984 Civic Award.

THE FORTY FOOT, SANDYCOVE

The former bastion for males only bathing.

142

BAILY LIGHTHOUSE, HOWTH

The first Baily lighthouse was built on the summit in 1667 following a patent granted by Charles II to Sir Robert Reading. The beacon was a coal burning brazier placed on top of a square stone tower. This rather unsatisfactory arrangement lasted until 1790 when sophistication arrived with Thomas Rogers, the man who pioneered the world's first use of lenses and reflectors at a lighthouse at Portland a year earlier. Rogers demolished the square tower and replaced it with a more familiar circular structure topped by a lantern. Oil lamps, which attained no more than 250 candlepower, were the light source.

The location of this beacon had never been a happy choice as, ironically, when it was most needed it was itself often shrouded in low cloud or mist and lost to view. The present lighthouse was built on Dungriffin promontory in 1814 and the old Baily fell into disuse.

Experiments with coal gas flames and improved lenses, which were to revolutionise the efficacy of lighthouses around the world, were carried out at the Baily by John Wigham from 1865. Up to the end of the last century the light was a steady beam but in 1902 a rotating optic was introduced. Vaporised paraffin replaced gas in 1908, until it was ousted by electricity and a new optic in 1972.

The strength of the present light is 1,200,000 candlepower and it can be seen on a clear night from a distance of 26 miles.

HOWTH

Howth's fishing tradition predates the 12th century but until the completion of the piers in 1812 the village had remained remote and isolated overland from Dublin.

In addition to their long, hard and often frustrating hours spent at sea, trawlermen have to contend with fog, gales and occasional breakdowns. Although there are hundreds of square miles of virtually flat and muddy seabed in the Irish Sea, the unwary can get their nets fouled on rock outcroppings or in holes 70 fathoms deep. In the featureless undersea world the charts also reveal some man-made hazards. Shipwrecks include the trawler Sheralga, which was dragged down when her nets became entwined around a skulking submarine. There is also the wreckage of aircraft, some containers which fell overboard from a storm-lashed ship and even six mobile homes not originally designed for fishy inhabitants.

The fleet fishes for cod, plaice, whiting, haddock, sole, hake and prawn for the home market. Mackerel and herring are usually destined for export, mostly to Eastern Europe.

KILLINEY HILL

A massive obelisk on the summit of Killiney Hill bears an inscription which reads "Last year being hard with the poor, the wall around these hills and this were erected by John Mapas, Esquire, June 1742". The year referred to had brought a severe famine in the wake of an extremely harsh winter — the prolonged frost had frozen the Liffey and some old prints show Dublin's citizens amusing themselves on the ice. Mapas commissioned his "folly" to offer relief employment to the starving poor of the district.

The hill was laid out as Victoria Park in 1887 to celebrate the 50th year of the Queen's reign.

Across the little valley to the north lies Dalkey Hill, surrounded by Mapas's wall and surmounted by a curious little castle-like building. The hill's summit is reached either by a steep pathway or by a dizzy, twisting series of steps which skirt past precipitous granite walls. These facings are the remains of the quarry used to supply the stone for the construction of Dun Laoghaire Harbour.

BULL ISLAND

Today we take Bull Island and Dollymount Strand for granted, but 170 years ago it just didn't exist. In 1809 work started on building a two mile long causeway, the North Bull. Its completion four years later significantly helped to improve the navigation channel into Dublin Port and at the same time caused the build-up of Bull Island.

The causeway itself began some distance from the shore and a wooden bridge was constructed to allow access for materials and workers.

The present bridge dates from 1907 and except for top decking replacement in 1962 and a major refurbishment in 1985 it has survived intact since then.

The centre carriageway is 9 feet 9 inches wide and there are 21 spans of approximately 24 feet each.

The bridge and road are privately owned by the Dublin Port and Docks Board and are closed to the public one day each year, usually in February.

There were plans in the 1950s to replace the bridge with a concrete counterpart, but happily this unique and quaint old curiosity is still with us.

The sand dunes and salt marshes of the 5 km long North Bull Island contain a wide variety of plants, animals and up to 40,000 wildfowl and wading birds which migrate from their Arctic breeding grounds during the winter months. An Interpretive Centre was opened on the island by Dublin Corporation in 1986 following the designation of the undeveloped part of the island as a UNESCO Biosphere Reserve in 1981.

HELL FIRE CLUB, MONTPELIER HILL

According to local legend, a wandering priest inadvertently stumbled upon a meeting of the notorious Hell Fire Club at their lonely mountain retreat and was forced to witness their macabre festivities. The cleric noticed that a sinister looking black cat with fiendish eyes was the object of reverential treatment. In a sudden burst of energy he broke free from his captors, grabbed the feline creature and flung it with great force against the wall. Before the enraged gathering could react the priest uttered an exorcism which tore the cat apart and ejected a demon which then shot up through the roof, brought down the ceiling and scattered the assembly.

Whatever about the truth of this chilling tale, the Hell Fire Club was real enough. Based on a, by then, suppressed English antecedent, the Club was founded in Athy in the 1730s by young bucks from the nobility and the officer corps. Moving to Dublin, the members met in many haunts, especially in the taverns around Dame Street and Cork Hill and they were renowned for their evenings of licentiousness, blasphemous toasts and devil worshipping.

Its supposed headquarters on Montpelier Hill was built around 1720 as a hunting lodge for William Conolly, the speaker of the Irish Parliament. Upon his death in 1729 it was sold and was subsequently purchased by the Hell Fire Club in 1735. After the demise of the Club in the 1740s it appears to have been abandoned.

The former lodge is now only a ruin but a very substantial one all the same. The walls, constructed from an old cairn, are over two feet thick. The stone vaulted roof, replacing an earlier one blown off by a storm withstood a huge bonfire lit on it in 1849 to welcome Queen Victoria to Dublin.

It is well worth the bracing climb through the pine scented Hell Fire Wood (just past the Kilakee House Restaurant) up to the summit of the hill. With the magnificent hulk at your back the view is at once unexpected and truly spectacular.

PUBLIC TRANSPORT

Dublin has a well developed system of public transport comprising of electric and diesel suburban trains and an extensive bus network but has, as yet, no city centre underground.

On the 11th December, 1986 Córas Iompair Éireann (CIE) was restructured into a holding company controlling three operating companies each with a distinct mandate. Iarnród Éireann — Irish Rail provides the state's railway service including the Dublin Area Rapid Transit (DART). Bus Éireann — Irish Bus operates the road passenger service outside Dublin and Bus Átha Cliath — Dublin Bus is in charge of the capital city's bus fleet. The companies have full individual autonomy except in matters of overall financial control and in rival competition issues where the CIE board will exercise supremacy.

FIRST RAILWAYS

Ireland's first railway and the world's first suburban line was inaugurated when the locomotive Hibernia puffed its way out of Westland Row Station at 9 a.m. on the morning of the 17th December, 1834. William Dargan was the contractor for the new Dublin and Kingstown Railway Company and apart from contending with a difficult terrain he had to deal with obstinate landlords who refused to allow tracks to be laid over their lands. A compromise was reached when substantial compensation was paid to the landlords. The railway company also agreed to build piers, bathing places, and pedestrian bridges for the use of the landowners and most of these curiosities are still to be seen today.

PEARSE STATION
(formerly Westland Row)

MALAHIDE RAILWAY STATION

The line through Malahide was launched by the Dublin and Drogheda Railway Company in 1844. As well as being an intermediate stop for many long-distance trains, Malahide also grew in importance as a suburban halt.

Although excluded from the Dublin area electrification scheme, Malahide is fully connected to the new Continuous Automatic Warning System. The nostalgic old levers and telegraphy in the signal box have been replaced by a computerised panel and a print-out machine.

The environmental setting of the station is quite exquisite. The evocative architecture of bygone days is still very much in evidence, and is further enhanced by the imaginative array of evergreens and shrubbery.

Malahide could be made into a showpiece station and restored to all its former glory. Perhaps period lamp standards and wooden fencing along platform number one could be reinstated? As the station is closed on Sundays could it not be used as an enticing starting point for steam engine excursions on a regular basis during the summer?

Commercial success as both a tourist and a commuter attraction would then encourage its future preservation.

CONNOLLY STATION, AMIENS STREET

Initially proposing to site their new terminus opposite the GPO on Sackville (now O'Connell) Street, the Dublin and Drogheda Railway eventually chose Amiens Street. Even relatively small railway companies sought to have grandiose termini and Amiens Street was no exception. William Deane Butler designed the building which displays an Italianite style facade of Wicklow granite.

The foundation stone, containing contemporary railway documents, newspapers and coins, was laid on the 24th May, 1844 — Queen Victoria's birthday — by the Lord Lieutenant, Earl de Gray. The high elevation of the line necessitated the construction of 75 supporting arches over the short distance between Amiens Street and the Royal Canal.

The various railway companies functioning in the north-eastern part of the country were amalgamated in 1876 to form the Great Northern Railway and Amiens Street became its headquarters. Another important date, 1891, saw the establishment of the Loop Line between Amiens Street and Westland Row.

Secure from the fate of its redundant sisters, Broadstone and Harcourt Street, Connolly Station (renamed in 1966) continues to flourish. Daily visits from the trains of Northern Ireland Railways contribute a unique flavour.

HEUSTON STATION, KINGSBRIDGE

Constructed in 1844, Kingsbridge Station was the monumental showpiece of the Great Southern and Western Railway Company, an amalgamation of some two dozen smaller regional concerns.

Except for the modern facilities at the head of the platforms the station still echoes the Victorian age and in recognition of this some notable films have been shot there in recent years.

BROADSTONE STATION

Baron Heytesbury, the Lord Lieutenant, cut the first sod at Broadstone in 1846.

In earlier days passenger boats on the Royal Canal started their leisurely journeys from Broadstone Harbour, which was linked via an aqueduct over Constitution Hill to the canal proper at Mountjoy Prison. The Midland Great Western Railway bought the Royal Canal, lock, stock and barrel, and built the railway alongside the waterway almost as far as Mullingar. The little harbour was filled in, the aqueduct became a connecting road to Dominic Street, and the splendid station, designed by John Skipton Mulvany, was completed in 1851.

Solidly Egyptianesque to the front, with an impressive long Greek-styled colonnade to the side, the station was intended to and did exude confidence and assertiveness.

The line closed down in 1931, and the station took on the appearance of a lonely monument whose passive dignity seemed to mourn the lack of scurrying crowds and shunting locomotives.

Now Broadstone hums again with a different activity, for it has become the headquarters and main depot for the 1,000 coaches of Bus Éireann.

ST. STEPHEN'S GREEN CENTRE

Ireland's largest retail development, costing circa £60 million is due for completion in 1988. The South King Street and Mercer Street elevations will reflect the brickwork style of the Gaiety Theatre. Developers: Power Securities and British Land Company plc. Architects: Power Design.

Plan prepared by Patrick and Maura Shaffrey for the City Centre Business Association on how Henry Street should look if shop fronts were more in tune with the rich architectural character of the buildings they occupy. Projecting plastic signs would be banished, use of unpainted solid aluminium shutters would be discontinued, individual shopfront design either modern or traditional would have to conform with certain general principals and facades would have to be well maintained and enhanced by flower and plant arrangements. This plan was first publicised in March '86 and already several owners have responded positively.

DUBLIN BUS, O'CONNELL STREET

Numbers 59 and 60, Upper O'Connell Street contain the management offices for the Dublin city bus services.

The modern block was built in 1961 and its interior features some stained glass work by Evie Hone. The adjoining older building was formerly the offices of the Dublin United Tramway Company.

Dublin's public transport goes back to around 1840 when an omnibus service was inaugurated. These vehicles seated ten passengers on the roof and twelve inside and were pulled by two horses. Early attempts at a tramway system failed including an experimental line laid on Aston's Quay by the aptly named George Francis Train.

In 1871 the Dublin Tramway Company obtained powers from Parliament to buy up the various omnibus firms and a year later it commenced running horse-drawn tramcars to Terenure. Other rival companies quickly followed but by 1881 they were all amalgamated as the Dublin United Tramway Company who could now muster 186 trams and over 1,000 horses.

Horse power was often no quicker than walking pace so in 1886 the DUTC began to electrify the network and became the outstanding pioneer of modern electrification in the United Kingdom.

At the peak of their operation there were 330 trams, with most of them using Nelson Pillar as their main hub. In 1912 they carried 57 million passengers. During and after the Second World War the DUTC went into a sharp decline and the last tram ran to Dalkey on 10th July, 1949.

Dublin Bus carries in excess of 160 million passengers per annum and operates over 800 buses on 132 routes with a total network length of 510 miles (821 kms).

DUBLIN AREA RAPID TRANSIT

DART began operating on the superbly scenic coastal Howth to Bray railway line in 1984. In one fell swoop, the high speed, reliable, safe, clean and late working transport system changed the commuting, social and commercial patterns for thousands of citizens.

Housing estates, apartment blocks and office developments sprang up in close proximity to the line and its presence must influence future planning.

Work started on electrifying the line in 1980. Sixty bridges had to be reconstructed and to preserve some old bridges between Dun Laoghaire and Sandycove the permanent way was lowered by over half a metre for a distance of one mile (one and a half km) to gain the necessary extra clearance.

Controlled by computers at Central Control in Connolly Station DART has 40 two-car train sets, each capable of carrying 500 passengers. At peak the system carries 25,000 people per hour with the two-car units usually joined to make six-car trains carrying the equivalent of 3 jumbo jet loads.

The trains were built by Linke-Hofmann-Busch of Germany and are highly energy efficient.

149

AER LINGUS

On 27th May, 1936 the first commercial flight by Aer Lingus took off from Baldonnel and headed for Bristol. This flight was operated by the airline's only aircraft, a five seater de Haviland Dragon DH84 named Iolar. The original Iolar was lost during World War II but fortunately a sister aircraft was traced, restored to operational condition by a dedicated team of Aer Lingus personnel and made ready to fly to Bristol in 1986 to commemorate that first flight.

Today Aer Lingus is a major European carrier with a fleet of mostly Boeing jets supplemented by four turbo-prop Shorts 360s. The airline has carried over 50 million passengers since 1936 and has an annual turnover of £500 million.

The drawing shows Iolar parked close to one of the airline's three Boeing 747s.

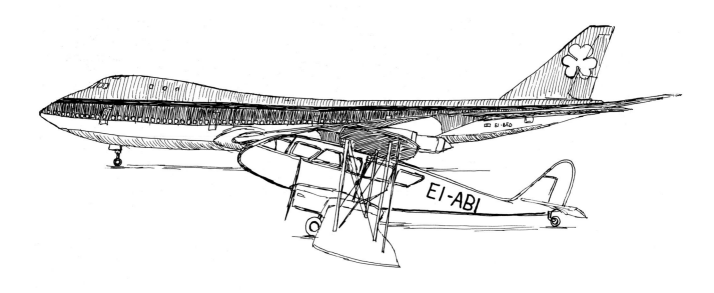

LORD CHANCELLOR'S COACH, NEWBRIDGE HOUSE, DONABATE

Lord Fitzgibbon, the Lord Chancellor, had his resplendent gilded coach paraded before the people of Dublin in 1791. The gigantic vehicle, which needed six horses for traction power, was built in London at a cost of £7,000. It was restored in 1982 aided by sponsorship from the Bank of Ireland and the Charles E. Merrill Trust of New York.

HOWTH TRAM

To spirited day trippers of those seemingly bygone sunny summers of yesteryear the Howth tramway was the high point of a visit to the peninsula. With bells clanging, wheels grating and trolley poles sparking the swaying vehicles groaned their way up steep gradients and willingly plunged into grass meadows and gorse filled cuttings. Opened in 1901 the five and a quarter miles long Hill of Howth Tramway was built by the Great Northern Railway to link the scattered communities of Howth with the railway stations of Sutton and Howth. Although it was busy during the tourist season the line could not be adequately supported by the small population in the winter and it was finally and with undignified haste closed down in June 1959. Dublin had lost a major attraction and Howth had lost a friend.

The trams had been more than a means of transport to the widely scattered homesteads around the Hill. They were a way of life. The crews delivered messages, watched out for the welfare of the elderly, made unscheduled stops for regulars and even provided alarm-clock calls with their bells for known sleepyheads. Dependable, but not always predictable, the service weaved and threaded its way into the legends and folklore of Howth.

Immediately after the closure the trams were disposed of. One now reposes in the Transport Museum in Belfast, another stands under the Californian sun in Perris, Orange County, and a third still labours on along the Blackpool Tramway. The number 9 was rescued by architect Jim Kilroy who has, with the help of members of the Transport Museum Society of Ireland, restored it to perfect condition. When a track system is laid it is planned to run the venerable old vehicle around the grounds of Howth Castle thus forging a real link with treasured memories of the past.

TRANSPORT MUSEUM, HOWTH CASTLE

Presently housing over 25 vehicles the number will be doubled when the second stage of the museum is completed. Retired public service, commercial, emergency and military transports are represented and they provide a nostalgic but important link with the past and show the quality and ingenuity of their engineering.

Shown in the drawing is a Howth Tram (number 9), a horse drawn Merryweather steam fire engine (manufactured 1889) and Merville Dairies' last operational milk float which was withdrawn in 1978.

The museum is open to the public at weekends.

ROYAL CANAL

Trundling its way towards Glasnevin Cemetery the funeral cortege in James Joyce's "Ulysses" passed over the iron Cross Guns Bridge which spans the Royal Canal and the adjoining railway bridge.

John Binns quarrelled with his fellow members on the Grand Canal Board and he angrily vowed that he would build a second canal. In 1790 work started on his new waterway which in the event never seriously challenged its southside rival and lack of sufficient business pushed the venture into serious financial difficulties.

The canal fell into gradual decline until it was finally closed in 1961 by CIE, the then proprietors. In 1986 the Office of Public Works was vested with the ownership so we can now hope to see the locks restored and the canal turned into a worthwhile water amenity set amid pleasant linear parklands. To this end the OPW has commissioned a study to be undertaken and is expected to publish a management plan in the near future. In the meantime much credit must go to various voluntary groups who have carried out restoration projects to sections of the canal.

THE GRAND CANAL

The Grand Canal was constructed in 1772 and provided a comfortable passenger link between Dublin and the Shannon. Before the advent of the railways the 80 mile (128 km) long Grand Canal carried tens of thousands of passengers every year. After the arrival of the steam locomotive passenger traffic disappeared but cargo barges continued working on the canal right up to the middle of this century.

As with its Northside cousin the Royal Canal, the Grand Canal is now in the possession of the Office of Public Works who are expected to carry out landscaping improvements and restoration work to the locks and banks.

MILLTOWN

This plant-enshrouded, twin-arched stone bridge is claimed to be the city's oldest existing span south of the Liffey. Now exclusively used as a pedestrian crossing, it once carried horse-drawn vehicles over the normally placid but sometimes torrential Dodder river. A tiny recess midway along the bridge, and still extant, allowed pedestrians room to step aside against oncoming traffic.

The cobblestone pathway had become damaged over the years but, much to the disappointment of the locals, it was resurfaced with tarmacadam instead of being restored. There are active plans to upgrade the landscaping here as part of a linear park running along the banks of the Dodder. Their implementation will not come too soon for this historic and potentially beautiful setting, which is thickly overgrown with wild vegetation and overlooked by an ugly and all too obvious scrap-yard. Perhaps when this work gets underway the cobblestones could also be restored.

O'CONNELL BRIDGE

O'Connell Bridge, reconstructed in 1880, has the distinction of having its length and width in almost equal proportions.

Twelve bridges span the Liffey from Parkgate Street to the Link Bridge.

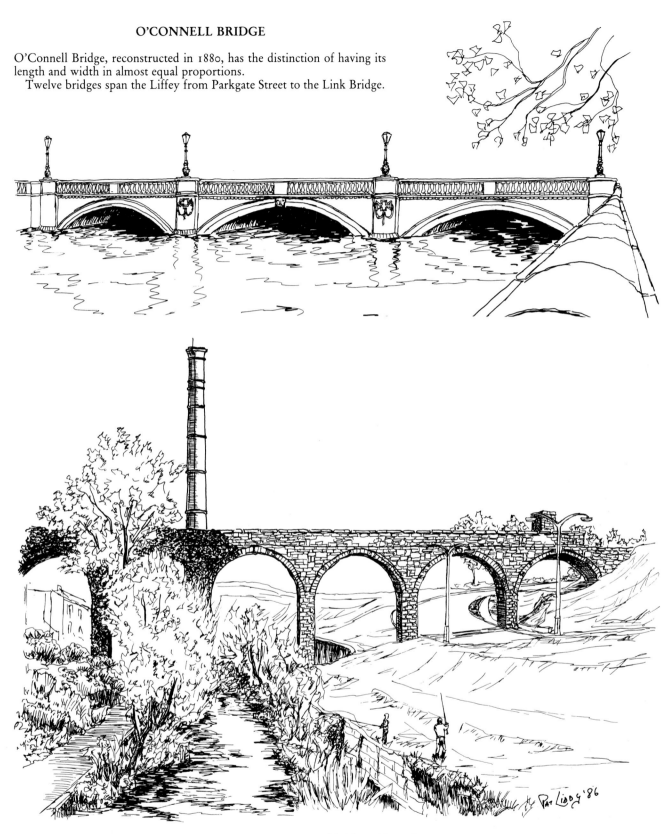

HARCOURT STREET LINE

Although truncated at both ends, the stately old stone viaduct, bestriding the River Dodder at Milltown, endures as a monumental vestige to the closed Harcourt Street railway line. Its lonely vigil is shared by other curious remnants including occasional iron footbridges, crossings, the remains of stations and the patch and cuttings where once the tracks were laid.

Falling revenues convinced CIE to terminate the line on 31st December, 1958, just a month short of the hundredth anniversary of the opening of the Harcourt Street terminus.

153

EAST LINK BRIDGE

Dublin's first toll bridge this century has been a huge success and has effectively reduced travelling times between north-eastern and southeastern parts of the city. It has also opened up the possibilities and potential for future development around the Lower Liffey districts.

ROYAL IRISH AUTOMOBILE CLUB

In 1901, when petrol was only two shillings (10p) a gallon and the motor car was beginning to assert itself on Irish roads, a number of prominent car owners met in the Metropole Hotel and formed the Irish Automobile Club "for the furtherance of automobilism in Ireland". One of the original committee members was Dr. J. F. Colohan, who is reputed to have been the first person in Ireland to own a motor car.

The club's first headquarters were in the Shelbourne Hotel but were in turn moved to the Earlsfort Rink and then Anne's Lane before finally coming to roost at 34, Dawson Street in 1906. The adjoining premises were acquired three years later and pursuing a somewhat conservative policy, the results of which can now be relished, it was never considered necessary to carry out structural "modernisations". The appearance of the building appears much the same today as it did 80 odd years ago, and many of the interior fittings and furnishings have been jealously preserved.

During the Great War many of the members generously donated their vehicles, often accompanied by their drivers, to serve as ambulances on the battlefields. In recognition of this service King George V bestowed Royal Patronage on the Club in 1918.

It organised the first and only Irish Grand Prix series from 1929 to 1931.

Chapter Twelve

A New Image

Time and tide waits for no man or city. Like their inhabitants cities mature and grow old and the ageing process is not always dignified. Buildings become neglected or fail to stand the test of time and fall into decay. Whole blocks may suffer the ravages of redundancy or else be pressganged into unsuitable usages leading eventually to their demise.

Dublin is no stranger to the process of degeneration and in fact may have suffered more than most. Past architectural glories were often never more than a stone's throw away from rancid slums. Fashion sometimes dictated the surrendering of a fine street to tenement occupation. In the last hundred years the lack of adequate maintenance of many notable buildings led to their untimely destruction. Certain unscrupulous developers contrived to ensure that unwanted buildings on their speculative sites fell into sufficient disrepair to warrant their removal. Sadly the structures that usually replaced them were of little value architecturally or environmentally.

Planning debacles led to further mistakes and road widening schemes, contrived in a time when the car ruled supreme and was to be given access priority through the city, have left serious scars of derelection.

From a historical perspective it must be admitted that modern developers are not the only ones who have swept aside the labours of previous generations. Great architects and builders of the 18th century undoubtedly erected fine edifices but in so doing they saw no relevance in the destroyed and substantial remains of the surviving medieval walled city. Conservationism was not a key issue then. A century later when Victorian enterprises scythed through Georgian terraces there were no words of protest. However, the replacement buildings of these periods were of pleasing design and were very much welcomed at the time which is more than can be said about some of the more recent creations.

The task now should be to safeguard and enhance what remains of our legacy while at the same time embracing exciting or worthwhile new ventures providing they are not the cause of any avoidable or unnecessary demolition. They should also fit into or complement existing streetscapes and contribute to the revitalisation of Dublin particularly in the designated inner city areas.

Many buildings no longer fulfil their original role and their only chance for survival may be adaptation to new functions. Conservationists will have many occasions to dispute proposed changes but all the parties involved should endeavour to quickly reach a satisfactory compromise to save buildings from lying empty or to enable them to achieve a reasonable revenue earning potential for owners. Otherwise noses may be cut off to spite faces.

Thankfully there is a perceptible growth in the awareness of many strands of society that the future of Dublin is now an important issue.

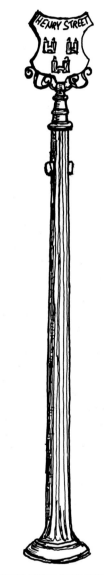

NEW "HENRY STREET"
NAME STANDARD

Corporate, municipal, governmental and individual response to the challenge of renewing the city is at last awakening but the pace needs quickening and the dangers of regression are all too real. To encourage a return of investment, confidence and a desire to live in the inner city its problems of asscessibility, law and order and environment will have to be tackled head-on.

This chapter presents a representative collection of successful conversions, significant modern developments and even some controversial examples.

IDA CENTRE, GRAND CANAL DOCK

Leading a chequered career this tower block, built in 1862, was variously a sugar refinery warehouse, a distillery warehouse and an iron foundry before the Industrial Development Authority adapted it for use as a craft centre in 1978. It received the international Europa Nostra award which is the equivalent of an Oscar for conservation projects.

THE CASINO, MARINO

When Lord Charlemont returned from his Grand Tour of Europe he resolved to build a fine villa with accompanying garden temple or casino on the style he had seen in Italy. Charlemont decided to spare no expense to make his casino a building of note. He employed Sir William Chambers, the leading palladian architect of the day, to draw up the plans and construction was supervised by the Italian sculptor Simon Vierpyle. The famous Dublin sculptor Edward Smyth worked on the stone carvings. The end result was a building which is acknowledged to be among the best pieces of Palladian architecture in Europe.

The building is a clever exercise in optical illusion. It appears small and dainty in the distance containing perhaps a single large room. In fact it is over three storeys high and contains 16 rooms. Upper storey windows are hidden by balustrades and the roof urns serve as chimneys.

Lying derelict for years the Casino was magnificently restored by the Office of Public Works and was opened to the public in 1984. *(See illustration page 59.)*

ROYAL HOSPITAL, KILMAINHAM

For the most part we are conditioned to viewing our main public buildings as they bravely assert themselves over the close intrusion of their lesser neighbours. However, Sir William Robinson's masterpiece, built between 1680-84, lies in splendid isolation and indeed the view along the long, tree-lined western approach is quite spectacular.

The four sides of the building are built around a quadrangle and although the outer facades are somewhat different in composition from each other they form a unified whole. The style is unmistakably French in character, not unsurprising as the hospital's initiator, James Butler, Duke of Ormonde, conceived the idea after seeing Louis XIV's Les Invalides in Paris. The continental flavour is reinforced by the addition of an extensive area of light coloured gravel placed around the perimeter of the building. Preceeding Chelsea by two years the Royal Hospital and Les Invalides were the world's first two retirement hospitals or homes for old or invalided soldiers. It closed in 1928 and fell into near ruin.

Restoration of the hospital itself has been carried out with great integrity and with over 300 rooms involved from the Great Hall to the humblest dormitory the task was singularly difficult. Fortunately Robinson's plans and all subsequent records were still extant and during work on the Great Hall itself the original oak floor and panelling were uncovered. Innovative work to conceal modern facilities was carried out and included concealing the ultra modern kitchen in the basements, the heating under the floor and the lifts in the chimney shafts.

The huge restoration task took from 1980 to 1984 and cost £20 million (construction 300 years earlier had cost £24,000). In recognition of the achievement and its "distinguished contribution to the conservation of Europe's architectural heritage", the Royal Hospital was awarded the prestigious Europa Nostra award for 1985. The building is especially important as it was Ireland's first classical building and marked the real beginning of Dublin's architectural development.

Open to the public at weekends or at other announced times the Royal Hospital houses exhibits from the National Museum, hosts major exhibitions and offers guided tours and various entertainments. *(See illustration page 59.)*

KYLEMORE RESTAURANT, O'CONNELL STREET

A key position at the corner of O'Connell Street and North Earl Street, this fine building was purchased by Kylemore Bakeries in 1987 and no time was lost in taking out the previous shoddy frontage and replacing it with finely carved wood and decorative glass.

GUINNESS HOP STORE, CRANE STREET

The former hop warehouse was extensively refurbished and is now used as an exhibition centre and it also houses the extensive archival and museum collections of the brewery.

McGRATH'S RESTAURANT, UPPER O'CONNELL STREET

Encouragement that individual members of the business community are prepared to make a personal financial commitment to the improvement of Dublin can be gleaned from examples such as this. A fire had left the building in a ruinous state and the new owner, Brendan McGrath, rebuilt the inside completely and added some points of interest to the exterior. The brickwork and fittings on the interior floors are imaginatively worked out and should add that elusive quality, atmosphere.

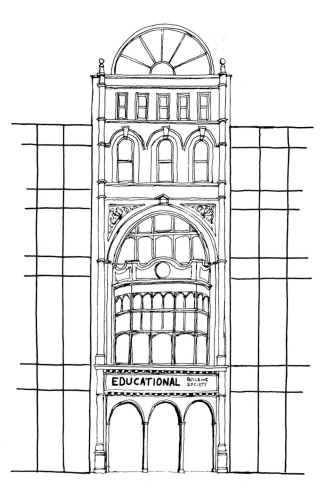

IRISH DISTILLERS, SMITHFIELD

Subsequent to the giant distillery in Bow Street closing in 1972 the old spirit store was converted in 1980 for use as the Group Administration Headquarters. Behind the building is the intriguing whiskey museum which is situated in another adapted warehouse.

EDUCATIONAL BUILDING SOCIETY, WESTMORELAND STREET

The old Paradiso Restaurant was incorporated into this modern glass fronted block. Architects were Sam Stephenson and Associates.

BELGARD CASTLE, CLONDALKIN

Imagine yourself, as a visitor to a company headquarters, driving past the impressive walled entrance and along a magnificent tree-lined drive which slices through an estate teeming with wildlife including fox and pheasant.

Crossing the flagged courtyard you might encounter shuttling executives mingling with strutting peacocks.

Such an experience is no fantasy but, to their constant amazement and delight, awaits all visitors who come to do business with Cement Roadstone Holdings at Belgard Castle, Newlands, Clondalkin.

The company bought the estate in the sixties and the preservation and restoration of the mid 18th century Georgian mansion has been the inspiration of directors Tom and Donal Roche.

REVAMPING HOTELS

Hotels built in the 1960s and 70s were mostly of a highly functional design and little consideration or expense was allocated to making them visually attractive or interesting. In an attempt to remedy this deficiency a number of the bigger hotels have had huge conservatory-type entrances and foyers affixed to their fronts and the results are a definite improvement. The two examples shown here are Jury's Hotel, Ballsbridge and the Burlington Hotel, Upper Leeson Street.

NATIONAL COLLEGE OF ART AND DESIGN

The National College of Art and Design was originally founded nearly 250 years ago and in the early 1980s moved from Kildare Street into the converted Power's Distillery in Thomas Street. It was an inspired adaptation of an old industrial building (by architects Burke-Kennedy, Doyle and Partners) bringing with it life to the Liberties and a continued source of creative inspiration to the students.

CENTURY HOUSE, HAROLD'S CROSS

Redundant churches have become inviting candidates for conversion to office use. Successful conversions like this one for the accountancy firm of O'Connor, Leddy, Holmes are in a way helping to preserve old buildings which might otherwise be demolished.

159

MODERN SHOP FRONTS

Modern materials as well as the more traditional kinds can also be successfully used in providing simple clean lines to shop fronts providing they are unobtrusive to the surrounding environment and avoid the shoddiness usually associated with plastic and aluminium.

IRISH PERMANENT, GRAFTON STREET

This refurbishment of an old chemist's shop took place in 1987.

POWERSCOURT TOWNHOUSE CENTRE, CLARENDON STREET

This is an exciting shopping and craft centre development by Power Securities of Lord Powerscourt's Town House (1774) and the courtyard enclosed by the old offices of the Commissioners of Stamp Duties. The imaginative refurbishment was nominated by the Irish Government as a National Demonstration Project for submission to the Council of Europe as part of its 1981 European Campaign for Urban Renaissance.

AMERICAN EMBASSY

Ultra modern in appearance the American Embassy actually dates back to 1964 when there was nothing else like it in Ireland. The designers, American John MacL. Johansen and Irishman Michael Scott, drew their inspiration for the unusual design from ancient Celtic motifs.

METEOROLOGICAL CENTRE, GLASNEVIN

Built in the late 1970s its shape was as much influenced by a concern not to interfere with the right of light to nearby houses as by any symbolic reference to ancient sky gazers and their pyramids.

SWAN CENTRE

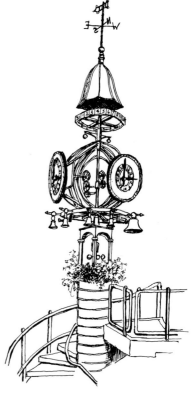

Swan Centre was built by developers Sisk Properties and has been highly acclaimed at home and internationally. The shopping complex has an entry in the 1987 Encyclopedia Britannica as "one of the world's significant projects". Architects to the £10 million project were John O'Reilly and Partners.

The drawing shows the delightful central feature of the centre, the chiming clock. This precision instrument was made by the firm of Heinrick Perrot near Stuttgart in West Germany.

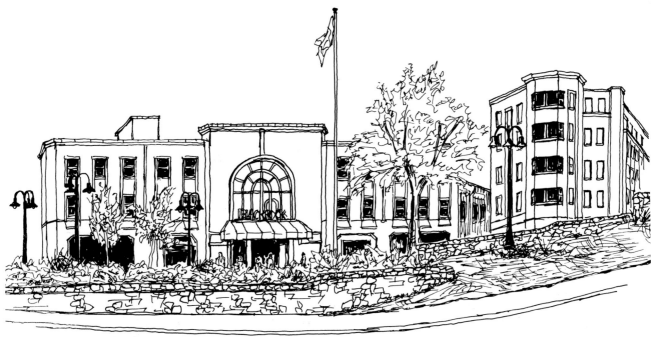

BLACKROCK CENTRE

Fergal Quinn is possibly one of Ireland's best-known businessmen who skilfully combines success with a high popularity profile. His supermarket chain, Superquinn, has twelve locations in the Dublin area, comprising both supermarkets and shopping centres, and Blackrock Centre, built in the early 1980s, is the largest and best-known.

Blackrock Centre is a worthy example of the efforts some companies are making to match quality, style and a sense of place with site efficiency and the means to profitable trading. It respects its Victorian neighbours while still developing its own very up-to-date style and charm. The Centre consists of a large Superquinn supermarket and some forty other shops which are arranged on two levels facing into an open courtyard, and the atmosphere is relaxed and intimate with the feeling of a village square. Blackrock Centre's success has earned international acclaim — it won the "Shopping Centre of the year" award in 1985 from the British Council of Shopping Centres. Architects were Keane, Murphy and Duff.

162

CENTRAL BANK, DAME STREET

Architects were Sam Stephenson and Associates. The building is unique in Dublin for its method of construction in that each floor was first built separately on the ground and then raised to hang suspended from the central core.

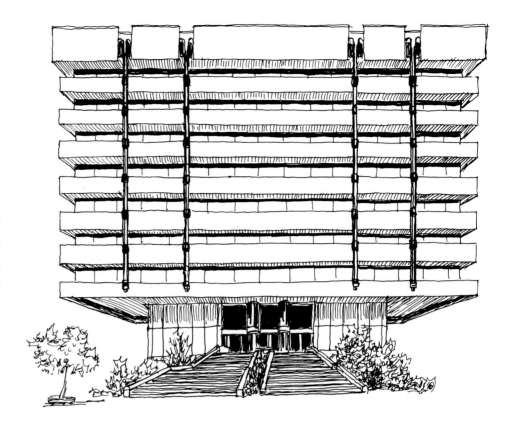

IRISH LIFE CENTRE, LOWER ABBEY STREET

Commenced in 1973 the three phases of this complex when fully completed will have cost around £40 million.

163

INVESTMENT BANK BUILDING, LOWER LEESON STREET

Developed by Power Securities for the Investment Bank of Ireland this new building, designed to match the existing facades along Fitzwilliam Street, attempts to link the Georgian tradition with modern functional requirements.

BANK OF IRELAND HEADQUARTERS, BAGGOT STREET

Architects for this building, first opened in 1972, were Scott, Tallon, Walker.

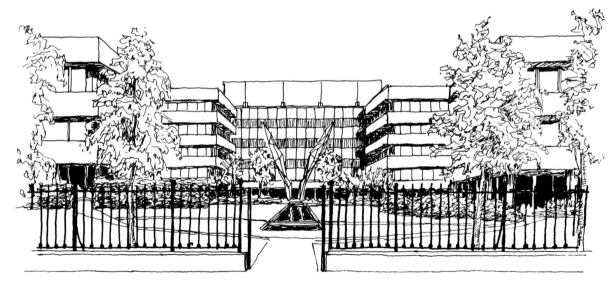

GROUP HEADQUARTERS, ALLIED IRISH BANKS, BALLSBRIDGE

First occupied in May 1979 this complex was designed by Robinson, Keefe and Devane.

164

CIVIC OFFICES, WOOD QUAY

After nearly four years of acrimonious argument and litigation, sit-ins and mass protests, work finally commenced in 1981 on the foundations of the controversial Civic Offices at Wood Quay. Designed by Sam Stephenson the twin tower blocks soon rose over the hotly disputed territory and the first Corporation office staff arrived in 1986. Already costing £23 million the project includes a planned two more blocks but it may be quite some time before they are built.

From 1977 popular opinion had sought to preserve in situ the substantial archaeological remains found on the site in an area that had earlier been identified as the cradle of Viking and medieval Dublin. Several stays of execution had been achieved and archaeologists from the National Museum urgently but painstakenly carried out the excavations that were to reveal an incredible amount of information about the ancient city.

BORD NA MÓNA

Bord na Móna headquarters, Baggot Street, was designed by Sam Stephenson and features John Behan's sculpture "The Turf Cutter".

MODERN HOUSING

In the past decade apartment blocks and townhouses, more than the traditional estates of semi-detached housing, have occupied the energies of developers. Competition in this sector is fairly fierce, a factor which has pushed up the quality of design.

Two examples built by Sheelin Homes Ltd., Glasnevin Hill (left) and Merrion Village (right), illustrate the imaginative use of brick and natural surroundings in creating unique designs.

ARTANE AND BEAUMONT FAMILY RECREATION CENTRE, KILMORE ROAD

One result of the outstanding achievement of the local community in raising £1.5 million by voluntary effort is this highly pleasing and imaginatively designed community centre. For the quality of both interior and exterior design and its massive but well proportioned scale it must rank as unique for a community centre not only in Ireland but anywhere in these islands. The architect was Duncan Stewart.

166

Chapter Thirteen

Great Expectations

Something is genuinely stirring in the heart of Dublin. Talk is slowly giving way to action. Government ministers now tend to look less frequently over their shoulders at the reaction of provincial voters when they express a concern for the future of what is, after all, the nation's capital. There is more universal support for the notion that life must be restored to the inner city.

Special areas have been designated for Government tax incentives and already schemes totalling hundreds of millions of pounds are under way. The retail world is reponding with developments such as St. Stephen's Green Centre, The New Ireland Assurance complex along Nassau Street and Friends Provident's Royal Hibernian Way. Existing stores such as Clerys, Arnotts and Roches are planning multi-million pound improvement schemes.

Attention is now being focused on the quays of the Liffey, the river that first gave birth to Dublin. The giant Custom House Docks Development is being augmented by several smaller but none-the-less significant schemes as far upriver as Sarsfield Quay. Largely abandoned or under-utilised areas like the Grand Canal Basin and Smithfield are being spoken of, as one Corporation official put it, "as the skeletons of great architectural spaces".

There are, however, serious problems that need to be tackled, for instance, areas of social deprivation may present difficulties in attracting the mixed class developments that would benefit the area as a whole. The Custom House Docks project could become isolated from instead of being integrated into the surrounding dockland community to the detriment of both.

On balance, though, it is a time of historic opportunity.

Drawing by Gerry Lombard on how the Custom House Dock might look when it is completed.

CUSTOM HOUSE DOCKS

At a cost of around £300 million this is easily the most significant development that Dublin has seen this century. Renewing derelict dockyards has proved to be very successful in other countries and there are special reasons why it should work very well here too.

For one thing the 27 acre site is so close to the centre of the city that it may be considered as such. The layout of the 18th and 19th century docks themselves lend towards their continued use as a valuable water amenity. Two of the giant warehouses (stack A and stack C) are notable for their construction. Stack A has probably the oldest cast iron supported roof in the world and its cellars are vast. Stack C has interesting timber trusses and an outstanding basement with 72 chambers of exquisite barrel vaultings.

It is proposed to preserve stack A, at least the vaults of stack C, St. George's Dock, parts of the inner dock, the cut stone entrance, segments of other buildings and the lock gate. Cranes, hoists, capstans, cobbles, brickwork and other items will be salvaged for creative re-use.

Ventures being planned for the docks include: A huge Financial Services Centre, offices, apartments, shops, an art gallery, a multi purpose conference centre cum leisure arena and a riverfront hotel. It is also planned to moor an historical ship in one of the docks. The present dockside road will be diverted to run through the middle of the development allowing a pedestrianised quayside. Creating pedestrian precincts is a stated priority for the scheme. The docks have been designated for special tax incentives and have been placed under the control of the Custom House Docks Authority.

All in all it is an important and exciting development which offers a unique opportunity to add to the social, economic and environmental qualities of Dublin and moreover should act as a catalyst for opening up the rest of the redundant quaysides for imaginative improvement.

Some of the latest developments from the city centre.

Important development for High Street (Christchurch Square) on either side of Tailors' Hall comprising office, retail and residential space. Developer: Hillview Securities. Architects: Horan, Cotter and Associates.

View of planned extension to Westbury Hotel on Clarendon Street. Architects: Henry J. Lyons and Partners.

Proposed development for mixed shopping office and residential use
along the lower end of Fishamble Street and Exchange Street. Architects: Conroy, Crowe, Kelly.

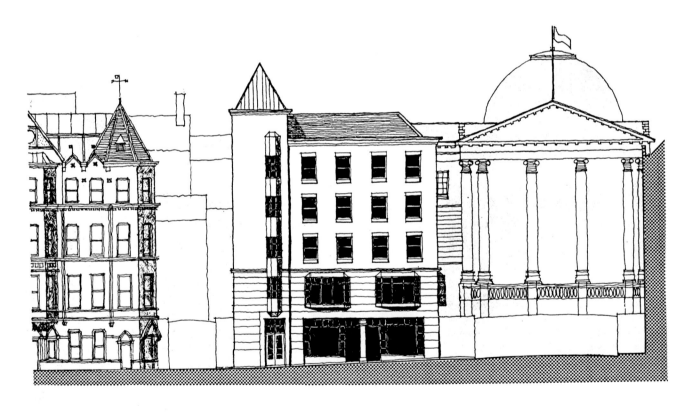

Office and retail development for Essex Street. Developers: Hillview
Securities. Architects: Horan, Cotter and Associates.

Office development at No. 3, Upper Ormond Quay incorporating the surviving ground floor facade of a Presbyterian Church demolished in 1959. Architects: Grafton Architects.

Architects Patrick Rooney and Associates have prepared plans for three inner city housing schemes at Mountjoy Square, Sean McDermott Street and Sarsfield Quay (illustrated).

HA'PENNY CENTRE

The £3 million development for the Bachelors Walk and Liffey Street corner. Developer: Hillview Securities Ltd., Architects: Burke-Kennedy Doyle & Partners.

THE HA'PENNY CENTRE

The writer will now exercise an author's privilege and list some of the things he would most like to see happen over the next few years. Space limitations militate against anything but a highly subjective, hopelessly inadequate and thoroughly random catalogue. Certain items are attainable with relatively little expenditure and others might require a longer lead-in time but all are within reach for "where there's a will there's a way".

Short term

* Brighten the city by painting light colours on drab and dirty concrete and cement facades. Place flower boxes on window ledges/balconies.

* Floodlight suitable exteriors and nicely plastered first floor ceilings of Georgian buildings.

* Keep main roads free of illegal parking and the city might not require unnecessary road widening.

* Establish local Garda sub-stations in Henry Street and Grafton Street.

* Encourage "built-in" window shutters and outlaw unpainted aluminium shutters.

* Stiffer protection for listed buildings. In 1985, according to An Taisce, 80 out of 1,320 listed buildings were demolished or radically altered.

* Complete the landscaping of the Royal Hospital and the Casino.

* More, many more, litter bins.

* Establish a depot to receive large and small pieces salvaged from demolished period houses including slates, chimney pots, cut stone, setts, internal fittings, railings etc.

* Complete a register of skilled craftsmen in traditional trades.

* Plant dense rows of trees along unattractive main roads in the inner city especially on the north side.

* Don't plant trees to obscure classical buildings from the front.

* As an investment towards future enhancement plant a double line of trees down the Lower Quays.

* Cultivate more wooded areas. A fifth of wall-locked West Berlin is in woodland.

173

* When fully de-commissioned. Resite into a Public Park the beautifully decorated external metalwork of the bigger gas holder on Barrow Street. It is a magnificent piece of Victorian Industrial Engineering.

* Locate multitudes of seating precincts in the central city area. Seats can be circular or backless to discourage lounging.

* Remove advertisements from the Loopline Bridge — it is bad enough that it obscures the Custom House from O'Connell Bridge.

* Develop derelict site beside Carlton Cinema in O'Connell Street. It could include an arcade to Moore Street which was first suggested away back in 1857!

* The Lord Mayor's term of office should be extended for a minimum period of 3 years.

* Restore and landscape both canals as quickly as possible in the Inner City.

* Make it a caring city by providing adequate and well maintained shelters for the homeless.

* Restore the glasshouses in the Botanics as a matter of priority.

* Appoint a minister with special responsibility for Dublin who could more effectively pull all the public and private sector agencies together to form a cohesive strategy for the capital.

* More extensive creation of bicycle lanes.

* Promote new uses for the growing number of abandoned hospital and church buildings rather than allow their demolition.

* Expand the size and role of the Civic Museum.

Longer Term

* Extend the DART system to Tallaght from Heuston Station and link this terminus and Connolly Station by an underground — this was first mooted in 1864!

* Develop the rest of the under-used dockland and especially the Grand Canal Basin at Ringsend where there is a possibility for a huge marina and housing for up to 2,000 people.

* Reclad the exteriors of poorly designed modern buildings in a more acceptable fashion.

* City centre circular route tramway system (with tracks that have already been specially developed to prevent cycle wheels getting lodged in them.

The Steyne Stone *(see page 1)* needs more imaginative treatment than simply to leave it standing on a concrete base. One suggestion might be to create a little water feature and the prows of Viking ships to indicate what the stone represents. The pedestal could provide informal seating.

The city badly needs a Tourist Interpretation Centre and a showplace for Dublin craftsmanship. An appropriate building would be O'Connell Street's last surviving Georgian mansion and now lying empty and in danger of becoming a ruin — the former Catholic Commercial Club.

Support is needed for the preservation and renewal of Henrietta Street (Dublin's oldest near-complete Georgian Street), North Great George's Street (an almost intact Georgian Street with several houses still used as private residences) and Harcourt Terrace (the city's only Regency-style street).

Enhance the central pedestrian walk along O'Connell Street by restoring it to something like what it was 200 years ago. Balustrades would give it visual protection from traffic and prevent jay-walking which often leads to accidents. A fountain (there was also one here in a former, more elegant century) could be erected near the old Nelson's Pillar site.

This drawing is not depicting some continental city but in fact is an accurate representation of the type of houses commonly found in Dublin between the 15th and 17th centuries. On the left is an oak framed cagework house (this example was demolished in 1812) and on the right are some "Dutch Billies" named after the followers of William of Orange who brought the style to Ireland.

To re-establish an effective link with the past why not design some appartments and houses in these styles and locate them in an historic site, say somewhere along the Quays?

The following contributions were submitted by a cross section of the city's key decision makers who kindly accepted the invitation extended to them to submit their views on and hopes for the future of Dublin.

The Way Forward

Many of the world's cities can be summed up in a single phrase, an individual building or a distinctive skyline.

Not so Dublin.

Ireland's capital can be evoked, but never summed up.

It is a marvellous mix of the cosmopolitan and the parochial, of the modern and the traditional. Its textures go from the porous softness of granite to the warm mathematics of red brick.

In atmosphere and architecture, Dublin is not a place of consensus, but of controversy and contradiction.

Every new statue has its aficionadoes and its antagonists. Every new development is seen from one side as providing endless promise — and from the other side as offering the ultimate threat. Everything that bespeaks pace and colour and lively commercialism to one generation suggests deterioration and crude exploitation to another. Natives constantly criticise the city — and instantly unite in passionate dismissal of non-natives who have the impertinence to agree with their criticisms.

No matter who you talk to in Dublin — native or 'blow in' — you find each has a different mental map of the city, some highlighting busy shopping areas and eating places, others majoring on formal architectural landmarks. In the same way, each of Dublin's writers has portrayed a different city. For Sean O'Casey, Dublin was about patriotism and poverty. For Robert Collis, it was about dearth and disease. For James Plunkett, it was about working people and their leaders.

For all of them, Dublin was a city of characters.

As it moves into its millennium, Dublin continues to be a city of characters, because it is still built on a human scale.

It must grow and develop in a coherent, organic way. A key element in that growth must be the creative re-interpretation of areas of the city which have out-lived their initial pattern of use. A classic example is the Custom House Docks area, which is being re-developed as a base for a financial services centre, for retail shopping, for hotel and residential development and as a location for buildings dedicated to culture. All this, while preserving its waterways, the best of its architecture and its distinctive ambience.

As the Minister responsible, I believe that Dublin's built environment must celebrate and preserve what is superb, facilitate the functionally innovative and reject the tawdry.

It's not a simple task.

*But then, nothing to do with Dublin **ever** is simple . . .*

From little acorns . . .

PADRAIG FLYNN TD,
MINISTER FOR THE ENVIRONMENT.

The Challenge

The Chamber of Commerce has been part of Dublin for two of the ten centuries of the millennium. The Chamber itself emerged from an act of piracy: the good ship **Ouzel**, *owned by Dublin merchants, was pirated on the high seas. Five years later she sailed up the Liffey to the astonishment of Dubliners, won back from the pirates by the original crew in an African port. The subsequent arbitration to decide the division of spoils gave birth to the Ouzel Galley Society, later to develop into the Dublin Chamber of Commerce, the first chamber in these islands.*

The Chamber is, therefore, a product of that great enterprising era in the city — the late 18th century — the period of the Wide Streets Commission and the most productive phase of the architect James Gandon. Gandon did most to beautify Dublin, the gems in his crown being the Customs House, the Four Courts and Carlisle (now O'Connell) Bridge.

It would be nice to report that the infant Chamber welcomed his noble new Customs House but they would more likely have been to the fore in condemning the move down river because it lessened the importance of the then city centre, Capel Street and Essex Street.

Dublin's 18th century renaissance sets a headline for today's Dubliners. The challenge facing us now, and dramatised by the millennium, is to add our contribution to the continual work of renewal which our city needs. Dublin has suffered in the past century from neglect, from an absence of commitment to its development as a worthy metropolis.

Some national policies have discriminated against the capital. To some extent the current difficulties the city faces are products of those policies.

The millennium is a time to examine our consciences about Dublin. The city needs our special attention. This can best be achieved by a partnership of government, local and national, with the leaders of business and other committed citizens putting resources to work so that we may reposition Dublin as the flagship of Irish enterprise and tourism, a fitting setting for displaying Ireland at its best.

James Malton, no mean judge of line, form and ambience judged the Dublin of 200 years ago as ranking "with the very finest cities of Europe for extent, magnificence and commerce". We must set our sights no lower for the year 2000.

DENIS J. SHELLY,

President:
DUBLIN CHAMBER OF COMMERCE.

Dublin — The Future

THE ISSUES

All the ingredients of shopping issues in contemporary western cities are to be found in the Dublin Sub-region. There is growth of the population and of its purchasing power and widespread shopping dispersal from the centre to the suburbs.

In such a situation it is necessary for the planning authorities to pursue retail planning as a part of their overall development planning. A pattern of shopping centres should be proposed and implemented as part of the development planning and retailing system seen as a whole. The aim should be to achieve for consumers, in proximity to such centres, a balance satisfying all their requirements for everyday/weekly needs and range of choice.

The possibility of the undermining of the shopping role of the City Centre could be regarded just as the substitution of shops in the one part of the County (the suburbs and satellite towns) for another (the City Centre). But these are not substitutes for each other. The satellite towns can provide only centres of suburban interest. The City Centre offers services unique to Dublin and Ireland.

It is by their centres that most towns are remembered. These centres of commerce in town or city tell the story of urban development and indicate the varying prosperity of the place through the ages. Towns were seldom designed and built at one time; they have grown, been extended, altered or torn down according to the needs, the fashion and the prosperity of the day. A total lack of uniformity is almost always the rule; the resultant mixture of styles and materials contributes to the richness of our city centres.

The 20th century has been less than sympathetic to the commercial streets and centres of our towns and has seen the erosion of character which is so important to a town.

Today, nearly 20 years after the 1960's renewal process, there is general agreement that the quality of urban environment has suffered a loss and that the gains of redevelopment have not made up for the losses.

SHOPPING OPTIONS FACING DUBLIN

The Consumer's Options: *However important the City Centre is for retailing it cannot provide for all the shopping in Dublin and dispersed centres are needed. But the questions arise as to how far retailing and services should be allowed to disperse from the Centre and build up in the satellite towns, before the City Centre itself is undermined; and what Dublin's strategic policy should be towards the classic dilemma of dispersal and concentration in shopping?*

The full answer to these questions can only be found in the carrying out of retail planning within the scope of development planning.

Shoppers will only frequent shops which can easily be reached by their mode of transport and they will require a degree of choice so as to have the opportunity to purchase a range of goods in one shopping trip. Thus, their criteria can be summarised in terms of "convenience" and "choice". Therefore, "shoppers" can usefully be sub-divided into three categories, each of which requires to be satisfied and reflects the different types of shopping trips.

These are,

—*convenience, e.g. daily or weekly trips to buy food and household items in everyday use,*

—*convenience/durable, e.g. regular trips to purchase food and the more common clothing or household requirements,*

—*comparison/durable, e.g. irregular excursions to obtain items demanded more occasionally and bought usually after comparison of products.*

The Spatial Options: *The theoretical spatial distribution of shopping provision in an urban area can usually be described in terms of concentration in one focal point (usually a city centre) at one extreme and dispersel at the other.*

THE OPTIONS IN THE DUBLIN SUB-REGION

(i) *Concentration in the City Centre;*
(ii) *Dispersal throughout the established centres;*
(iii) *Concentration in the satellite towns.*

Each option has distinct advantages to some sectors of the Sub-region, but is undesirable for others. If consideration is given to the specific shopper objectives a balanced option emerges. This is:

(1) *the location of convenience and convenience/durable shopping in areas where there is population growth and inadequate present facilities, i.e. suburbs including the satellite towns;*

(2) *the concentration of new comparison/durable shopping floorspace in the location where there is the opportunity to extend the existing range and choice in a position most accessible to the whole population of the Sub-region either by car or public transport, i.e. City Centre.*

THE FUTURE

The past neglect of our Capital City is a sad reflection on our sense of pride as a nation and upon the lack of will and commitment of our politicians.

Shopping in the 21st century will be a leisure activity. It is important to recognize the changing patterns of social behaviour presently taking place in society which is progressing towards this evolution in the use of Towns and Cities. Standards of Order, Control and Environment will become more important as the customer demands better service, well designed products and leisure activities. The need for easy, better access (by car or public transport) a pleasant environment (pedestrian streets, attractive shop fronts) and a feeling of safety (better law enforcement against shoplifters, pickpockets, illegal traders, disruptive demonstrations, subversives), will become a priority.

Dublin, like all other cities will have to face this challenge of the Future. Since 1980 some progress has been made and the debate about the future of our Capital City is now a populist issue.

TOM COFFEY,
Development Manager for the CCBA.

Possible Directions for Financial Institutions

Before considering the possible future direction of institutional investment in the city centre, it is important to understand where the financial institutions get their funds. Their money does not come from internal sources, but from "the man in the street", either through the pension scheme in his job or from his own decision to take out life assurance. The financial muscle of the institutions comes from the accumulation of large numbers of small contributions, which they then invest. They compete with one another for the custom of "the man on the street", and do this by aiming for the best possible return on the invested funds.

The return on investment in property has not been as good in recent years as the return from shares in public companies or even loans to the Government. Property values have actually fallen at a time when the value of company shares has often doubled or trebled and Government stocks have shown a return of 14% per annum. Because investment in property would prove less profitable than investment in stocks and shares, the financial institutions and pension funds have cut back on their involvement in property, to the extent that such investment in 1986 was about £10 million, whereas in 1980 it was close to £70 million.

A change in attitude towards property as an investment vehicle depends on a recovery in the Irish economy and a reduction in the overhang of vacant buildings. Such a recovery would lead to higher property values, at which stage investor confidence would be restored and funds would be channelled back into property. It is more than likely that substantial funds would be involved in such a move, with fund managers seeking to increase their property holdings and balance their portfolios. Indeed, the property market itself is approaching the point where such a move may be on the way. One of the reasons why property values fell in the early 1980's was the number of buildings which were developed but not occupied in the last boom at the end of the 1970's, but most of these buildings are now occupied. There are currently signs of a scarcity of high-quality commercial floor space, and potential tenants are beginning to compete with one another for the available good buildings. A continuation of this trend would soon lead to investment managers recognising the advantage of holding property in their portfolios.

The question then remains: when funds start to flow into property again, where will investment happen? There are many reasons to feel that the City Centre will form the focus for much of the activity. While the 1960's and 1970's were the years of the suburban shopping centre and suburban office buildings, the suburbs have since become somewhat discredited as a location for investment, while the City Centre has at the same time become more attractive. Access by public transport has been made easier with the introduction of the DART, bus lanes and other developments, and will continue to improve as a result of the

... big oaks grow.

work of the Dublin Transport Authority, the streamlining of the bus service, and maybe even an extension of the DART to other areas. The problems of security and environmental quality are also being tackled. The level of crime in the city has been substantially reduced, and shop owners, in co-operation with Dublin Corporation, are taking practical steps to improve the environment. The Government are also doing their bit for the environment with work like the refurbishment of the Custom House and Dublin Castle, while the establishment of the Custom House Docks Development Authority is another example of Government commitment to the City Centre.

Prospects for the City Centre are brighter now than they have been for many years. There is a renewed climate of interest in and commitment to revitalisation of the heart of Dublin. Property invest-ment managers are fully aware of this, and realise that the City Centre is the place to hold and develop property in the 1990's. Substantial investment in the City Centre is to be expected during the next decade, and this investment will be to the benefit of all concerned: the fabric and life of the city will be enhanced, attracting greater numbers to enjoy better amenities; the city will be better able to take its rightful position as a tourist capital; and "the man in the street" will see improvement in the performance of pension funds and life assurance policies and will reap the benefits of this improvement.

BILL NOWLAN,

Assistant General Manager — Property
IRISH LIFE ASSURANCE PLC.

Irish Life Assurance have recreated a street in Viking Dublin which is located in the Crypt of St. Audoen's Church, High Street. The exhibition is Irish Life's contribution to the Dublin Millennium.

Conclusion

The writer, it may be safely assumed, is imbued with an incurable sense of optimism about the future prospects for the city. The purpose of this volume is to share the feelings of hope with the widest possible audience for without a certain amount of enthusiasm and confidence it will be all the harder to muster the necessary resilience and the will to win against the inevitable adversity that lies ahead before Dublin is finally shaped into a capital worthy of Ireland and a city everyone can be proud of again.

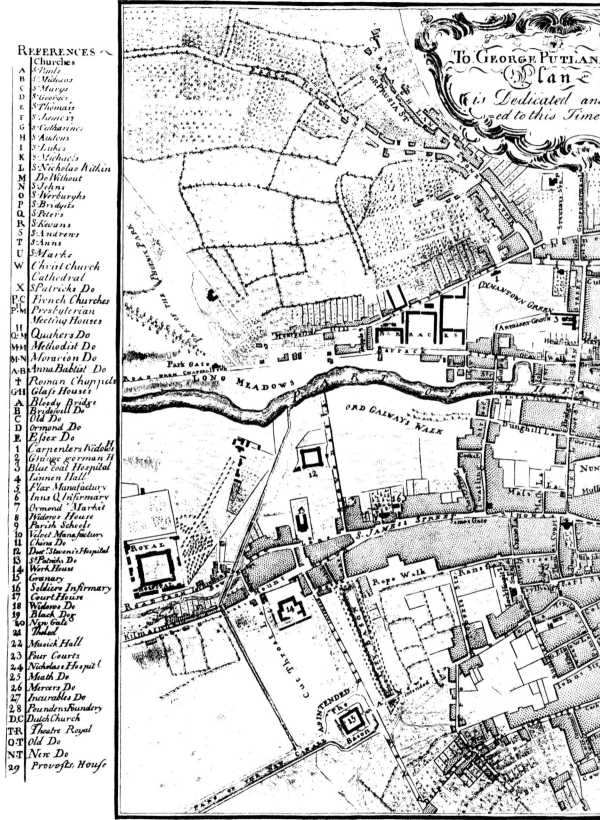

TO GEORGE PUTLAN...
Plan ...
is Dedicated an...
...ed to this Time

REFERENCES

Churches
A	S! Pauls
B	S! Michans
C	S! Marys
D	S! Georges
E	S! Thomas
F	S! James's
G	S! Catharines
H	S! Audeons
I	S! Lukes
K	S! Michaels
L	S! Nicholas Within
M	Do Without
N	S! Johns
O	S! Werburghs
P	S! Bridgets
Q	S! Peters
R	S! Kevans
S	S! Andrews
T	S! Anns
U	S! Marks
W	Christ Church Cathedral
X	S! Patricks Do
F.C	French Churches
P.M	Presbyterian Meeting Houses
Q.M	Quakers Do
M.M	Methodist Do
M.N	Moravian Do
A.B	Anna Babtist Do
†	Roman Chappels
G.H	Glass Houses
A	Bloody Bridge
B	Bridewell Do
C	Old Do
D	Ormond Do
E	Essex Do
1	Carpenters Widows
2	Grange gorman H
3	Blue coat Hospital
4	Linnen Hall
5	Flax Manafactury
6	Inns Q Infirmary
7	Ormond Market
8	Widows House
9	Parish Schools
10	Veloet Manafactury
11	China Do
12	Doct! Stevens's Hospital
13	S! Patricks Do
14	Work House
15	Granary
16	Soldiers Infirmary
17	Court House
18	Widows Do
19	Black Dog
20	New Gate
21	Tholsel
22	Musick Hall
23	Four Courts
24	Nicholas Hospit!
25	Meath Do
26	Mercers Do
27	Incurables Do
28	Pounders Foundery
D.C	Dutch Church
T.R	Theatre Royal
O.T	Old Do
N.T	New Do
29	Provosts House

Engraved for and Sold by L. FLIN

A Scale of

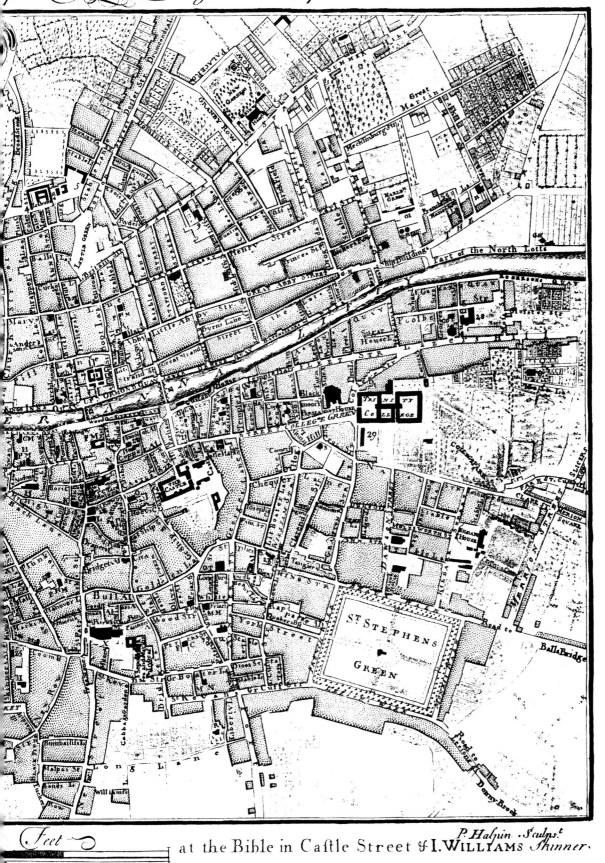

Feet

4000

at the Bible in Castle Street & I. WILLIAMS Skinner.

P. Halpin Sculps.t

(Reproduced by courtesy of Civic Museum)

Index